Language Learning and Teaching in a Multilingual World

NEW PERSPECTIVES ON LANGUAGE AND EDUCATION

Founding Editor: Viv Edwards, *University of Reading, UK*
Series Editors: Phan Le Ha, *University of Hawaii at Manoa, USA* and Joel Windle, *Monash University, Australia.*

Two decades of research and development in language and literacy education have yielded a broad, multidisciplinary focus. Yet education systems face constant economic and technological change, with attendant issues of identity and power, community and culture. This series will feature critical and interpretive, disciplinary and multidisciplinary perspectives on teaching and learning, language and literacy in new times.

All books in this series are externally peer-reviewed.

Full details of all the books in this series and of all our other publications can be found on http://www.multilingual-matters.com, or by writing to Multilingual Matters, St Nicholas House, 31-34 High Street, Bristol BS1 2AW, UK.

NEW PERSPECTIVES ON LANGUAGE AND EDUCATION: 65

Language Learning and Teaching in a Multilingual World

Marie-Françoise Narcy-Combes,
Jean-Paul Narcy-Combes,
Julie McAllister, Malory Leclère
and Grégory Miras

MULTILINGUAL MATTERS
Bristol • Blue Ridge Summit

DOI https://doi.org/10.21832/NARCY2975
Library of Congress Cataloging in Publication Data
A catalog record for this book is available from the Library of Congress.
Names: Narcy-Combes, Marie-Francoise, author. | Narcy-Combes, Jean-Paul, 1947- author.
Title: Language Learning and Teaching in a Multilingual World/ Marie-Francoise Narcy-Combes, Jean-Paul Narcy-Combes, [and three others].
Description: Bristol; Blue Ridge Summit: Multilingual Matters, 2019. | Series: New Perspectives on Language and Education: 65 | Includes bibliographical references and index.
Identifiers: LCCN 2018046188 (print) | LCCN 2018054243 (ebook) | ISBN 9781788922982 (pdf) | ISBN 9781788922999 (epub) | ISBN 9781788923002 (Kindle) | ISBN 9781788922975 (hbk : alk. paper)
Subjects: LCSH: Language and languages--Study and teaching. | Multilingualism.
Classification: LCC P51 (ebook) | LCC P51 .N34 2019 (print) | DDC 418.0071—dc23

British Library Cataloguing in Publication Data
A catalogue entry for this book is available from the British Library.

ISBN-13: 978-1-78892-297-5 (hbk)
ISBN-13: 978-1-78892-761-1 (pbk)

Multilingual Matters
UK: St Nicholas House, 31-34 High Street, Bristol BS1 2AW, UK.
USA: NBN, Blue Ridge Summit, PA, USA.

Website: www.multilingual-matters.com
Twitter: Multi_Ling_Mat
Facebook: https://www.facebook.com/multilingualmatters
Blog: www.channelviewpublications.wordpress.com

Copyright © 2019 Marie-Françoise Narcy-Combes, Jean-Paul Narcy-Combes, Julie McAllister, Malory Leclère and Grégory Miras.

All rights reserved. No part of this work may be reproduced in any form or by any means without permission in writing from the publisher.

The policy of Multilingual Matters/Channel View Publications is to use papers that are natural, renewable and recyclable products, made from wood grown in sustainable forests. In the manufacturing process of our books, and to further support our policy, preference is given to printers that have FSC and PEFC Chain of Custody certification. The FSC and/or PEFC logos will appear on those books where full certification has been granted to the printer concerned.

Typeset by Deanta Global Publishing Services Limited.
Printed and bound in the UK by the CPI Books Group Ltd.
Printed and bound in the US by NBN.

Contents

Introduction   xi
     Epistemological Stance   xi
     Some Important Definitions   xii
     Context   xiii
     Chapter Organisation   xiv

Part 1: Reference Theories: Interrelationships and Complementarities   1

1   Neurophysiology, Cognition and Language   3
     Neurophysiology and Cognition   3
     Language, Cognition and Knowledge   4
     Language and Modularity   5
     The Age Factor   5
     Musical Development and Language Development   6
     Effect of Disciplinary Knowledge on L2 Production   7
     Situated Cognition   7
     Attention   8

2   Language and Cognitive Development in a Plurilingual Perspective   9
     Neurophysiology and Plurilingualism   9
     From Codeswitching to Codemeshing and Translanguaging   10
     The Present Situation of Plurilingual Education and Research   13
     From Additive and Subtractive Bilingualism to Dynamic Bilingualism   14
     The Benefits of Plurilingual Competence   15
     Language(s) and Identity   16

3   Multilingual Practices   18
     Translation   18

	Multilingual Education	19
	Content and Language Integrated Courses	20
	Multimodality/Multiliteracy	22
	Plurilingualism and Teaching	23
	The Multilingual Teacher's Specific Competence	24
	Requirements for the Education/Training of Teachers	24
	Teaching and the Native Speaker	25
4	Psycholinguistics and SLA: Useful Constructs Revisited	26
	Action and Interactions in Language Learning	26
	The Information Processing Model	27
	The Dual-Processing System of Language Production in L2 and Formulaic Language	28
	Connectionist Models of Language and L2 Competition Model	28
	Psycholinguistic and Sociolinguistic Factors in Multi/Plurilingualism: Emergentism and the Dynamic Systems Theory	29
	Plurilingualism in the Connectionist Paradigm	29
	A Dynamic Framework of Emerging Language	30
	Attention in Language Learning	31
	Focus on Form, Focus on Forms and Focus on Meaning	32
	Mediation and Metareflection	33
5	Cultures, Affects and Identities	35
	Perception	35
	Transculturing	35
	Emotions	36
	Motivation	40
	Construction of the Agent	43
	Conclusion: Speaking as a Specific Situated Action	45
6	The Potential of Information and Communication Technology for Language Learning	47
	Recognised Benefits of ICT for Language Learning	47
	Informal Learning	49
	Open Educational Practice	50
	ICT and Computer-Mediated Communication	50
	Defining Telecollaboration and Its Scope	53
	Conclusion	54
7	Context	55
	Introduction	55
	Definitions	56
	Why Context Should be Taken into Account	57
	Context Indicators	60

Validity of the Construct	62
Universal Values and Local Contexts	63
How to Understand Contexts	63
Objectivity of the Analysis	64
Conclusion	65

Part 2: Multilingual Practices in Action — 67

8 Organisation of the Study — 69
   Introduction — 69
   Methods — 72

9 North America — 74
   Case 1: Translanguaging Practices in New York State Schools — 74
   Cases 2, 3 and 4: A Five-Phase Approach to Translanguaging in Schools — 76
   Case 2: Translanguaging in a Social Studies Class — 78
   Case 3: Translanguaging in a Bilingual Classroom in New Mexico — 78
   Case 4: Translanguaging in a Science Class — 79
   Case 5: Translanguaging Practices in a Bilingual University in Puerto Rico — 82

10 Africa — 85
   Case 6: Promoting National Languages with French at Primary Level — 85
   Case 7: Benefits of Using the Home Languages in Primary Schools — 87
   Case 8: Translanguaging in a Mathematics Class in English-Speaking Africa — 88
   Case 9: Informal Learning of Italian by TV Viewers in Tunisia — 89

11 European Large-Scale Projects and Intercomprehension Networks — 91
   Case 10: A Website for CLIL Teachers in Italian High Schools — 91
   Case 11: Online Intercomprehension Learning Programme for Romance Languages (Example 1) — 92
   Case 12: Online Intercomprehension Learning Programme for Romance Languages (Example 2) — 93
   Case 13: Online Intercomprehension Learning Programme for Romance Languages (Example 3) — 95
   Case 14: Developing University Students' Academic and Professional Vocabulary through Reading Intercomprehension and ICT — 96

      Case 15: Promoting Regional and Minority
      Languages through Intercomprehension at
      Primary and Secondary School Level   97

12 European Small-Scale Projects   100
      Case 16: An ICT-Supported Translanguaging
      Approach to Collaborative Writing   100
      Case 17: Promoting Bilingualism and Biliteracy in
      a Two-Way Immersion Programme   103
      Case 18: Implementing a Plurilingual CLIL
      Programme in a University in a Monolingual
      Region of France   104
      Case 19: A Binational Course in Applied Linguistics
      (France and Germany)   106
      Case 20: Promoting Plurilingualism in a University in
      Denmark   107
      Case 21: Multilingualism in a Ukrainian University   110
      Case 22: Writing Class for Students from Different
      Countries   111
      Case 23: Plurilingual Language Awareness and
      Self-Recognition   113
      Case 24: A MOOC that Relies on Plurilingual
      Reflection   114

13 Telecollaboration   117
      Case 25: Telecollaboration between Quebec and
      Australia   117
      Case 26: Telecollaboration between a French and
      Irish High School   118
      Case 27: Telecollaboration between Speakers of the
      Two National Languages in Belgium   119
      Case 28: Telecollaboration between Learners of
      Distant Languages   120
      Case 29: Preparing for International Exchanges
      through Telecollaboration   121
      Case 30: Telecollaboration for Intercomprehension   121
      Case 31: Telecollaborative Teacher Training Courses   122
      Case 32: The Benefits of Asynchronous
      Telecollaboration   123
      Case 33: Corrective Feedback in Telecollaboration   124
      Case 34: Identity Construction in
      Telecollaborative Practices   124

Case 35: Telecollaboration to Enhance
Pragmatic Competence   124
Case 36: Bringing Telecollaborative Practices to
Primary School Children   125
Case 37: Effects of Tandem Practices on Corrective
Feedback   125

14 Learning Languages in Multilingual Contexts:
   Where are We Now?   129
   Contexts   129
   Teacher Education and Training   136
   The Consequences of So Many Different
   Situations and Positions   137
   Implemented Learning Systems   138
   Assessment and Evaluation   142
   Factors Enabling or Inhibiting the Development
   of a Bi/Plurilingual Programme   143
   Consistency with the Theoretical Data   145

15 When Theory and Practice Meet   147

**Part 3: Designing Contextualised Language
Learning Environments in a Plurilingual Perspective**   **151**

16 Multilingual Language Learning and ICT   153

17 Designing Courses and Tasks in a Multilingual
   Perspective   157
   Towards a New Approach   157
   Curriculum as Interaction   159
   Content and Language Integrated Learning (CLIL)/
   Bilingual Education in Curricular Development   160
   Types of Language   161
   Implications for Learning Activities   161
   Social Situations   162
   A Flexible Approach to CLIL-Oriented TBLT   163
   Teacher Education and Language Awareness   164
   Practical Framework   164

18 Modelling the Work   167
   Tasks   167
   Learning Environments and the Teacher's Role   171
   Teacher/Tutor's Role and Community of Learners   172
   Individualisation/Socialisation of Learning   173

Discontinuity and Changes in LLEs	173
Synthesis	175
Concluding Remarks	176
References	179
Index	202

Introduction

Plurilingualism has taken an increasingly dominant position in the field of language learning in Europe and in other areas where many languages are in contact (Coste, 2001). Around the world, the majority of people live in multilingual societies, so plurilinguals should be considered the norm (Jessner, 2006), especially as more and more supposedly monolinguals are in fact language learners.

This book starts with the state-of-the-art research in language learning, then sets out to investigate how research into the implementation and development of language learning environments (LLEs) and tasks compares with that of descriptive second language acquisition (SLA) or applied linguistics. We identify what we call 'intervention' as what is implemented in the different social contexts following careful didactic analysis of a situation. This covers a wide range of activities including the design of teaching materials, the implementation of LLEs and teacher training. 'Intervention' in this sense goes beyond the scope of what is sometimes called 'pedagogical engineering'. We intend to show that 'intervention' should start as a bottom-up movement, then top-down, following careful thinking about the transferability and the relevance of the theoretical and practical choices, then bottom-up again during the implementation and the working of the system (e.g. follow-up, assessment). A theoretical framework that can help understand the specific contexts and plan and monitor the action accordingly will be presented along with checklists and guidelines.

Epistemological Stance

Following the Douglas Fir Group (2016), we examine through a transdisciplinary lens the problems that researchers and practitioners have to face when they need to implement any type of learning environment. Applied linguistics (or didactics) cannot provide all the answers, so other fields must be explored including psychology and neurophysiology (emotions and cognition), psycholinguistic and sociolinguistic dimensions of multi/plurilingualism, as well as interconnections between emergentism, the dynamic-systems theory and socio-interactionist/sociocultural theories (Vygotsky, 1978). We will turn to fields such as education, sociology (especially of education), economics of education, language policies and behavioural psychology for vital clues to the problems arising in learning environments and provide language educators with references to overcome their lack of familiarity with these fields. However, taking them on board requires some methodological and epistemological reflection which may not be easy for practitioners who need guidelines in order not to waste too much precious time. An attempt is made to answer important questions such as: how much theory is enough for adequate professional knowledge and in which form?

Some authors distinguish between the concept of a 'named' language and that of the language system (*productions*) of individual speakers expressed as discourse. 'English', 'Spanish', 'Chinese', 'Arabic', etc., name socially invented categories that do not necessarily overlap with the linguistic productions of individual speakers. Named languages are recognised as having material and social reality, but not linguistic reality (García & Kleyn, 2016; Otheguy *et al.*, 2015). We will endeavour to show that this legitimises the practices of plurilingual speakers and encourages educators to leverage learners' full language repertoire and translanguaging capacities to support their understanding of content and develop their language performances in a learner-centred, educational philosophy (see Chapter 2). We would be tempted to do the same for culture. Named cultures are associated with nation-states seen as a monolithic bloc, which we know they are not.

Some Important Definitions

Researchers have become aware that situations where people speak more than one language are more frequent than when they only speak one. In Otwinowska and De Angelis (2014: 35), the problem is expressed clearly. Using first language/second language/third language (L1/L2/L3) as a sequential order of acquisition may be confusing as it is not adapted to situations where multiple languages are used at the same time. Hammarberg (2014: 37) suggests another terminology: primary, secondary, tertiary language and primary, secondary, tertiary language acquisition, which would take the individual's development more into account. The Douglas Fir Group (2016) also has an interesting view, calling 'additional languages' all the languages that are not connected to the initial socialisation of the speaker. While using the term 'home languages', García and Kleyn (2016: 14) refute the notion of L1 and L2 preferring to annotate the features (F) of the speaker's full linguistic repertoire with a nominal number (n). We would prefer to use 'initial' instead of the more affectively connoted 'home' and for practical reasons, though referring to initial and additional languages (IL and ALs), we may sometimes refer to AL1, AL2,

AL3 when the ranking makes sense to understand the phenomena under investigation.

Regarding multilingualism and plurilingualism, we will follow the Council of Europe's (2001: 168) position. Multilingualism refers to the presence in a geographical area, large or small, of more than one 'variety of language', i.e. the mode of speaking of a social group whether it is formally recognised as a language or not. In such an area, individuals may be monolinguals speaking only their own variety.

Plurilingualism is the ability to use languages for the purposes of communication and to take part in intercultural interaction, where a person, viewed as a social agent, has proficiency of varying degrees in several languages and experience of several cultures. This is not seen as the superposition or juxtaposition of distinct competences, but rather as the existence of a complex or even composite competence on which the user may draw (Council of Europe, 2001: 168). We are aware that other definitions of plurilingualism are used (Canagarajah & Ashraf, 2013) that are less usual in the European context.

Bilingualism will refer either to plurilingualism limited to two languages (we will specify if it is additional or not) or to multilingualism also limited to two languages (we will specify whether it is official, diglossic, educational, etc.).

Diglossia can be said to be a specific instance of multilingualism. It refers to a context where a given language community uses two languages: the first is (one of) the community's dialect(s) and the second may be an older or a more elaborate version of that dialect (cf. Arabic, Czech), or a distinct yet closely related variant (e.g. *Hochdeutsch*) (Causa, 2002). Diglossia may have implications on the acquisition of other languages, as the official or educational diglossia does not always correspond to individual practices (Ferguson, 1959; Fishman, 1971). Polyglossia applies to countries where more than two languages coexist with a complementary distribution based on functional criteria. Contrary to multilingual situations, there is a definite functional distribution which is not necessarily based on the relative prestige of the different languages. Luxembourg (Luxemburgish, French, German, Portuguese and English) and Singapore (Mandarin, Bahasa, Malaysi, Malay and English), for instance, are polyglossic countries. Countries such as India and Pakistan have even more complex situations (Canagarajah, 2013; Leconte *et al.*, 2018), as do most countries in South Eastern Asia, Africa and South America with more or less support from their governments (see i.e. Canagarajah & Ashraf, 2013; Haddad, 2008; Leconte *et al.*, 2018; Sandberg, 2017).

Context

Implementing instructional action means that the context has to be understood, as have the different stakeholders' competences and beliefs.

The complexity of multilingual, diglossic or monolingual contexts and their effect on language development are such that they must be analysed with well-adapted tools in order to go beyond traditional analyses based on one or two clearly defined languages.

In terms of social contexts, the Douglas Fir Group (2016) describes micro contexts of social action and interaction, meso contexts of sociocultural institutions and communities and the macro level of ideological structures, which corresponds to what the Council of Europe (2001) also defines.

We should add that a homoglot context is a context where the language to be learnt is spoken, while it is not spoken in a heteroglot environment. Context can also be institutional, guided or unguided, individual or collective. Time (contact time, learning phases, personal history of learning AL) also needs to be analysed as do individual and collective work and interactions.

Chapter Organisation

In Part 1, we show that the focus of our reflection should be both on the interactional dimension of language learning and on the cognitive organisation it enables (Bouchard, 2009). We briefly explore the above-mentioned fields in order to highlight the points which influence LLEs and tasks. Our assumption is that those fields and the various theories deal with phenomena that can be viewed as the crystals of a kaleidoscope (see Chapter 4 of Bertin et al., 2010). There are many such crystals and they are studied in so many different fields of research that linking them in a fluid text is not always easy and often artificial. Dealing with them as separate individual crystals is the choice we have made. Each tilt of the kaleidoscope will lead to a different interpretation of how these phenomena can be organised or explained. In the past 10 years, advances in research have modified our conception of some of the crystals. New crystals have been found to be important and new patterns of the crystals are now possible. This part will eventually lead to a checklist of the crystals worth collecting in order to construct appropriate LLEs.

The opening chapters (1–7) in Part 1 present the theoretical underpinnings that precede and influence our choice of case studies in Part 2 and proposed LLEs and tasks in Part 3. They are central to understanding multilingualism. Chapter 1 reviews the interplay between neurophysiology, cognition and language and attempts to uncover the cognitive and neural mechanisms that support language development. Chapter 2 examines this further, but more specifically from a multilingual perspective. We start by examining the relationship between neurophysiology and plurilingualism. The chapter then moves on to consider codeswitching and translanguaging processes of a multilingual's cognition. We draw on recent research to highlight the current situation of plurilingual education and the cognitive advantages of plurilingualism.

Chapter 3 builds on Chapter 2 by focusing on the shift in multilingual practices and how they are now emphasising holistic approaches that highlight the interrelationship between languages and the benefits of making full use of the plurilingual repertoire. We first examine translation, Content and Language Integrated Learning (CLIL) and multiliteracy approaches. Then, we explore practices from the teacher's perspective outlining the specific competences and training requirements of multilingual teachers.

Chapter 4 revisits useful constructs from psycholinguistics and SLA research that we believe are effective for setting up tasks in a plurilingual approach if the underlying theories are reinterpreted. We describe interactionist, information processing, connectionist and dynamic systems models, as well as the role of attention, mediation and metareflection in language learning.

Chapter 5 attempts to understand the social and cultural dimensions that contribute to multilingual learners' personal development and how this impacts their language development, their identity and actions. We examine the constructs of perception, emotions and motivation and how learners can develop personal agency.

In Chapter 6, we investigate the potential of information and communication technology (ICT) for language learning, highlighting the benefits as revealed by recent research. We describe new learning practices that rely partly on ICT including: informal learning, open educational practices, computer-mediated communication and telecollaboration.

The concluding chapter of Part 1 (Chapter 7) recognises the role of context in understanding language and language learning, but also the complexity associated with trying to analyse context. This leads us to propose a framework of contextual indicators at the macro, meso and micro levels, which are used in our analysis of the various case studies presented in Part 2.

Part 2 (Chapters 8–15) is devoted to a qualitative review and meta-analysis of multilingual research projects in line with our theoretical and practical positions. We bring together 37 case studies from across different contexts, principally in North America, Africa and Europe as the team of authors is more familiar with these areas. The cases do not cover all the multilingual areas in the world and Chapter 14 will show how our findings relate to multilingual settings in other areas, such as Asia and South America. The case studies are purposely varied by age group, educational setting, learning approaches and scale, as well as sociocultural and international contexts. We describe our methods in Chapter 8 and provide a useful summary of the case studies to guide the reader. The case studies in Chapters 9–12 are organised according to their geographical location as mentioned above. Within this overall organisation, we also examine CLIL, translanguaging and intercomprehension learning programmes, as well as very specific studies on just one aspect of language development. In addition, Chapter 13 looks specifically at telecollaboration projects. After offering a synthetic overview of what the case studies reveal and shedding light on data from studies of the situation in Asia and South America (Chapter 14), we proceed to propose in Chapter 15 a checklist of the factors to be taken into account when organising LLEs and designing tasks. These factors are the crystals we described previously.

Part 3 aims to bridge the gap between theory and practice as we consider the implications of the case studies and of our theoretical foundations and propose a flexible and adaptive framework for setting up learning environments and designing tasks. The framework takes into account the crystals and the effects of contextual, cultural and/or individual variations. Chapter 16 takes a look at innovative ICT-based multilingual LLEs and provides an extensive list of essential tools, systems and tasks. Chapter 17 highlights aspects of our flexible approach including how teachers and learners can collaborate to co-construct tasks and learning environments and how variability and the sociocultural needs of learners can be taken into account in the designing of courses and tasks in a multilingual perspective. The closing chapter provides a model for this flexible, task-based framework, describing teacher/learner roles and interactions with context, culture, technology and tasks, as well as the relations between all these poles and the dynamic nature of the system. It also examines the way macro/social tasks and micro/training tasks can be designed and implemented.

Part 1
Reference Theories: Interrelationships and Complementarities

In this part, we examine the theories underpinning our understandings of language and plurilingualism, which serve as the theoretical framework for Parts 2 and 3. We consider the multifaceted processes of the multilingual's language development and their interrelationships drawing on a number of disciplines including neurophysiology, cognitive psychology, psycholinguistics, sociolinguistics and second language acquisition. The roles of ICT and context are also discussed.

1 Neurophysiology, Cognition and Language

Turning to neurophysiology first is consistent with our position to refer to theories about living and learning that have neurophysiological validity (see Churchland, 2002).

Neurophysiology and Cognition

Cognition can be defined as the whole range of mental activities and processes related to producing knowledge and to the functions that implement them. The objective of cognitive neurosciences is to understand how and for what purpose the different regions of the brain interact (Lachaux, 2015). However, cognitive processes in the brain cannot be observed directly through neuroimaging, but rather are inferred and reconstructed. Only behaviours and productions can be directly observed. There are thousands of research studies but no unified theory (Démonet et al., 2005), and experimental conditions may bias the results. Since Damasio's (1994) work, researchers have questioned the location of cerebral functions (Démonet et al., 2005; Duffau, 2016; Nielsen et al., 2013, among others). It now seems very unlikely that the newborn child's brain is completely organised in specialised modules. Parts of the brain become more and more specialised as it is exposed and responds to the environment. In adulthood and throughout life, the external and internal connections of a synaptic network constantly evolve according to the stimuli. They reinforce or inhibit the efficacy of certain brain areas depending on what is experienced (Finn et al., 2015). The conception of the brain in which the activity of the areas corresponds to specific functions has evolved towards a more connectionist model. In this model, functions are not localised in a restricted part of the brain, but involve neural networks that are distributed throughout or in parts of the brain (Marendaz, 2015). Thus, it is not the brain areas that matter, but the deeper networks that are distributed throughout the brain and operate in parallel, evolving constantly in a complex and dynamic game of reconfigurations.

As a consequence, an adult brain appears highly structured and functionally specialised (Kail, 2012). However, even when there is injury to the brain, plasticity enables it to compensate for the loss and other parts of the brain take over.

While the human brain adapts to its environment, its structure and function are self-determined according to genetic and epigenetic constraints (Rancillac, 2014). Individual brain anatomical differences are very important (Duffau, 2016), even regarding language (Kail, 2012). Thus, the lateralisation of connections in the brain is an individual rather than a universal phenomenon (Levy, 1969).

The data collected do not fully validate the fact that some people have a hemispheric preference even though it appears that there are specialisations. Lateralisation may increase slightly as people get older (Démonet et al., 2005), though without significant differences between people and genres (Nielsen et al., 2013). The role of the right hemisphere tends to be predominant at the beginning. The left then takes over. However, the right hemisphere plays a predominant role in remediation (Démonet et al., 2005). Interactivity has become an increasingly predominant concept (Anderson, 2014).

Rancillac (2014) links language to other cognitive abilities such as perception or working memory, which means that it is difficult to separate language skills from other cognitive abilities (Kail, 2012). This confirms the fact that language/discourse and knowledge/content cannot be dissociated (Narcy-Combes, 2005), and we will soon see that society/culture cannot be dissociated from the previous elements as well.

For LeDoux (2003), what is innate simply means that the connections are in place from birth, and Dehaene (2007) reminds us that the fetus can perceive the sounds of languages spoken in its environment which may influence the organisation of the brain. Research on language acquisition needs to take into account both internal individual parameters and exposure to the environment.

Language, Cognition and Knowledge

Discourse, similar to cognition, is part of human social practices and can only be understood through action (Maingueneau, 2009: 44). If we consider speaking as an action, then the result of speaking should present the same features as the result of any action, i.e. be contextually, socio-culturally, historically and personally marked. This will be dealt with in more detail in Chapter 2. The mutual connection between language and cognition has been put forward by Lupyan (2012), among others. He argues that language, and more specifically linguistic labels, rapidly modulate putatively non-verbal processes. Gentner et al. (2013) examined spatial cognition in deaf children with minimal exposure to formal language and showed that spatial language is critical for the development of seemingly non-linguistic spatial skills.

Language and Modularity

Randall (2007) points out that an initial research question was to investigate whether knowledge of language was treated in a specific module of the brain and if language production was the result of the addition of several parallel monolingual competences when the speaker is plurilingual. The current dominant assumption is that forms of modules develop, especially for lexicon, grammar or phonology. However, the innate, preprogrammed character of these modules is not validated, so the lateralisation of language in the left hemisphere (Broca area) is neither innate nor irrevocable (Kail, 2016). It naturally occurs during development. Therefore, the network of language areas has encapsulation, automation, functional specialisation and rapid acquisition properties, which make it work in a way that may look similar to modularity according to Fodor's (1986) definition, but is in fact far more complex, to a point that is too abstract for the purpose of this book.

The Age Factor

Chomsky's and Fodor's modular position justified the construct of a *critical period* after which acquiring another language would not be easy. This construct has been questioned. As Singleton (2005) pointed out, there is no sufficiently precise evidence of the limitative effects of this so-called critical period. However, according to Narcy-Combes *et al.* (2008), there is evidence of some kind of phonological process of high efficiency and preferential treatment in initial language(s), which some call a phonological 'sieve' (Troubetzkoy, 1939). According to Miras (2014), it is a phonological phenomenon, not a phonetic one, refuting the fact that there would be 'deafness' to sounds of additional languages (ALs). The brain no longer preferentially processes sound data that are irrelevant to the language(s) it is accustomed to hear, and this as early as when the child is 2 years old (De Boysson-Bardies, 2005). At about 6–7 years old and beyond, what some researchers call filters, nativisation (Andersen, 1983) or assimilation (Piaget, 1970) is due to the fact that individuals process data according to internalised personal processes. The effects can be felt syntactically first and that can be quickly settled. Articulation difficulties linked to automatisation are significant but can be compensated for. The development of logical operations leading to adult cognitive functioning may become a hindrance to 'natural' learning. Then, between 9–10 and 13–14 years old, nativisation occurs in any field of knowledge, though change is still possible through regular training and more and more analytical learning (Gaonac'h, 2006). Gradually, the abilities associated with cognitive development open new ways of learning. The coexistence of multiple languages may complicate things, but it also maintains brain plasticity.

Ellis (2008) and Gaonac'h (2006) argue that learning an initial language and learning an AL are two different things even at a very early age without any really daunting obstacle. The initial language determines the working memory processes (Cutler, 2000), which vary according to the languages. Studies on age effects have often focused on contexts involving immigrants massively exposed to the target language, which is obviously very different from the school context (Kail, 2015). They show that the earlier the child becomes bilingual, the narrower the zone in the brain devoted to language becomes. This zone will be used later to learn ALs (Kail, 2015). When data measure the effect of learning conditions on outcomes, the benefit of early learning disappears (Gaonac'h, 2006). Adults are sometimes more effective, even for pronunciation, given equal exposure and practice time and considering these variables are the most relevant. Furthermore, adults tend to start faster while children, when allowed plenty of time to learn, then catch up with them.

There are sensitive thresholds:

- early language acquisition and adult learning are initially different in nature as the neuronal substrates vary and evolve differently over time;
- teaching language the 'natural' way cannot be done at primary school level as the learners are already too old for it and caretakers not so available;
- how and how long individuals are exposed to the AL are more important than how old they are;
- language classes in monolingual schools do not offer the best conditions for efficient early language learning in terms of exposure.

In a 'natural' environment, adults and young learners will develop different second language (L2) learning strategies and modes that depend on their age on arrival in a resettlement country. 'Natural' learning will work until the age of 7. Beyond that age, learners will benefit from institutional support. Only adults develop strategies that are specific to the AL learning situation.

Musical Development and Language Development

Listening to a new AL is often intuitively supposed to be facilitated by musical education. Music education does, indeed, contribute to aural memory development, and thus to the capacity of identifying and reproducing new sounds mainly at a phonetic level but also at some phonological level. Bolduc *et al.* (2014) have shown that a better sense of rhythm leads to better segmentation of the sound chain. A musical programme for preschool children highlighted that a music awareness workshop not only favoured the development of reading and writing, but also, more broadly, intelligence, attention, information processing and communication. Improvements take a long time (about two years), but are sustainable. In line with the stance of researchers exploring multiliteracies (cf. Chapter 3), Auzéau (2017) and Miras (2014) have recently argued that using music may positively impact language development at some point. Yet, the approach cannot be generalised and needs more empirical and critical research. Drama, however, proves more successful with every one according to these authors and Carson (2012), for instance.

Effect of Disciplinary Knowledge on L2 Production

Language expresses some form of content, which will necessarily influence its production. At lower levels of proficiency, utterances may be constructed with disciplinary concepts used as labels without the adequate syntax and forms required in such discourse. Interaction will be made more difficult for the interlocutor(s) since they must reconstruct the cohesion. Learning skills are not affected by the change of language and may compensate for language difficulties (Bertin *et al.*, 2010; Cummins, 2007).

As we wrote in Bertin *et al.* (2010), advanced mastery of content leads to better mastery of the rhetorical structures of the discourse in fields in which cultural differences do not influence these structures to a great extent (Pacteau, 1999). Automaticity and fluency of AL production depend more on instances/chunks than on lexical or morphosyntactic units, which may explain the great influence of familiarity with the content on performance. Such familiarity favours instance/chunk-based production (Bygate *et al.*, 2001), which in turn increases fluency, but not accuracy or complexity (Bygate *et al.*, 2001). A learner who is well read in a given field will sound more proficient in the AL in that field than a specialist of this AL who is ignorant of the domain (Bertin *et al.*, 2010). It is easier to produce discourse if the memory effort is reduced, which accounts for the important role of rehearsal in academic or professional production (Derix *et al.*, 2014; Rodríguez-Fornells *et al.*, 2009). Frames and scripts are easily transferable from one language to another in specific domains only, which is limiting. Prior knowledge of disciplinary content has a positive influence on performance in new languages and can speed up the learning process (Bertin *et al.*, 2010). However, teaching new content in a new language may not prove so beneficial if translanguaging is not possible (see Chapter 2). Starting from documents in the learner's other language(s) proves beneficial (García *et al.*, 2016).

Situated Cognition

Knowledge is situated (Hutchins, 1995) and results from coordinated reflection and construction processes between human beings, artefacts and the environment where time plays a role. Humans think in collaboration with other human beings and through tools and devices provided by the context (Salomon, 1997). This is very close to Siemens'

(2005) 'connectivism', which aims at giving a global vision of knowledge construction as a network of connections, but eventually does not cover everything. Distributed cognition is being mobilised when a contextual element is identified as significant by an individual in action and is constantly co-constructed (Lave & Wenger, 1991). Human cognition is thus grounded in human interactions with the physical and social environment at the micro and macro levels so that it can be said that 'cognitive structures develop within perception and in action' (Kitayama *et al.*, 1997; Pecher & Zwaan, 2005: 1) and the education systems should take this fact into account.

Attention

Since cognition is situated, the individual must pay attention to what takes place in the interaction but needs to rely on internal processes as well. The focus of attention is determined by the pervasive competition between stimulus-driven or bottom-up mechanisms and goal-directed or top-down mechanisms (Egeth & Yantis, 1997). Importantly, attention can also be guided in a top-down way by internal goals (e.g. rules, instructions and plans), as well as by moods (emotions) and motivational states (e.g. feeling anxious or hungry) (Xue, 2016). Lachaux (2011, 2015) argues that the aim of attention is to prioritise an element of the external or internal world so that it can receive the major part of cognitive resources. He also reveals that individuals do not pay attention to something when it is not important or when something else is more important. The role of attention and the difficulty in controlling it must be understood. Three systems are at play (Lachaux, 2011):

- A first system directs attention to salient facts such as a loud noise or a fly interrupting our reading.
- A second system attracts or diverts attention according to internal or external emotional factors, even going as far as creating positive or negative obsessions that hold attention captive.
- A third system enables us to direct attention consciously to what seems particularly important. This can only be possible from adolescence. Attention is constant when concentrated on a single objective (the link with emotions will be dealt with further on). This implies that learners should feel the need and desire to direct and maintain their attention and feel emotionally comfortable.

2 Language and Cognitive Development in a Plurilingual Perspective

In Chapter 1, we dealt with language in general, but our focus is plurilingualism. This, as we will now see, has changed some perspectives.

Neurophysiology and Plurilingualism

Functional neuroimaging has been used to explore the neural counterparts of the plurilingual ability to address two important questions (Démonet *et al.*, 2005):

(1) Are two different languages implemented in the brain through a common neural network or several spatially segregated neural networks?
(2) What are the characteristics of the cerebral organisation of language in bi/plurilinguals?

Various responses are explored in Kail (2015). Kim *et al.* (1997) showed that initial and additional languages (ILs/ALs) are represented in separate parts of the brain in individuals who have acquired an AL in early adulthood, while they overlap in subjects who have been exposed to both an IL and IL2 or an AL in early childhood. However, when late bilinguals have reached a high level of proficiency in both languages, a common neural network can also be identified. This aligns with finding reported by Kail (2015) and Perani *et al.* (2003).

Yetkin *et al.* (1996) suggested that a less frequently used language yielded larger cerebral activations than a more regularly spoken language. The level of attained proficiency and the duration of exposure to a second language may be more important factors than age of acquisition to account for the cerebral representation of language networks in bilinguals. This supports critical period studies and translanguaging theories as previously mentioned in Chapter 1.

A qualitative evolution of the psycholinguistic system due to brain plasticity can be observed as the learner progresses in the acquisition of an AL (or more). So, gradually the multilingual speaker's languages form subsets within the same cognitive system (Paradis, 2004). These subsets get activated simultaneously to varying degrees according to the needs of reception and production and are never totally deactivated (Grosjean, 2008). In line with this, Otwinowska and De Angelis (2014) recall the holistic nature of the plurilingual speaker's competence, as mentioned by Grosjean (2008) and Wright (2015). De Bot and Jaensch (2015) sum up the situation by saying that early studies on the localisation of languages in the 'plurilingual' brain suggested both shared and language-specific neural substrates for different languages. However, more recent studies concluded that the same brain areas subserve the different languages of multilinguals and that more brain tissue is involved in processing languages that are less developed and automatised. Consequently, using another language is initially more costly in terms of resources. They conclude by pointing to the absence of signs that an AL2 is processed differently from an AL1, but at different levels of command.

From Codeswitching to Codemeshing and Translanguaging

Codeswitching

In different situations, speakers may resort to the different subsets of their competence in flexible ways in order to communicate with a given interlocutor. Interlocutors may switch from one language or dialect to another, making use of their respective capacity for expression in one language and of comprehension in another. Knowledge of different languages may help an individual to go through a written, or possibly oral, text in a new language by recognising words belonging to a common international repertoire despite the influence of the unknown language on these words (intercomprehension of Romance or Germanic languages in Europe, for instance, see Causa [2002] and Chapter 11: Cases 11–15 of this volume). Depending on the situation, the speaker may adopt a monolingual mode, endeavouring to use one language when interacting with monolingual speakers, or a plurilingual mode, allowing the mixing of languages and codeswitching when in the company of other bilinguals (Grosjean & Li, 2013). The term 'codeswitching' refers to switching back and forth between language codes that are regarded as separate and autonomous (Causa, 2002). Codeswitching was often considered a violation and a disruption of monolingual language use and is still frequently stigmatised (Causa, 20). According to Causa (2002), codeswitching may occur between sentences (intersentential) or within a single sentence (intrasentential) and may be more or less phonologically or linguistically adapted depending on the degree of bilingualism of the speaker. It follows then for the receivers that codeswitching refers to the description of the message they perceive. This position considers language only from an external perspective that looks at bilinguals' language behaviour as if they were two monolinguals in one, while, for the speaker, it results from internal processing that does not necessarily separate the codes in the same way. This enables speakers to solve communication problems or to mark their identity. It is also a way to determine boundaries between different social groups or languages as highlighted in various sociolinguistic studies.

Ferguson (2009: 231–232) referred to codeswitching for 'constructing and transmitting any knowledge' and for 'classroom management'. Both Lin (2014) and Ferguson (2009) considered that codeswitching can also have an interpersonal function in social interaction in the classroom and can be used to negotiate identities, as exemplified in Asia and Africa for instance (e.g. Wei & Martin, 2009). Causa (2002) states that distinguishing between codeswitching, borrowing, lexical assimilation and mixing languages is not always easy and Herdina and Jessner (2006) argue that the distinction between codeswitching and transfer has not been methodologically validated and that transfer, codeswitching and codemeshing are different positions on the same continuum. In codemeshing, the local, vernacular, colloquial and world dialects of one language are mixed. It goes beyond social and cultural differences. This aligns with the assumption that language production in plurilinguals implies the partial activation of a language other than the expected one with more or less efficient adaptations to the target language (Grosjean, 2008).

Williams and Hammarberg (1998) distinguish two roles played by the known languages when acquiring an AL (AL2 here). During the AL2 communication process, an active language can play either an instrumental role or a supplier role. As far as the learners are concerned, the instrumental role facilitates their reflection while the supplier role supports their creativity. In natural settings, this kind of mutual mediation may result in communication based on many languages (see Translanguaging below), oversimplified forms and mimics and gestures to reach the common objective as was evidenced in Lebanon for instance (Wehbe, 2017). De Angelis (2005: 11) shows that the representations of learners can also lead them to dismiss the IL as irrelevant to learning an AL2 in terms of their perception of correctness and association with foreignness.

Translanguaging

New positions have radically changed traditional conceptions of what it means to learn a language, breaking with the established goal of mastering two or three different languages learnt separately to reach native-like competence. Plurilingual speakers acquire and use their languages while engaging in language practices and call on all their resources in a given social context, shaping this context in communicative interaction (Canagarajah, 2011; Kramsch, 2006). The use of two or more languages in interaction involves 'simultaneous and reciprocal affordances for language learning' (Martin-Beltrán, 2010; see also van Lier, 2004). We would say that affordances should be seen as the properties of an object that define its possible uses whether it was designed or not for that use.

As the constructs of translanguaging and codemeshing are centred on the speakers and their practices, they are more relevant when language learning and teaching is concerned. Translanguaging was first used by Williams (1996) to refer to a pedagogical practice in Welsh bilingual schools where input was in one language and the task in another language. To go beyond the monoglossic reference of codeswitching, García (2009) broadened the scope of translanguaging and described it as a process that involves multiple discursive practices and is the norm in multilingual communities. Wei (2011: 1223) argues that translanguaging 'includes the full range of linguistic performances of multilingual language users for purposes that transcend the combination of structures, the alternation between systems, the transmission of information and the representation of values, identities, and relationships'. According to García *et al.* (2017: 2), translanguaging refers to 'both the complex language practices of multilingual individuals and communities, as well as the pedagogical approaches that draw on those complex practices to build those desired in formal school settings'.

As a consequence, 'to translanguage is to speak naturally and freely, without regard for the restrictions established by the boundaries of named languages, without heed for the constraints that give dual names and borders and limits to the bilinguals' unitary competence' (García & Kleyn, 2016: xi). A strong version of translanguaging is one in which bilingual people do not speak languages, but rather selectively use their repertoire of linguistic features. The weak version (Cummins, 2007) supports named language boundaries, but calls for the softening of these boundaries.

Canagarajah (2011: 403) also uses the term 'translanguaging' for the 'general communicative competence of multilinguals' but prefers the term 'codemeshing' for the realisation of translanguaging in texts to highlight the mixing of 'communicative modes and diverse symbol systems (other than language)'. Some scholars go even further: Otsuji and Pennycook (2010: 244) challenged the notion of discrete language and used the term 'metrolingualism' to refer to creative linguistic conditions across space and borders of culture, history and politics, as a way to move beyond current terms such as 'multilingualism' and 'multiculturalism'. The situations in countries such as India (Canagarajah & Ashraf, 2013; Leconte *et al.*, 2018) and Lebanon (Wehbe, 2017) among others, justify this position and may lead to new combined approaches to language learning in schools in which languages are separated, as suggested in Leconte *et al.* (2018). We will also argue that intercomprehension is a particular case of translanguaging. As Ollivier (2013) shows, research has fragmented and incomplete notions of what intercomprehension competence involves. It is a long-standing practice, as Sheeren (2016) rightly reminds us (for more details, see Ollivier, 2013). The Council of Europe, in particular, has tried to rekindle interest in intercomprehension (see Doyde, 2005, for instance), and numerous projects have been implemented, as will be seen in Part 2, without great changes in teaching practices outside these projects.

Translanguaging transformative impact in instruction

A number of scholars have pointed out the transformative nature of the translanguaging process (García & Kleyn, 2016; Wei, 2011, 2017). According to García and Kleyn (2016), three dimensions of educating bilingual children can be transformed through translanguaging:

- instructional pedagogies;
- assessment;
- programme types.

Specifically, with respect to instruction, teachers will modify their attitudes and behaviours in three ways (García & Kleyn, 2016). Firstly, the teacher will develop a stance that often goes against conventional views about what should happen in schools. García and Kleyn (2016: 21) identify two stances: the 'scaffolding stance', which sees inclusion of the child's full repertoire as only temporary and the 'transformative stance', which posits that the child's full repertoire will transform language hierarchies in school. Secondly, teachers will strategically design and plan translanguaging instruction. This requires (i) constructing collaborative/cooperative and student-centred approaches; (ii) collecting and developing varied multilingual and multimodal instructional resources; and (iii) using translanguaging pedagogical practices (García & Kleyn, 2016). Finally, teachers must be prepared to 'shift' their design, which implies changing the course of instruction in order to respond to individual children's language repertoires.

Institutions could offer a varied choice of languages to enable learners to develop a plurilingual competence that would include intercomprehension of related languages (Ollivier, 2013). Besides, if we accept the fact that learning a language is a lifelong activity (we prefer the notion of development), what matters most is to foster motivation, capacity and the confidence to face a new language experience outside the world of formal education.

The Present Situation of Plurilingual Education and Research

Current educational policies and practices are still linked to the idea of language separation (see García *et al.*, 2017; Hélot & Erfurt, 2016; Paulsrud *et al.*, 2017; Wehbe, 2017), even in complex multilingual societies such as India, Pakistan and Malaya (Leconte *et al.*, 2018), not to mention Africa (Haddad, 2008; Sandberg, 2017), despite attempts at altering the situation. However, classroom language practices do not always match official policies, and translanguaging (often simply seen as mere codeswitching) is a very common phenomenon in multilingual contexts (see Translanguaging in Chapter 2) as people more or less consciously realise it can provide better access to the curriculum and has the function of differentiating classroom activities (e.g. Haddad, 2008; Sandberg, 2017; Wei, 2011). This is confirmed by research showing that, when required to ignore one of two languages, bilingual subjects have been shown to resort to a pre-semantic phonological selection of the target language. Such research highlights that ignoring one language is costly in cognitive terms (Price *et al.*, 2010), and very likely in affective terms as well, since children are happier when the situation changes (see Sandberg, 2017, concerning Nepal).

Most studies on multilingual practices focus on two languages, but studies that involve three or more languages are particularly informative because they show different strategies and directions in the use of languages that are not evident when only two languages are involved. For example, the study of multilingual practices by Chinese children in a French immersion programme in Canada, reported by Moore (2010), showed competencies in the three languages, as well as codeswitching in different directions in a multilingual and multicultural context. This will necessarily happen in countries such as India and Pakistan (Canagarajah, 2013; Leconte *et al.*, 2018). In many areas of the world (Asia and Africa in particular), multilingual encounters involving three or more languages can often be found outside the school context in the linguistic landscape (Gorter, 2006; Haddad, 2008; Shohamy & Gorter, 2009). However, in this case, studies are more complex to carry out.

From Additive and Subtractive Bilingualism to Dynamic Bilingualism

Cummins (2007), among others, draws a distinction between additive bilingualism in which the IL continues to be developed and the initial culture (IC) to be valued while an AL is learned; and subtractive bilingualism in which the AL is added to the detriment of the IL and IC, which no longer develop as a consequence. Subtractive bilingualism can be experienced on a large scale in Southern Asian countries for various reasons (e.g. Canagarajah & Ashraf, 2013; Haddad, 2008) and in African countries also (e.g. Sandberg, 2017). Learners working in an additive bilingual environment are more likely to succeed than those whose IL and culture are devalued by their schools and by wider society, as exemplified in the Odisha region (Eastern India) for instance (Leconte *et al.*, 2018).

Potentially subtractive bilingualism may lead to some form of rejection of the AL. Depending on the individual learner's context or on the general context of the course, this may play an important role and will be assessed prior to the course.

Rejecting the linear nature of additive and subtractive bilingual models, García (2009) introduced the concept of dynamic bilingualism in order to take into account the complexity and multimodality of communications in the 21st century (see multimodality/multiliteracy in Chapter 3). It goes beyond the notion of additive bilingualism to reflect the translanguaging practices of bilinguals acknowledging that 'the linguistic features and practices of bilinguals form a unitary linguistic system that interact in dynamic ways with each other' (García & Kleyn, 2016: 16) in response to the communicative context.

The dynamic effects on the functional anatomy of language in bilinguals also involve attrition effects observed when subjects cease to use one of their languages, even when they actually renounce their IL. For instance, Pallier *et al.* (2003) showed that children adopted by French families forgot their IL and exhibited activation patterns no different from those observed in native French speakers when perceiving this former IL.

The Benefits of Plurilingual Competence

Cenoz and Gorter (2011: 339), in their exploration of recent trends in second language acquisition, multilingualism and education, highlight the most prominent trends as being the reaction against the monolingual bias that takes the *native speaker* as the reference and the study of multilingual practices in school contexts. Grosjean (2010: 20) referred to the 'equal and perfect knowledge' of two languages as a myth, especially because 'individuals seldom have access to two languages in exactly the same contexts in every domain of interaction' (Valdés, 2005: 414). Multilingual speakers use languages according to their communicative needs and the communicative context.

Mastering more than a single language is a common and socially important feature in human societies and has many advantages. Cook (2003, 2007) described how learning an AL has an influence on the whole cognitive system with some multilinguals achieving a very sophisticated, but different knowledge of a target language that goes beyond the common competence of many native speakers. Cenoz and Gorter (2011: 340) argue that 'because of their rich experience with languages, multilingual speakers of a language can also manifest a greater creativity and language playfulness'. In Otwinowska and De Angelis (2014) and Cenoz (2015), among others, evidence is offered of the cognitive advantages of plurilingualism. They argue that a monitoring system enables speakers to manage the available codes whereby languages in the repertoire are drawn upon depending on the interlocutor, the context and the topic. However, all of the available resources are resorted to adequately. In addition, contrastive awareness sensitises plurilinguals to cross-lingual differences, which in turn facilitates reading. Plurilinguals are also more successful at metalinguistic and epilinguistic tasks (Bialystok, 2009), as evidenced in India when learners work in different languages at school, translanguaging between languages in their textbooks and classroom discourse (Canagarajah, 2013).

When plurilinguals select a code or codeswitch, they do so in relation to the sociocultural context they find themselves in and with an intentionality they can explain. Automaticity and intentionality are interrelated.

Bialystok (2009) argued that there are positive neurocognitive effects throughout life. Her studies found that the age-related decline of grey matter is slowed down and Alzheimer's disease symptoms have a later onset in plurilinguals than in monolinguals as a more distributed functional connectivity in the frontal areas is maintained. Creative thinking as well as conceptual mobility are greater as working memory is called upon through different proceedings, and there is a positive impact on maths abilities as well.

Abdellilah-Bauer (2014) and Abdellilah-Bauer and Bijeljac-Babic (2015: 54–55) remind us that early bilingualism can have positive effects if connected with affects:

- hiring a nanny who speaks another language is arbitrary, thus inefficient;
- no language is better than another for child development and any language is as good as another one;
- it takes years of continuous practice to maintain an AL (see From additive and subtractive bilingualism to dynamic bilingualism in Chapter 2).

Language(s) and Identity

If individuals are to be taught the local language, their IL should be valued and their practice encouraged. Komorowska (2014) shows the links between identity, ethnicity, language and culture and emphasises that openness requires that the group feel solid in its bearings and identity. Studies reveal the diversity of situations in different countries (see e.g. Hélot & Erfurt, 2016), which suggests that potential resistances and difficulties should not be overlooked. It is best to pay attention to who the people are and how they feel as shown by instances in Nepal and Cambodia, where the specific needs of the local people were taken into account and the organisation of classes adapted to their working hours (Sandberg, 2017).

Otwinowska and De Angelis (2014: 33) are among those who argue for a multidimensional conceptualisation of plurilingualism as individuals' investment in representations of languages and identities are much more symbolic, complex and ideological. This is supported by Otwinowska and De Angelis (2014: 33) who found that 'the participants' symbolic investments demonstrate how some of their real everyday social and linguistic practices challenge social categories through the complex and (sometimes) simultaneous ways in which they manage, negotiate and resist discourses of language and power'. For example, Cummins (2007) showed how important the school's use of identity texts are for children who speak languages other than that of the school at home and in their community.

3 Multilingual Practices

Individual plurilingualism and global multilingualism have led to specific practices both at the level of learners and of teachers. For a very long time, such practices were frowned upon. This chapter will complete Chapter 2 and show that educationalists are now emphasising the benefits of making full use of a plurilingual repertoire.

Translation

Dealing with two languages at the same time triggers greater demands on coordination and the inhibition of parallel lexical processing in the brain. However, even if translation has generally been reproved as a method for additional language (AL) learning for some time (Randall, 2007: 165–167), conscious or unconscious reference to the initial language (IL) is logically one of the dominant processes used by language learners since known codes cannot be totally deactivated (Bertin *et al.*, 2010; Grosjean, 2008). Evidence is given by Bozhinova *et al.* (2017) that some form of translation can be an effective support for writing tasks and oral production if learners are trained to use it adequately and see its shortcomings. Translation into or from an IL (or any other language) can be seen as an efficient means of saving working memory space, as shown in a study of learners of French using think aloud protocols on a reading comprehension task (Kem, 1994, in Randall, 2007: 166): (1) there was little difference between more proficient and less proficient learners in the degree to which they used translation; (2) the difference between the two groups appeared to lie in the 'size' of the chunks they translated: less proficient readers translated word for word, but more proficient readers processed larger chunks of text and then translated them into English; (3) the students, especially the more proficient ones, reported that translation allowed them 'space' to take in longer stretches of text. Language is processed for meaning, not form (Narcy, 1990), so the meaning of these larger chunks, once translated into the IL, can be stored more economically. Such practices seem to become the rule in some classes in multilingual regions of the world, in particular in India (Canagarajah &

Ashraf, 2013, see also OEP site: www.TESS-India.edu.in for practical cases in India[1]). Translation becomes a collaborative means of discovering the languages of all the children in a group and of translanguaging.

Multilingual Education

Research on bi/plurilingualism in education, including heritage languages, minority languages and immigrant languages or languages in postcolonial settings, has often focused on multilingual practices (e.g. Valdès, 2005). However, despite the pedagogical advantages associated with a more flexible type of bilingualism (see e.g. Blackledge & Creese, 2010), fluidity between languages has not been encouraged whether it concerns the switching or meshing of languages or the integration of languages in the school curriculum (cf. Bozhinova et al., 2017). This is despite the long-known Linguistic Interdependence Hypothesis (Cummins, 1994), which argues that certain IL knowledge and competences can be positively transferred during the process of AL acquisition as illustrated in an African study reported in Haddad (2008). An evaluation in Niger demonstrated the power of transfer in either direction by testing students in 'mother tongue'-based bilingual classes and French (AL) submersion classes in both languages. The highest scores were attained by bilingual students tested in the IL and the lowest scores by submersion students tested in the AL.

This common underlying proficiency (Cummins, 1984) between the languages of bilinguals enables them to transfer academic and linguistic concepts from one language to the other. This research provided the impetus for the expansion of all types of bilingual education in the 20th century. However, the two languages were very often taught at separate times, for separate subjects and/or with separate teachers who were in separate rooms, thus advocating double monolingualism (Cummins, 1984), even if practices exemplified codeswitching. The translanguaging practices of Welsh educators (Williams, 1996) were exceptions to this common practice of strict separation of languages and offered more scope than previous practices.

Multilingual education, defined as 'the use of two or more languages in education provided that schools aim at multilingualism and multiliteracy' (Cenoz, 2009: 4), often refers to schools with three or more languages in the curriculum. In this case, Elorza and Muñoa (2008) advocate a holistic approach, which implies an important degree of coordination among language teachers with a view to implementing an integrated language curriculum that highlights the interrelationship between languages. By focusing on the total language repertoire of plurilinguals, we can see how they process and use the different codes available and how their skills vary according to the codes and the interactions (Ortega, 2010).

As far as writing is concerned, as evidenced by Bozhinova *et al.* (2017), a multilingual and holistic approach provides interesting insights about relationships between the languages and can also have important pedagogical implications and eventually improve academic results (Cenoz & Gorter, 2011). This is supported by García and Sylvan (2011) who show how translanguaging makes newcomer immigrant students more academically successful and more confident in their use of their languages in secondary schools in the USA. Wei (2011) focuses on British-born pupils of Chinese origin who attend Chinese language and culture classes and examines how they create their own social space by translanguaging. He also shows that multimodality enhances their creative and critical behaviour (Bozhinova *et al.*, 2017). Shohamy (2001) highlights the discrepancy between the official rejection of these practices and their contribution to the level of language creativity among plurilinguals, particularly immigrants. Conversely, McNamara (2012) questions the celebration of multilingualism and highlights its complexity.

Plurilingual competence develops in specific contexts. Other contexts, or traditionally monolingual contexts, cannot be expected to switch to effective multilingual practices without some form of conscious or unconscious reluctance. The move should then be educationally accompanied, which we will propose in Part 3.

Content and Language Integrated Courses

The way that institutions implement their idea of plurilingual learning and teaching is often reduced to creating learning environments where academic content (i.e. history, mathematics, etc.) is learnt through an AL. This is known as Content and Language Integrated Learning (CLIL) or content-based instruction (CBI) (Cenoz, 2015; Coyle *et al.*, 2010; Dalton-Puffer, 2007). It originates from immersion programmes in Canada in the 1970s and 1980s and has also been known in Europe as 'content-based language instruction' or 'bilingual education'. The approach benefited from the support of the EU as early as 1995 (Council of Europe, 1995). CLIL offers two main advantages for the development of language skills: the possibility of increasing the time that learners are exposed to the AL and the fact that they do so while being exposed to real-life situations. The main problem arises from the lack of teacher qualification and training in CLIL. Hence, they feel they are unprepared to do the job. In Europe, CLIL may concern foreign languages, with a dominance of English, French and German, or minority/local languages. However, despite European political support, there remain strong limitations to the generalisation of CLIL as no specific training or qualifications are needed other than the basic national teacher qualifications in most EU countries. Besides, the study of bilingual courses has revealed that teaching content through an AL remains inconclusive if the objective is for learners to acquire the AL (Dalton-Puffer, 2007). They achieve high proficiency in listening and reading, but sometimes produce a school variety of pidgin (Dalton-Puffer, 2007), which may not be what was expected. Other limitations include vague linguistic objectives, a lack of research on the links between disciplinary content and language and a lack of investigation on how the oral activities traditionally proposed enable the development of disciplinary knowledge. It is clear that disciplinary and language teachers should interact constantly.

Eisele-Henderson (2000) argues that high demands concerning content will result in linguistic performance loss, while low language proficiency will lead to utterances where disciplinary concepts are juxtaposed as labels, regardless of the forms of the AL. As seen in Chapter 1, language change does not affect cognitive skills that can compensate for language difficulties (Cummins, 1994). Consequently, a good knowledge of the field favours learners' AL performance, which is not necessarily transferable to another domain. However, because the automaticity and the fluidity of AL production depends on chunking rather than on separate lexical or morphosyntactic units, being familiar with the content makes the process easier (Bygate et al., 2001). Finally, familiarity with content generally increases the fluidity of the performance, but not its accuracy nor its complexity (Bygate et al., 2001).

As a consequence, teachers are concerned that teaching in the AL may slow down content learning and that a low proficiency in the AL may reduce the cognitive complexity of the content. In line with García (2014), we would suggest starting with the learners' IL to access content and help them towards reconstructing it in the language of instruction in school. In a biology course in Morocco, Amina Aberchoum and a team of teachers are experimenting with such an approach, which is the subject of doctoral research. The primary school pupils initially have biology lesson texts in Arabic, which they turn into French by copying and pasting the French elements that have been muddled up in another document. In a second phase, they have to find the adequate French elements in more complex documents. In Phase 3, they are given the lessons in Arabic and have to write them in French. Finally, they are just given the theme and have access to websites to find what they need to write the lesson in French. In Phases 3 and 4, they can use all the information and communications technology (ICT) tools necessary just as in Case 16. So far, the experiment has only reached Phase 3. Training tasks are suggested individually. The teachers involved have found it more difficult to adapt than their pupils who enjoy the collaborative, more active and creative work.

It is also important to take into account that CLIL or CBI courses initially took place in contexts that were favourable to their development, such as immersion classes in Canada or Val d'Aosta (Gajo, 2001), and that the measurement of the effect of contextual variables is necessary before transferring the approach to other locations. Meaningful and culturally relevant content seems to be what counts most, as we will advocate further on, as well as a more learner-centred approach to favour individual or collaborative development (see Chapter 2 for the example of projects in Cambodia and Nepal reported by Sandberg [2017]). Adjunct CLIL (Dalton-Puffer, 2007), where language teachers and content teachers work together to deliver a class, favours the development of the AL in parallel with disciplinary work. The question remains as to whether or not one teacher can ensure the teaching of both content and language.

Multimodality/Multiliteracy

Another important aspect that cannot be disassociated from multilingualism is multimodality (Cope & Kalantzis, 2009). The widespread development of digital technologies and communications media has given rise to multimodal literacy, which is based on 'the affordances provided by gesture, sound, visuals, and other semiotic symbols, including, but not limited to, language' (Cenoz & Gorter, 2011: 340). Where written text was once a 'pervasive source of knowledge and power' (Cope & Kalantzis, 2009: 361), now speech and writing are intertwined with other modes of meaning such as images, diagrams, pictures, icons, video and colour to the extent that traditional boundaries are blurred. For Cope and Kalantzis (2009), this has had the effect of reducing the privileged place of the written textual in Western culture, so that full communication is no longer possible by means of language alone but needs to include visuals and other modes. Specifically, the authors propose a breadth of mixed modes that encompasses written and oral language, as well as visual, audio, tactile, gestural and spatial representations of meaning. At the same time, literacy should be considered as multiple literacy practices that vary across languages and social, cultural and religious contexts.

Research on multiliteracies (Dagenais, 2012; New London Group, 1996) took an ideological and political stance right from the start, moving away from academic literacy to less standardised, less elitist forms of literacy. As practitioners, we are faced with similar phenomena in France and Africa where various examples have shown that starting from forms of literacy closer to the learners' sociocultural environment fosters access to academic proficiency (see case studies of this volume). Similar examples can be found in other contexts, as shown in Haddad (2008) and Sandberg (2017) covering projects in Asia, Africa and South America. The assumption is that because learners start from what they know, destabilisation and rejection can be avoided. Learners can make sense of their environment from a great variety of modes (Dagenais, 2012), so using the modes they enjoy and are familiar with will help them to gradually adapt to the educational and social expectations that they will then be able to understand and accept. This in turn will enable them to deliver a final product that meets external standards initially by alternating or even mixing codes (Bozhinova *et al.*, 2017). Through the social tasks that are part of the multiliteracy approaches, learners meet people from the real world, whether online or face to face, which contributes to making the work they do at school meaningful. As they become actors in their social environment, the needs for training and practicing will emerge from their action.

Taking into account their profiles does not mean that learners should remain as they are, opportunities must be offered for them to go further without giving up their own background knowledge (Marquilló Larruy, 2012). Combined with ICT, multiliteracies shed light on what is possible. The development of critical cognitive skills and technical knowledge and skills is necessary to access, manage, integrate, assess and create information in an environment that is particularly adequate for the development of higher-order capacities (Penloup, 2012). When exposed to ICT, learners from any social origin will have access to different kinds of literacies (traditional or digital). Learning will be made easier due to the resources available and the possibilities for individual and/or collaborative work. Because these are real-life communication situations (Penloup, 2012), learners pay greater attention to how their utterances will be received by their partners, thus triggering a social incentive to comply with standards.

Plurilingualism and Teaching

In such a complex, multilingual world, Ziegler (2013) highlights two main challenges for current schooling contexts and language teachers:

- language is presented as the reified object of teaching and raises cultural and power issues in classroom practices;
- teachers have to deal with learners who are both learners of the language classroom and also plurilingual individuals with their respective linguistic biographies and practices.

As major actors in bringing about change and managing the diversity of today's societies, language teachers have a social and political influence. They have a part to play in fostering collaboration between learners and the co-construction of knowledge with due regard to diversity and multilingualism (García, 2014). Some initiatives show a move away from language teaching for the sole purpose of interpersonal communication. More research is still needed to solve these problems, as well as to see how ICT can be integrated and how the digital divide between learners and language teachers can be resolved or compensated for (Dornisch, 2013). As can be seen, we are now turning to the teachers in order to see how their role and training are affected by the changes.

The Multilingual Teacher's Specific Competence

The language teachers involved in plurilingual education promote 'the ability not only to approximate or appropriate for oneself someone else's language, but to shape the very context in which the language is learned and used' (Kramsch & Whiteside, 2008: 664). As such, teachers will need an understanding of the various resources that a speaker accesses when engaging in talk and interaction, and more specifically, the teacher will need to be sensitive to issues of identity as enacted through language in a multilingual interaction within a specific community or context of speaking.

School, then, 'as a social event' and 'language as a social event' (Andrews, 2006: 53), would take into account the way learners' identities are expressed through transcultural habitus, plurilingual resources and languages. In that respect, participants in language teaching are addressed as agents who resituate, 'inhabit' (Durus, 2009: 7) and 'rehistorizise' (Kramsch & Whiteside, 2008: 667) the resources, which are available to them at any given time, which is in line with what the New London Group (1996) proposes.

Requirements for the Education/Training of Teachers

Our own research has highlighted that, when background and theoretical knowledge is collaboratively co-constructed and mediated (through observation and self-observation), trainee teachers become aware of behaviour and context-induced effects, particularly in international courses (Narcy-Combes & Narcy-Combes, 2014; Narcy-Combes & Xue, forthcoming 2018). Otherwise, it seems difficult to initiate the necessary distantiation. Scholarly knowledge or observation may induce significant discourse changes. However, they do not totally alter practices (Fantognon, 2014). For reasons of face, assessment through self-confrontation is more effective than peer or tutor comments. Teachers' skills are said to be incorporated into action (Lenoir, 2007) when they are not expressed explicitly, but teachers can become aware of what they have been doing when they reflect on their actions. That is why feedback and debriefing are important to prevent incorporated action to prevail unconsciously (Channouf, 2004). A self-confrontation mechanism allows teachers to discover their teaching activity from a different perspective (Cahour, 2014). The discrepancy between teaching and teachers' practice allows us to grasp the breach between the reflectivity of the actor before and after the action and the course of the action that is performed in a largely unconscious way (Cicurel & Narcy-Combes, 2014; Jack et al., 2013; Xue, 2016).

Studies reporting the implementation of language teaching in multilingual regions of the world all point to the need for adequate teacher education. Inadequate training increases the linguistic inequalities between students that eventually leads to situations where some forms of plurilinguism lead to social dominance while others confirm exclusion (see Castellotti and Moore [2010] for Europe and Leconte et al. [2018] for India).

Teaching and the Native Speaker

As highlighted previously (see Chapter 2: The Benefits of Plurilingual Competence), the concept of ideal native competence as a goal has also been challenged by scholars working on 'English as a lingua franca' (Canagarajah, 2007; Seidlhofer, 2007). When English is used as a lingua franca, the norms are no longer those of British or American English. However, in school contexts, the idea that non-native speakers are deficient communicators is still widespread.

The concept of 'incompleteness of L2 acquisition' (Schachter, 1990) and the interlanguage theory (Selinker, 1972) have long sensitised researchers and teachers to the need to adapt their objectives to learners' proficiency by proposing attainable goals. Lamy and Hampel (2007: 59) quote Lemke's view of identity as 'performance', and his opposition to the conventional model of language learners as monoglots seeking to become 'fluent' in an 'idealised L2'. This has now been taken on board by the Council of Europe and the various levels of competence described in the Common European Framework of References for Languages (CEFRL; Council of Europe, 2001). The CEFRL is a testimony to how a unitary language competence leads to language productions that fulfill socially acceptable functions at different levels of attainment and goes against the myth of native speaker usage (Jenkins, 2007). The same position is held in many other regions of the world, but is not always followed by teachers and parents (see Sandberg, 2017, for instance). However, research into plurilingual practices and approaches does not yet answer all the questions raised by AL learning, and some of the older theoretical propositions can still help learners and teachers.

Note

(1) Open Educational Resources. *Multilingualism in the Classroom*. India: Teacher Education through School-Based Support. See www.TESS-India.edu.in and www.open.edu/openlearncreate/mod/resource/view.php?id=64965 (accessed 10 July 2018).

4 Psycholinguistics and SLA: Useful Constructs Revisited

Despite our clear commitment to a plurilingual approach, we believe that some 'monolingual' research has led to results that may still prove productive in setting up tasks in a plurilingual approach if their foundations are reinterpreted.

Action and Interactions in Language Learning

Bertin *et al.* (2010), Karimvand (2011) and Randall (2007) have formulated state-of-the-art papers that serve as a basis for what follows. Psycholinguistic approaches, mainly interactionist, conceive language learning (LL) as a cognitive and individual process in which knowledge is constructed as learners are:

(1) exposed to comprehensible input (Krashen, 1982);
(2) given opportunities to negotiate meaning (Gass, 1997);
(3) receive negative feedback (Long, 1996) pushing them to reformulate their utterance.

There is no agreement on the type of input needed, much less on how such input is processed in order to become acquired (Gass, 1997). As a reaction against Krashen's (1982) input hypothesis, Long (1996) proposed the interaction hypothesis (IH) (comprehensible output), which asserts that manipulation of the input through interaction is necessary for language development. According to Long (1996), input comprehensibility increases as learners interact and use different types of interactional modifications (comprehension checks, confirmation checks and clarification requests) to overcome communication breakdowns.

Long refers to the concept of noticing (Schmidt, 2001) and hypothesises that postmodified input (recast seen as a reformulation of the learner's preceding inadequate utterance) is more effective than premodified input (models of the correct forms taught beforehand) (see Attention in Chapter 1).

Long's interactional theory has common features with studies that described interactive methods for the organisation of exolingual communication to ensure intercomprehension and to support learning. Py (1989) redefined input in interaction and through the notion of intake highlighted that some interactive negotiations, which occur when a misunderstanding arises, are an opportunity for the learner to select and reorganise the input data. In such situations, de Pietro *et al.* (1989) hypothesise the emergence of potentially acquisitional sequences (PASs). Subsequent research hinted that the acquisition effect of negotiations is difficult to verify (Matthey, 1997) as they have only a small place in the discursive activity of learners and are largely limited to solving difficulties at the lexical and grammatical level. This concerns a 'classroom situation' with teacher-led activities. However, other contexts might offer more opportunities for interaction, even if in real-world situations learners are not always in a position to notice the gap or obtain more adapted input through interaction with other speakers of the additional language (AL) through conversational adjustments from their interlocutors. In addition, even if they are not always able to process, analyse and memorise what has been adjusted, there are many cases when they do.

The interactionist theory, as applied in 'classrooms', is what Block (2003: 4) calls 'a technical model of interactions'. Interaction also needs to be analysed in social terms and we will see how this reflection can help us define social tasks, on the one hand, and subsequent training (micro) tasks on the other hand. For Bange (1992), the most favourable situations for AL acquisition correspond to those in which the learners' communicative objectives do not lead them to avoid obstacles, but to seek ways to manage them interactively. This has important implications for task design. Thus, the development of language skills does not depend so much on language itself, but rather on how it is used for social purposes (Vygotsky, 1978), and on the learner's responsibility in the management of discourse (Bialystok, 1993). Respect for the learner's needs and possibilities is the cornerstone for acquisition in interaction (cf. the 'zone of proximal development' of Vygotsky [1978: 86]). If development is a result of frequency of exposure, only immersion, or the very active participation of learners, allows the necessary conditions for triggering the process.

The Information Processing Model

In the information processing model, human learning, in this case learning an AL, is viewed as the gradual construction of knowledge or skills and the ensuing practice that will lead to automatic recall for processing the AL. A distinction is drawn between declarative memory (what is known) and procedural memory (how it is processed) (Anderson, 1995; Randall, 2007). Processing needs to be transferred appropriately and, more particularly, data are best retrieved in situations similar to those in which they were encountered (Blaxton, 1989). This theory may explain some retrieval difficulties when AL data have been introduced in traditional classroom settings and the learners cannot see the connection with real-world activities. The distinction between declarative and procedural knowledge remains frequently quoted even if information processing as a theory has largely been discarded as we will see.

The Dual-Processing System of Language Production in L2 and Formulaic Language

Language production has often been seen as the result of a dual processing system that combines rule-based production, on the one hand, and exemplar-based production on the other. Rule-based production was largely associated with Anderson's (1995) model and Levelt's (1989) model of speech production, whereas exemplar (chunk)-based production was connected with Logan (1990) and the connectionist model (Ellis, 1993). Studies into the effects of formulaic language on AL acquisition led to conclusions that largely correspond to the theory of a dual system of language production (see Wray, 2002). Individuals will select their strategy according to the demands of formulaic sequences and to processing pressures, and the holistic system reduces processing effort. Corpora (oral or written) can help learners acquire these formulae, which can be seen as a way of overcoming the initial difficulties of rule-based production and of increasing the rate of acquisition. They can also be seen as favouring investment by enabling learners to produce more complex language faster. Mitchell and Martin (1997) noted that the early learning of an AL (in the case of French children in British secondary schools) consisted of rote memorisation of unanalysed chunks of language and that children who did not internalise and retain a corpus of phrases of this kind at this early stage were highly unlikely to make any real progress. More specifically, they never moved on from pragmatic communication strategies to grammatical control (Mitchell & Martin, 1997: 23).

Connectionist Models of Language and L2 Competition Model

In these models, the frequency with which learners encounter specific linguistic features in the input and the frequency with which features occur together are of paramount importance. Learners gradually develop their knowledge of a new language through exposure to the thousands of instances of features they hear or see. This knowledge is a network of neural connections between situations and linguistic elements in which the presence of one situation or one element activates complex automated processes (Randall, 2007: 21).

The competition model is closely connected to the connectionist perspective. Each language gives 'cues' that signal specific functions. Languages use multiple cues, the importance of which varies with each language (Lightbown & Spada, 2006: 42). In English, word order will be a major indicator of the relationship between sentence components. Italian and Spanish rely more on morphological markers and French on pragmatic markers. Learners need to be sensitised to the appropriate cues in the language they are learning. This model can help anticipate some working memory and intercultural difficulties.

Psycholinguistic and Sociolinguistic Factors in Multi/Plurilingualism: Emergentism and the Dynamic Systems Theory

Studies in developmental psychology and in psycholinguistics offer a model in which linguistic features and processes emerge from interactions between the children's sociocognitive capacities, their personal characteristics and the specificities of their initial language (IL). What is universal in language acquisition is not a potential innate grammatical module, but a basic sociocognitive operational principle shared by all human beings and involved in learning (McWhinney, 2006). The usage-based or emergentist approach focuses on demonstrating that language can be learned from both input and communicative interaction (Tomasello, 2003) and emerges from interactions at all levels from the brain to society (Ellis, 1998). It emphasises the richness of interactions and argues that language and 'simple learning mechanisms suffice to drive the emergence of complex language representations' (Ellis, 1998: 631).

Plurilingualism in the Connectionist Paradigm

To date, there are few connectionist studies on plurilingualism. Hernandez et al. (2005) developed a competition model of how children can distinguish and build up multiple language systems based on experience. They argue that children are able to construe modular multiple grammars based on the competition between cues and predict entrenchment of units belonging to the different languages to be learned. Ellis (2008) shows that frequency factors account for several aspects of second language (L2) learning as well as language change. He also shows that, for emergentists (emergentism is a connectionist theory), knowledge of the IL results in learned attention to language whereby the processing of the AL proceeds in IL-tuned ways (Ellis, 2008) (cf. nativisation, Chapter 1). The plurilingual's languages and cultural schemata interact, both facilitating and complicating the learning of new languages at the level of forms, concepts and form-meaning mappings (Jarvis & Pavlenko, 2008; Kail, 2015). The more 'similar' these IL forms, concepts and form-meaning pairings are to those in the AL, the easier it may be for AL learners to learn them. However, even slight variations and subtle differences across languages can complicate the development of apparently similar AL forms, concepts and form-meaning mappings. This is in line with assimilation or nativisation (see Chapter 1). These cross-linguistic influences are pervasive, but they are also bidirectional. They are dynamic and variable, rather than deterministic or constant (Jarvis & Pavlenko, 2008).

A Dynamic Framework of Emerging Language

The Complex Dynamic Systems Theory (CDST) of language development is a recent contribution to the field that completes emergentism by relying on the concept of dynamic development over time (Lowie, 2017). Each step in the developing language system depends on the previous state of that system in dynamic interaction with other relevant (sub) systems. However, the development of an AL is not restricted to the combination of predetermined items. It involves establishing complex interrelations between history, context, perception, intention, action and reaction, while attempting to stabilise the result through social action. There is no such thing as specific learning mechanisms, but rather networks that come together based on a logic whose complexity escapes us. This is far from technical thinking (cf. Block, 2003), our rationality is limited and does not escape our history or our emotions.

Lowie (2017) reminds us that in language development, the subsystems (such as phonology, syntax and lexicon) that are most relevant for LL are closely interconnected and their mutual influence may change from one moment to the next. At early stages of language acquisition, syntax may be heavily dependent on lexicon, while at later stages of acquisition, lexical development may require the acquisition of syntactic structures. Similar links can be postulated about the relationship between lexical and phonological knowledge. Development can also be affected by embodied roles and the communicative structure of the interactions (McWhinney & O'Grady, 2015). This explains why language and gestures are strongly interrelated and why body language constitutes an integral part of multimodal communicative interaction (Wehbe, 2017).

For Lowie (2017), the dynamic interaction of subsystems also helps to explain that the different languages in a multilingual language user are interrelated in a complex way as evidenced by translanguaging practices and activation of all the codes, etc. (see above and Grosjean, 1989). Language development viewed through the emergentist lens can be seen as 'a process embedded in the context of language use, and integrated in cognition, the body and the world' (Lowie, 2017: 3), which implies that the effects of context and individual histories have to be taken into account. All this corroborates the highly individual and nonlinear nature of language development. Thus, it is difficult, if not impossible, to generalise about changes for groups of learners over time. This is reflected in emergentist research into dynamic development, which makes notable use of individual case studies (see De Bot *et al.*, 2007; Lowie, 2017).

As a consequence, a high degree of variability is observed in language use and language acquisition (Lowie, 2017). The learner expresses new forms and revises them according to the way interlocutors respond. The amount of variability typically coincides with changes in development. An increase in the amount of variability is commonly followed by a developmental jump (Spoelman & Verspoor, 2010). Due to the learners' limited resources (attention and focus) when one subsystem develops, the other subsystems are affected. Khreim (2008) showed that a long and intensive period of work on how to pronounce English led to renewed problems with grammar accuracy. Variability is necessary for change, while attractor states are a sign that the system is stable. In AL development, attractors are combinations of IL and AL subsystems, in which deep IL-related factors lead to IL-related attractors. This is in line with nativisation (see Chapter 1), even if the process is made more complex with plurilinguals. When a system is responsive to changes in the environment and is adaptable, it is likely to move away from attractors (Lowie *et al.*, 2014). So, variability must not be seen as negative, but as necessary for learning to take place. A great degree of variation shows that learning is going on, while little variation is likely to be connected with an attractor state. Investigating the links with affects would open new avenues. Tasks need to be designed so that learners feel the need to move away from attractor states by letting them see clearly that no change in their development is in some way detrimental to what they aim to do with the language.

Attention in Language Learning

For Schmidt (2001: 3), attention is 'access to awareness' and linked to consciousness. As we saw in Chapter 1, attention is limited and selective. Not all individuals evaluate its cognitive cost in the same way, which determines the attention they will devote to an object or task. Nativisation is an additional problem as learners are not capable of determining what they should pay attention to, hence the need for mediation and metareflection (see Mediation and metareflection in Chapter 4).

Simple grammar rules can be very demanding on attentional resources. Input processing is a matter of attention, in conjunction with what the communication situation highlights, although some associations can be acquired without much apparent attention. The processing is done on the basis of data such as perceptual salience, frequency, continuity of elements and various other parameters. Peer or tutor mediation will counteract the nativisation effects as perception occurs according to individual internal criteria:

- Explicit instructions favour attention: well-designed tasks enable fine-tuned input perception as learners put effort into them.
- Input can be taken up consciously (registration) or unconsciously: The uptake is efficient only in the first case, though this cannot always be feasible.

- Suppression (when the learner does not perceive some data) is a consequence of the more or less conscious selection that the learner operates by eliminating what is seen as not relevant. Mediation is required in this case.
- An AL is gradually developed through rules or exemplars capitalisation and the gradual awareness of the interface between the organisation of language constructions and the input while taking into account the context and the speaker's intention. Then, attention leads to noticing and is key to AL learning. Some task design should include the conditions required for attention to play its role. Those conditions should be validated in the field.

Focus on Form, Focus on Forms and Focus on Meaning

The need to raise awareness of language features for some forms of learning to take place has been justified. This can be done in many different ways that should be validated in the different contexts of use: awareness-raising exercises, recasts of different types and explicit correction with or without explicit reference to grammatical rules. The results of pre-teaching grammar have confirmed the validity of such practices (Randall, 2007). However, LL may gain from avoiding too linear or planned an approach. Moreover, grammar training can help cope with a limited amount of the required operations only (cf. Ellis, 1994: 73–117).

Long (1991), completed by Ellis (2001), described three basic teaching options as follows:

- The first is that learning can be based on meaning. By providing a rich corpus of appropriate language material, learners will acquire the language through use of the material in communicative interaction (Focus on Meaning).
- The second option is that learner output should be used to determine the examples of language form that will help students become more effective. This approach combines meaning and form (Focus on Form: FoF). Planned FoF involves the treatment of preselected forms in activities that focus the learner's attention on meaning, whereas in incidental FoF attention occurs incidentally without prior preselection. Incidental FoF is more flexible and less linear, but important aspects may be overlooked. FoF can be reactive (a problem has arisen in the learning situation) or proactive (when a problem is predictable).
- The last point made by Long (1991) is that learning can be based on the formal study of aspects of the language (FoFs) whereby the forms are presented to the learners either explicitly (teaching the rules) or implicitly (inference exercises).

FoF no longer seems adequate, as it does not correspond to how language development is now understood. However, incidental FoF can help us to understand how to organise some tasks, especially in academic settings, as Focus on Meaning is likely not to be totally effective and as metareflection can help learners if used wisely as we will now see.

Mediation and Metareflection

Seen as any form of interaction that helps learners in their development, mediation requires a metalanguage and access to linguistics or applied linguistics that may not be the best foundation for organising a curriculum or determining course content. Meta-knowledge relies on descriptions of the language that are systemic (linguistics), traditionally called 'grammar', or functional (the notions and functions of applied linguistics). A choice will have to be made in view of what is more appropriate to the learners' needs. What such descriptions offer will help learners understand the link between language and discourse and are likely to make noticing more successful. Well-designed interactive activities will ensure that output reflects the results of this form of training, as we will see in Part 3. Its success, however, depends on how the individual responds to it, bearing in mind that recourse to explicit knowledge in speech production needs to be quick and easy to avoid increasing the cognitive load (Gaonac'h, 2006). Interestingly, research shows that the spontaneous descriptions and interventions of peers are sometimes more successful than the scientific descriptions of the teacher (Rees, 2003). Research on writing (Bozhinova *et al.*, 2017) reveals that accuracy is achieved more easily when learners have all the tools they need at their free disposal.

The positive role of metacognition is unanimously recognised by second language acquisition (SLA) researchers. Roehr (2006) suggests process and experience-based ways to develop it. Learners' metalinguistic knowledge and their L2 linguistic proficiency correlate positively and significantly, even though the strength of the relationship varies between studies. The stability of metalinguistic awareness, regardless of the number of languages known and of the competence level attained in ALs, suggests an interlanguage metalinguistic awareness that transfers from one language to another without being influenced by attitudinal and motivational factors. However, as Cummins (2000) argued, there is no correlation between the metalinguistic skills development level and the final linguistic competence in production. Metalinguistic skills help but are not sufficient (see Motivation in Chapter 5).

Roehr (2006) formulates predictions as to when metalinguistic knowledge in AL learning is operative:

(1) Linguistic constructions that show comparatively systematic, stable and context-independent usage patterns are more amenable to explicit treatment. By contrast, conceptually complex AL form-function mappings will pose greater explicit learning difficulty.
(2) Use of metalinguistic knowledge will have different consequences on AL performance: (a) fluency may decrease, while accuracy and complexity may increase; (b) increased complexity will go with decreased accuracy and fluency; and (c) increased fluency is unlikely to be achieved with high use of metalinguistic knowledge.
(3) Use of metalinguistic knowledge will be related to individual learner differences (cognitive and learning styles, aptitude and working memory capacity).
(4) Use of metalinguistic knowledge and individual differences will be related to learners' affective responses. Analytic individuals are likely to benefit from explicit learning and teaching drawing on metalinguistic knowledge and will feel more comfortable. By contrast, more holistic-minded individuals may experience greater anxiety and will need specific training tasks to help them to cope in a more naturalistic way (Narcy, 1990).
(5) Use of metalinguistic knowledge in AL learning will be related to IL metalinguistic ability.

What was recalled in Chapter 4 can help practitioners to design both macro and micro tasks. The initial monolingual approach can be, and sometimes has been, adapted to plurilingual approaches. If becoming aware of how to express past time in a given language is needed, a complex webquest requiring learners to understand the link between a past event and present-day consequences may raise their awareness and lead them to compare the target language with the other languages with which they are familiar. Some form of more specific training may help learners infer the rules and apply them. Tasks requiring production may then confront them with how well they can handle the problem and when it actually matters to produce discourse that is grammatically adequate.

5 Cultures, Affects and Identities

This chapter will go beyond the individuals, trying to understand what contributes to their social and cultural development, how this affects their language development and, more importantly, who they are and how they act.

Perception

The personal side of action or of any experience is explained primarily by perception. Since action is a response to perceived problems in a given situation, the relevance of the problems will vary according to individuals. As Varela (1993: 30) points out, perception is not a duplicate of the outside world, but rather it 'passes through' the subjects and is dependent on them. We will see how emotions influence perception (see Emotions in Chapter 5). This perceptual functioning is also affected by the language(s) in the repertoire (Tan et al., 2008), which is used to express what is perceived. The paradox is that nothing is strictly social or individual: identity, society and cognition-action cannot be dissociated. Whether the action is collective or individual, two different aspects can be noticed: first, a stabilised or stabilising aspect partly frozen in time by the previously observed actional schemes and, second, an innovative aspect based on personal experiences. This may be complexified in the multicultural circumstances in which learners may feel at a loss. As a consequence, our conception of the cultural construction of individuals has been altered.

Transculturing

Suchman (1987) argues that because action is situated, it should not be separated from its circumstances to be rationally presented. Rather, the way people use those circumstances for intelligent action should be studied. As noted by Quéré (1999: 318–319), 'whoever is familiar with how people think and act in a given culture, their customs and practices, the artefacts they use, the methods and techniques they implement, can immediately perceive the object affordances'. It follows then that it is important for learners to be able to understand the habits of the people in the groups they intend or are forced to join.

After studying the effects of pluricultural experience on thoughts and behaviours, Baena (2006) proposes transcultural analysis as a register of the expansive dimensions of consciousness. By choosing 'transculturing', Baena and her colleagues highlight the importance of the action of transcultural experience on subject formation across an impressive spectrum of possible lexicons – from text to image, food, clothes, music, comics and film. She builds on analyses of experiences of migration or extended travel that follow upon the project of European colonisation, each reflecting some measure of choice, however minimal or subject to external imperatives. In the same line, Dervin (2011), who questions the validity of referring to named cultures only, describes mixed couples and questions analytical stereotypes for identities and cultures, arguing that behaviours, discourses on languages and beliefs are unstable, transient constructions that originate in the complex and varying interplay of cultural influences. In our reflection on multicultural interactions, we align with the researchers who focus on the cultural co-construction of the exchange, in which individual transculturing phenomena will play their part, rather than on interculturality. Interculturality remains at the level of metareflection (Puren, 2002). The level of action is more complex.

Yet, in many areas, such as South Asia, transculturing is put forward by educationalists (Canagarajah & Ashraf, 2013), as languages and cultures are blended. We would follow such practices and wholly agree with these authors when they remind us that this form of education does not reflect the dominant attitude concerning languages and cultures, even if Moore (2010: 322) argues that those phenomena are as old as humanity. Multilingualism has been catapulted to a new world order in the 21st century and a great many people feel threatened. However, today's multilingualism is enmeshed in globalisation, technologisation and mobility. People must learn to negotiate complex demands and opportunities for varied, emergent competencies across their languages. Understanding such learning requires the integrative consideration of learners' mental and neurobiological processing, remembering and categorising patterns, and moment-to-moment behaviours and use of language in conjunction with a variety of socioemotional, sociocultural, sociopolitical and ideological factors. The tasks that will be suggested to learners will have to take this on board, but educational situations are different from encounters in 'real' life, the interplay of emotions will change and due to the role of emotions this may be confusing. We will see that computer-mediated communication (CMC) can offer new situations to meet the demands of multicultural encounters.

Emotions

Emotions and cognition

Contemporary theorists have increasingly rejected the claim that emotion and cognition are categorically different (Damasio, 1994;

Pessoa, 2015) as recent imaging evidence demonstrates the overlap of emotional and cognitive processes in the brain. The distinction between the 'emotional' and the 'cognitive' brain seems fuzzy and context dependent as there is compelling evidence that brain territories and psychological processes commonly associated with cognition play a central role in emotion. Nevertheless, cognition and emotion have been viewed as oppositional forces (Damasio, 1994). Okon-Singer *et al.* (2015), among others, show that stress, anxiety and other kinds of emotion can profoundly influence key elements of cognition, including selective attention, working memory and cognitive control.

Research exploring the persistent effects of emotion on attention (Okon-Singer *et al.*, 2015) shows that emotional distractors disrupt cognitive control and working memory. Top-down attention, based on prior knowledge, plans and goals, is closely linked with working memory. Distracting emotional cues (more or less transient emotions) disturb working memory, which is no longer capable of maintaining the representations of task sets, goals and other kinds of information. Goal-directed attention and guiding behaviour can no longer be sustained (Miller & Cohen, 2001; Xue, 2016). As a result, congruent thoughts and actions are disturbed (Lerner *et al.*, 2015).

Interestingly, anxiety has two distinct effects. The first effect is to increase vigilance and early sensory cortical responses to innocuous environmental emotional stimuli. The second is to disrupt working memory, which may lead to behavioural avoidance because it increases misleading expectations of negative results.

We speak of social emotions insofar as the cultural environment impacts on emotions. De Leersnyder *et al.* (2015), for example, showed that first-generation Turkish immigrants in Belgium were emotionally close to Turkish people in Turkey, whereas second-generation individuals were closer to native Belgian people. Parents who rely on encouragement, affection and appreciation reinforce positive behaviour. Our research will describe targeted interventions with positive mediating styles in order to determine adapted tasks.

Languages and emotions

Emotions are physical phenomena in response to situations in the form of unconscious neural patterns whose early role was to ensure survival through adapted reactions (Damasio, 2003). We traditionally know six basic emotions: anger, disgust, fear, happiness, sadness and surprise. They induce behaviours and reactions that are cognitively or culturally sensitive. They precede and trigger feelings that correspond to an activation of neural networks that will be reactivated, often without the individual's knowledge. Damasio (2003: 138) reminds us that emotions and feelings are interdependent phenomena that can be grouped together under the generic term of 'affects'. Affects comprise a wide range of phenomena including emotions, feelings, moods, abilities and preferences.

What is remembered is not facts, persons and events, but neural patterns associated with these phenomena. These neural patterns form the basis of meaning-making practices that are symbolic (Kramsch, 2009: 70). Feelings result from perception and are lasting. Kramsch (2009) stresses that emotions, and therefore feelings, can be triggered by tiny details and this can create a sense of identity breakdown and discomfort when encountering an additional language (AL), as highlighted earlier by Guiora (1983).

Emotions determine how we manage information and make decisions that will guide our future (re)actions (Narcy-Combes, 2005). Learning an AL also means accepting not being able to rely on our automated guidance (see Ellis, 2008, and Chapter 4). It also affects the ego and requires adapted emotional and cognitive links (Guiora, 1983; Kramsch, 2009). Thus, it is not an emotionally trivial learning experience. Irrespective of their ages, learners are placed in a position of psychological vulnerability as they are required to express themselves with difficulty when they can do so easily in their first language (Horwitz, 1999). Following Guiora (1983) among others, Valdès (1986) determined an acculturation threshold, which implied stable self-esteem as noted in Chapter 2 with projects in Cambodia and Nepal (Sandberg, 2017).

Language teaching is thus conducive to the emergence of emotions through the selected learning methods and contents (Puozzo Capron & Piccardo, 2013). The humanistic methods of the 1970s and research about the affective filter (Dulay *et al.*, 1982) showed an interest (though still limited) in affects (see Arnold, 2000). Educational practices have an impact on emotional states and behaviours. Arnold (2000) argues that grammar-translation methodology reduces learner anxiety, while the communicative approach and the action-oriented approach increase it because personal investment is higher, which is not necessarily an argument in favour of grammar-translation. However, designing learning environments and tasks cannot ignore such facts when new approaches are offered. But such problems will be more complex and more difficult to solve in social life.

Language anxiety in different contexts

Language anxiety is a situation-specific expressed psychological phenomenon (Sevinç & Dewaele, 2016): while levels of language anxiety are typically much lower in the initial language (IL) of speakers who usually communicate in their IL (Dewaele *et al.*, 2008), anxiety levels can rise among those who use another language more frequently. An example would be the case of an immigrant context, where the language of the host society can penetrate immigrants' homes and limit the use of the home language, thus raising their anxiety when speaking it.

A few studies have investigated learners' language anxiety outside the classroom context (e.g. Woodrow, 2006). Similarly, Dewaele *et al.* (2008) reported multilinguals' language anxiety in all their languages in five different situations (speaking with friends, with colleagues, with strangers, on the phone and in public). Strong variations have been evidenced in language anxiety across situations. Multilinguals were found to experience very little anxiety in their dominant and weaker language(s) when speaking with friends, but reported feeling significantly more anxious when speaking with strangers in the language(s) they know less proficiently.

The level of education and gender differences seem unrelated to language anxiety (Dewaele *et al.*, 2008). On the other hand, higher levels of self-perceived language proficiency are often linked to lower levels of language anxiety (Santos *et al.*, 2017). Similarly, frequent use or the gradual increase in the use of an AL has been found to boost perceived competence and self-confidence and lower language anxiety (Dewaele *et al.*, 2008).

Language contact, language anxiety and immigrant context

Language is of central importance to the socioemotional outcomes of immigrant experience, even if the challenges that immigrant communities face in a language contact situation vary across contexts (Canagarajah, 2008) and across value systems underpinned by their culture. Language choice and practices, social and motivational factors, the sociopolitical status of the host country and sociocultural issues such as immigrants' attitudes and their general value system are some of the factors recognised as influential in the cases of language maintenance and shift. These are shown to reflect the psychological, social and cultural processes associated with habitual language use under conditions of intergroup contact (Giles & Johnson, 1987). Heritage language anxiety and majority language anxiety are prevalent in immigrants' daily life, and levels of both forms of anxiety differ across generations and in different daily life situations (Dewaele *et al.*, 2008). The immigrant context thus prompts tension between language pride and language panic. The most insecure social groups are considered to be those with a greater sensitivity towards prestigious linguistic forms, who desire to improve their social situation, especially the lower middle class and females (Labov, 2006). There are prestigious and disparaging forms of bilingualism as was seen in Chapter 3 (Canagarajah & Ashraf, 2013; Castellotti & Moore, 2010).

Raising bilingual children in a largely monolingual environment can be challenging. Education and the mainstream community should help reduce the social and psychological strain of complex negative emotions (e.g. shame, disappointment, frustration, stress and anxiety) that predominate and are not all language related. These are closely linked to perceptions of belonging and intertwined with identity, linguistic or social inequality and with acceptance by the ethnic and the mainstream community. Lack of success is often attributed to lack of motivation, thus blaming the learner for it. Motivation and agency do not just depend on the individual, but also on the social environment as we will now see.

Motivation

Different perspectives on motivation

Reeve (2014) highlights the link between emotions and motivation. There have been many studies concerning motivation in AL learning leading to different descriptions. Dörnyei and Ushioda (2009: 16) distinguished three steps in the historical evolution of this concept, the first two of which have been thoroughly investigated. The first is a socio-psychological paradigm, linked to AL acquisition and involving instrumental and integrative motivation (Gardner, 1985). Learners either see the practical benefits of the AL or want to integrate into a group/culture. The second is a cognitive-situated paradigm, which goes beyond the framework of our discipline and is associated with intrinsic and extrinsic motivation (Deci & Ryan, 2008). This paradigm, inspired by Maslow's (1954) theories, is completed by the attribution theory (Bandura, 2001) and aligns with mastery and performance-orientation theories (Brown, 2009). The third paradigm is linked to identity construction. It also goes beyond AL teaching methodology. The model takes into account the learners' wants, the social pressures imposed by institutions, tutors and key people in the learners' life, as well as the learning experience they engage in (Dörnyei & Ushioda, 2009: 18). Any conflicting points will explain the fluctuation in motivation. Dörnyei and Ushioda (2009) complements his reflection with references to the concept of investment developed by Norton Peirce (1995), that Reeve (2014) and Noels *et al.* (2016) refer to as engagement. Dörnyei *et al.* (2016), as do Mercer and Dörnyei (forthcoming), insist on the importance of triggering engagement in order to sustain initial motivation.

According to Bandura (2001), the most decisive drive for personal motivation is the confidence individuals have in their capacity to influence what they do. Personal beliefs (often implicit) play a decisive role in facilitating or hindering an individual's actions at school or outside school (Ushioda, 2008). So, what is important is to create the conditions for what is meant by motivation, not to measure it or wait for it (Reeve, 2014).

The achievement goal theory can help us to understand some of the conflicting positions. Motivation can be described in terms of two goal types: performance and mastery (Midgley *et al.*, 2001). When individuals desire to increase their knowledge and their understanding of a subject, the goal is mastery oriented (sometimes referred to as learning or task oriented). Teachers often have this goal orientation. Whereas, when individuals focus on demonstrating knowledge or competence or obtaining a reward that will fuel their ego, while sometimes avoiding hard work, the goal is performance oriented (Brown, 2009). Some learners may adopt this orientation towards their work. This will have to be taken into consideration since teachers and learners may have conflicting expectations.

Motives

Reeve (2014) reminds us of the need to understand how the internal processes that give energy, purpose and persistence to behaviours are triggered. A motive is an internal process that, when stimulated by a given situation, activates and maintains action towards a specific goal according to past and present conditions (Reeve, 2014). We can distinguish three types of internal motives. The first pertains to needs relating to conditions that are crucial for life, development and well-being. Maslow (1954) established a hierarchy that is worth reflecting upon in spite of its limitations (Narcy-Combes et al., 2015). The second relates to cognition and focuses on mental phenomena such as thoughts, beliefs, expectations, projects, goals, strategies, evaluations, attributions and the concept of self. The third type of motive is linked to emotions. This generates short flares of adaptive behaviours that direct attention towards the triggering event (see Chapter 5, Emotions).

Reeve (2014: 19) points out that people can harbour a range of different motives at any point in time, which can play a dominant or subordinate role in influencing behaviour. Subordinate motives can become dominant over time. Motives highlight the link between motivation and intention (Reeve, 2014). Specifically, motivation maintains intention during the course of the action. In a school environment, students do not necessarily have any initial intention or desire when asked to do something. This will have to be fostered. This corroborates the link that Bandura (2001) sees between intentionality and agency (see following sections).

External events and social environments

External environmental, social and cultural events can impact a person's internal motives. Social contexts correspond to general situations, a class or a working atmosphere, parental style or a culture that can trigger specific emotions in each case. Individuals often think that the force of their emotion or motivation is due to external events, whereas it arises from a conditioned physiological response (Schultz et al., 2000). Non-threatening mediation is needed to investigate why an inappropriate behaviour has been produced and to analyse the motivational effects of the sociocultural contexts and of the events on learners' motivation.

Motivation in context

Reeve (2014) argues that influence should not be mistaken for motivation. Influence is a social process through which an individual requires another to change his or her behaviour, thought or opinions. Persuasion, respect, conformity, obedience and leadership are all forms of influence. Motivation, on the other hand, is an internal process that gives an individual the drive to engage in and cope with a task.

Fostering learners' motivation implies creating or maintaining a favourable environment, meeting their needs, stimulating their behaviour, engagement and methods, while supporting them. People are motivated when their behaviour has vigour, purpose and is adapted, whereas influence leads people to respond favourably to a specific request and to do what someone else wants them to do, but it may not be as effective. The study of motivation should not lead to manipulating people, but stimulating and strengthening them to develop their commitment, performance and well-being (Reeve, 2014).

In contrast to Dörnyei and Ushioda (2009), Noels *et al.* (2016) propose a different way to connect the various theories. The theory of self-determination emphasises a need for competence, relatedness and autonomy (Deci & Ryan, 2008) and Gardner's (2010) socio-educational model shows that it is primarily integrative motivation that triggers orientation and intensity of efforts and thus commitment or investment, i.e. the degree of involvement of a person in a task (Christenson *et al.*, 2012). Seven aspects of the individual's behaviour reveal the presence, intensity and characteristics of motivation: effort, reaction time, persistence, choice, likelihood of response, facial expressions, gestures and body motion (Reeve, 2014: 14). The motivational process is supported or not by the perceived responsiveness of the interpersonal context to the person's psychological needs and that person's responses to the environment and emotions. Noels *et al.* (2016) confirm the important role of engagement, which research results show to be the most positive predictor of success. This is facilitated when every learner has something to actually do.

Positive reappraisals (providing positive feedback) make learners feel agentic and autonomous (Rogers, 1969). However, this is not sufficient. Self-determination (letting learners do things), agentic engagement (making them responsible) and resilience issued from positive reappraisals are not the only elements. Positive character traits, emotions and institutions are also influential, but traits cannot be easily changed. Language mindsets and beliefs play a significant part and the teacher and the institution should take them into account and measure them. Mediation can influence motivation without the mediator's knowledge. However, those who are in the greatest need of support may not obtain it. Research from the field of medicine (Schwarzer & Knoll, 2007) describes the enabling hypothesis, on the one hand, which assumes that social support enables self-efficacy, and the cultivation hypothesis, on the other hand, which argues that self-efficacy maintains and cultivates social support. The coping efforts of a target person are found to be predictive of the support he or she will receive from a potential provider. This should also be researched in education as teachers might unconsciously be tempted to provide less help to those who need it most.

Socioemotional selectivity, resistance to change and motivation

Socioemotional selectivity, as defined by Carstensen (1995), is also linked to motivational phenomena. The theory postulates that age differences in goals reflect shrinking time horizons. Individuals need to know what benefit they will reap from changing beliefs or behaviours. The older they become, the lower the benefits may look in terms of the efforts required. As a consequence, they may value past beliefs and behaviours unless they see the actual benefits or have some form of distantiation.

Low motivation is often attributed to resistance to change. Duclos (2015) questions the relevance of this construct by arguing that, in the educational field, the construct is not only invalid, but also useless as it gives the wrong impression. For Hall and Hord (2014) change is a process performed by individuals, not institutions, and will be facilitated by taking into account individuals, innovations and context. In fact, so-called resistance to change is the reverse of motivation when circumstances do not appear favourable to individuals. They are not motivated, but others believe they are resisting. Influence may then win, but not always...

Educational activities and motivation

Each discipline can develop pedagogical approaches that move away from teacher-centred collective activities and create the circumstances for learners to be motivated. We will come back to project-oriented teaching (Perrenoud, 1998), problem-solving (Sweller, 1988) and the task-based approach (Bygate *et al.*, 2001). Piccardo (2006) and Bozhinova *et al.* (2017), among others, confirm that working within a project-oriented approach can foster learner motivation and promote a desire for learning that goes beyond a purely instrumental vision of the AL. The learners need to feel in charge and active. This leads us to what turns the learner into an agent.

Construction of the Agent

Agency

'To be an agent is to intentionally make things happen by one's actions', according to Bandura (2001: 2), and this enables people to 'play a part in their self-development, adaptation, and self-renewal with changing times'. For individuals to develop personal agency, what is needed is the interaction between their behaviours, their individual characteristics and the environment. In addition, Bandura (2001) identifies four main skills:

(1) forethought (the ability to imagine, anticipate and plan for the future);
(2) intentionality (to act intentionally);
(3) self-reactiveness (to be able to motivate and control one's own activity);
(4) self-reflectiveness (the ability to reflexively examine one's own actions and thoughts and their consequences).

Concerning language learners, Van Lier (2008: 173–174) defines three features of agency that complete Bandura's definition:

(1) initiative or self-regulation;
(2) interdependence;
(3) a sense of responsibility.

Ushioda (2008) suggests that if students learning a language do not recognise themselves as 'agents' with control over their own motivation, their way of thinking and personal assessment of their own abilities may become negative.

Autonomy

Autonomy is linked to agency. In the study of autonomy within the paradigm of action and responsibility, Little (1991), similar to Freire (1970), stresses the impetus to take control and to do things for ourselves. Autonomy can be defined as a capacity for detachment, critical reflection, decision-making and independent action. However, interdependence is the essential aspect of our condition (Little *et al.*, 2017) and agency is at the level of actions, while autonomy is the psychological capacity that allows it (Little, 1991). This brings us back to Deci and Ryan's (2008) theory of self-determination, which argues that (1) human beings have an inherent tendency towards growth, development and integrated functioning and (2) this tendency requires adequate circumstances. In order to foster agency and autonomy, learning environments will have to empower learners while supporting them.

Identity

Lave and Wenger (1991: 115) argue that 'learning and a sense of identity are inseparable. They are aspects of the same phenomenon'. They also maintain that 'we not only produce our identities through the practices we engage in, but we also define ourselves through the practices we do not engage in' (Lave & Wenger, 1991: 164). Using the Lave and Wenger theory, Norton (2013: 173–187) referred to the concept of identity construction through practices and posited three modes of belonging: engagement, imagination and alignment. For Ellison (2013: 2), 'identity is enacted through social interactions with others and our relationships with them' and '…encompasses the way we think about ourselves'. This is what Lamy and Hampel (2007: 59) have in mind when they quote Lemke's view of identity as performance (cf. motivation). Bakhtin (1981) describes how individual identity fluctuates depending on and within contexts, or within sociocultural perspectives on language learning, which engage with how an 'L2 identity' may be constructed and mediated by language and language learners (e.g. Kramsch, 2000). Agency, autonomy and identity are powerful, multifaceted constructs that should not but often are overlooked.

Conclusion: Speaking as a Specific Situated Action

As we have already seen, individuals faced with the same situation will interpret it in a personal way (perception and emotion). 'In this permanent re-articulation of individual commitments and collective activities, language resources play a predominant role' (Fillietaz, 2005: 173). Discursive exchange allows participants not only to talk about an object or construct linked to the outside world, to follow what other colleagues think and do about it, but also to reflect collectively in order to attain a renewed understanding of a situation. Language is not only ingrained in situations, it determines them. If 'speaking' is an action, it possesses its fundamental characteristics, that is, it must be contextually, socioculturally, historically and personally marked. It is important that this be the case in the 'classroom'.

Communicating involves initially establishing at least one common code, and each language, transmitted from generation to generation through socialisation programmes, has its specificities that distinguish it from other languages (Knight & Power, 2011). Each sociocultural or socio-professional community, faced with the specific context that circumscribes its activities, brings to light its own means of communication aimed at serving the individual's social life (Halliday, 1975). As for the contextual aspect of language action, it can be seen in the understanding and interpretation of discourses that are inevitably inspired by the utterances of other speakers (see Introduction). However, when involved in identical situations, two individuals will not express themselves in exactly the same way (Bronckart, 2004: 17) because of their own history and personality. This will influence how tasks will be designed in order to sensitise learners to the complexity of these, sometimes conflicting, influences.

Communicating in other languages implies meeting speakers of these languages and practicing. However, traditional classroom situations do not necessarily provide enough opportunity for learners to be able to develop the intended competence. Information and communications technology now opens opportunities and there has been much research devoted to its role in language development.

6 The Potential of Information and Communication Technology for Language Learning

In Chapter 3, new learning practices relying partly on information and communication technology (ICT) were discussed. We will now turn to further research and results.

Recognised Benefits of ICT for Language Learning

The personal, linguistic, social and educational potential of technology for language learners has been largely acknowledged. The following list of benefits is drawn from the work of Bertin *et al.* (2010), Lancien (1998), Mangenot (2014, 2017) and White (2003), among others. The benefits should be seen as evidenced in learning contexts that correspond to what has been described in the previous chapters.

- *Self-paced learning.* ICT enables the learner to work either in a synchronous or asynchronous way, thereby facilitating individual time management (Bertin *et al.*, 2010).
- *Active learning.* Learners are more active in front of a computer than when sitting in class (Mangenot, 2002); they are actually doing things, therefore they are more likely to learn (Piaget, 1970).
- *Interactivity.* ICT promotes permanent interactivity (Mangenot, 2001) and customisation of learning without isolating the learner (e.g. Brudermann, 2010; Khalil, 2011).
- *Reduced urgency.* The urgency of decision-making and cooperation can be reduced especially in asynchronous situations.
- *Critical thinking skills.* Learners can access, cross-check and put information in perspective thanks to multicanality (sound, image, text) and multireferentiality, thereby developing critical thinking (Lancien, 1998).
- *Cross-cultural awareness.* Learners need to immediately take into account the effects of the strangeness of the messages in a different

code and come into direct contact with different people in their own world (see Helmling, 2007).
- *Creativity*. ICT brings flexibility and creativity to tasks as learners can create their own tasks (Bertin *et al.*, 2010; Mangenot, 2014) according to their personal objectives. Learners can collect and organise their learning materials following their teachers' instructions while relying on peer mediation, feedback and collaboration if they know how to check the reliability of resources.
- *Development of technical know-how*. Learners develop technical know-how in order to access data available on a given electronic platform.
- *Metareflection skills*. Analysing and reconstructing these data into coherent knowledge or know-how pushes learners to know how to learn and know how to reflect.
- *Needs analysis*. In creative and/or collaborative learning tasks, learners assess their language and learning needs (Bertin *et al.*, 2010).
- *Real-world tasks*. Computer-mediated communication (CMC) enables the implementation of genuine social tasks in a pluralistic context, which justifies the need to use a different language and highlights the potential obstacles (Bertin *et al.*, 2010; Grosbois, 2011).
- *Managing cognitive load*. The computer prevents cognitive overload by managing operations, thereby allowing the learner to focus on what really matters for second language learning (Bertin *et al.*, 2010).
- *Contextualised learning*. ICT changes the nature of tasks by making them more likely to favour contextualised training and at the same time allowing for more complex macro/social tasks (Bertin *et al.*, 2010).
- *Collaborative learning*. In the process, individuals build their own knowledge and fine-tune its management (intrapsychic level).
- *Interaction*. Interactions with so-called 'native' and advanced speakers, as well as peers and tutors, are more effective than teacher instruction not only in linguistic terms, but also in finding collocations and terms that are sociolinguistically appropriate in a given context (DuFon, 2010).
- *Mediation*. The computer is a transmitter of data and teachers are mediators who support learners in the transformation of data into knowledge.
- *Student-centred learning*. The decentred, multimedia character of new electronic media facilitates reading and writing processes that are more democratic, learner-centred, holistic and natural (Warschauer, 1999).
- *Building cooperation and citizenship*. ICT favours the role of school as a place where everyday matters are explained and accounted for, a social melting pot, a cultural resource centre for critical thinking, cooperation and the building of citizenship (Tricot & Amadieu, 2014).

- *New pedagogical practices*. ICT helps not only to renew pedagogical postures, but also to change practices towards theoretical models that complement each other (Brodin, 2002).

However, despite these favourable characteristics, Annoot (1996) cautioned against the somewhat exaggerated expectations that ICT arouses and Meirieu (2015), among others, emphasises that there are always drawbacks to using technology including fake news, constant connections and manipulation, and clearly some practices that replicate approaches that have largely been abandoned (cf. pattern drills, etc.).

We are now going to deal with the research concerning learning practices and environments that ICT makes possible.

Informal Learning

Informal learning (including online informal learning, e.g. Kusyk & Sockett, 2013; Sockett, 2012, 2014; Toffoli & Sockett, 2015) is an emergent process linked to a communicative intention that (1) does not follow a fixed schedule, (2) is not part of an organised learning activity and (3) where learners are not necessarily aware that they are learning. This is in line with Tissot's (2004) argument that learning results from everyday activities linked to work, recreation and family life, and with the European Union's definition that individuals might well be unaware that those activities contribute to their knowledge development. In contrast, Cross (2006) characterises informal learning as an intentional activity aimed at the development of specific professional skills through networking activities. The concept of incidental learning (Hulstijn, 2002) is useful to describe the nature of the phenomena, which Larsen-Freeman and Cameron (2008), among others, suggest calling 'development' rather than learning.

As an example, a study by Toffoli and Sockett (2015) found that many students in France are often in contact with English through viewing television series, listening to music and social networking (see also Chapter 10: Case 9 on Tunisian TV viewers). The effects can be felt in lexicon development and the increased use of language chunks acquired in informal contexts (Sockett, 2014). A recent report by the European Commission (2012) confirms that informal contact with a language plays a key role in its acquisition. It is therefore important to consider how institutions can evolve to take this into account in order to set up learning environments that remain relevant in a context where the learner can interact in the private sphere with other users of the languages learnt and obtain diversified resources that they can access through personal tools. Nevertheless, we have seen that there is a need for mediation, which can be catered for by meeting teachers in a physical or virtual resource centre, or during 'classes'.

Coroama (2013) has shown in a Romanian context how an approach based on the awareness of the relevance of resources and strategies used in informal and non-formal environments is likely to enhance student performance in additional language (AL) learning. She highlights the importance of the relationship between the different modes of language teaching and learning when they do not have the same status. This is in line with the ecological theory (Van Lier, 2004), which argues that a fourth environment (informal) would favour the synergy of resources and strategies. Multilingual environments provide great opportunities for informal learning that can be connected to work at school (see www.TESS-India.edu.in and Gorter [2015] for instances, respectively, in India and in the Basque country, or Khalil [2015] for Morocco).

Open Educational Practice

Open educational practice (OEP) (e.g. Zourou, 2016 online) is a result of a global open education movement that advocates increased access to and support for educational resources and learning opportunities. OEP has attracted growing interest from several types of stakeholders (practitioners, researchers, policy makers, public and private players). The key features of social networks, as summarised in Musser *et al.* (2007), are user participation, openness and network effects, which have led to their expansion in the field of OEP. However, Zourou (2016, online) notes that while social networks trigger user interaction, this is 'counterbalanced by issues regarding ownership, visibility across networks and their implications for identity construction'. In order for social networks to play a part in learning and disseminating OEPs, users need to create a community of practice to show each other how to adapt and use open educational resources (OER). This can obviously occur in multicultural and multilingual contexts and can be linked to the institutional learning environment in very much the same way as informal learning (see www.TESS-India.edu.in for language teachers in India, for instance).

ICT and Computer-Mediated Communication

ICT and project-based teaching

Project-based teaching (e.g. Perrenoud, 1998, among others) and problem-solving approaches (e.g. Sweller, 1988), as well as task-based language teaching (TBLT), based on collaborative group work are learner centred. They provide ways of learning by exploiting social documents available on the internet. Piccardo (2006) argues that this type of work can be enhanced by ICT use, which enables pair and small group work. The teachers then become partners who give advice and guidance. The following consequences ensue when designing the learning environment:

- respect for individual history and personality within their cultural environment;
- cultural/cognitive co-construction/distribution of knowledge;
- nonlinear experiences and developments;
- unpredictable individual development.

This aligns with the reflection on multiliteracies (New London Group, 1996) and the reflection concerning webquests (e.g. Catroux, 2006). Piccardo (2006: 32) argues that creation is the 'faculty – intrinsic to human nature (Vigotsky 1972) and capable of improvement – of rich and original reproduction, of personal restructuring of concepts and data, of autonomous non-banal use of every element of a different nature (text, and dissociation), all within a context of pleasure, humour and games'.

Collaborative writing and wikis

Writing is a production activity where creativity requires active involvement on the part of any actor concerned (Piccardo, 2016). It is a process that takes place over time and allows learners to work at their own rhythm, to plan ideas, to produce successive drafts, review them individually or collaboratively and revise them. Tutoring, digital tools and resources, as well as collaboration and interaction with peers or initial speakers of a language, need to be organised coherently within the learning environment in order to foster the gradual improvement of written production, awareness-raising, creativity and the empowerment of learners (see Bozhinova *et al.*, 2017). Piccardo (2006), among others, concludes that the computer not only supports the writing process through its structuring flexibility, multicode expression and the flexibility and ease of writing that it allows, but it is also a source of authentic resources, a tool for image, sound and word processing and a means of communication; it is perfectly adapted to the creative process.

A wiki is an asynchronous web-based environment where learners can collaboratively create, add, modify, delete and edit text at any time while the activity history is tracked by the system. Wiki use has been found to improve the efficiency and cohesiveness of group work (e.g. Clougherty & Wells, 2008) and the quality of interactions between students in a group (Kuteeva, 2011). In addition, the giving and receiving of peer feedback via a wiki helps some students to begin a process of self-reflection and critical thinking new to them (cf. Bozhinova *et al.*, 2017). Research also shows that the standard of students' writing during wiki collaboration improves in all areas because of students' increased awareness of a peer audience that gives social legitimacy to the work (Kuteeva, 2011).

As wikis encourage critical thinking and self-reflection, they connect with constructivist theories of learning. However, the successful employment of wikis to catalyse the move from 'knowledge representation' to 'knowledge construction', as Morley (2012) argues, requires careful guidance or scaffolding by the tutor and peers (Narcy-Combes & Xue, forthcoming 2018). Google Docs and similar tools may prove more adequate in institutional blended courses. Zhou *et al.* (2012) suggest that Google Docs holds potential for out-of-class collaboration and can influence students' perceptions of group work in particular. In their study, students' responses were overwhelmingly positive with respect to the influence of Google Docs on their collaborative experience. The authors also noted that students adjusted their means of communication to use the tools they found most effective for collaboration, relying less on traditional tools such as email, text messaging and Facebook in favour of increased use of Google Docs.

Unlike traditional transmissive practices in which learners merely listen, collaborative writing (e.g. Google Docs, Framapad, wikis, blogs and webquests) improves comprehension of the content that learners read. This comprehension is assessed by producing written material, so learning that involves writing has an advantage over learning that merely involves listening or reading. Self-generated material has also been shown to be easier to remember (Slamecka & Graf, 1978). Editing a wiki makes the course material personally relevant, another factor that has been shown to enhance memory for study items. Such an approach is in line with a 'constructivist' approach to education (Bruner, 1966) and easily opens the door to flipped or inverted pedagogy without necessarily going as far as flipped schooling (see e.g. Knewton, 2017). Indeed, as lectures and private study provide access to the information and content covered by a course, the use of a wiki to further collect and organise information on course topics could augment students' understanding (Slamecka & Graf, 1978).

Wiki-based (webquest) courses place the responsibility for collecting and structuring information about the topic on the students, who actually do something instead of passively attending to a lesson (Narcy-Combes & Narcy-Combes, 2014). Successful collaboration, however, is not always achieved through wiki use. There is some evidence that difficulties arise when students present different levels or different kinds of wiki participation. Wheeler *et al.* (2007) document various phenomena linked with wiki writing (among them, what is called 'social loafing', where some students hardly contribute at all, while others write and edit their own pages, without attending to the contributions of others or are over-reliant on tutor assistance). However, Bozhinova *et al.* (2017), among others, show that, when used with adequate preparation, mediation and support, collaborative writing leads to interesting results.

Speaking

Lin (2015) reports that the ever-growing interest in the development of AL oral proficiency in CMC has resulted in a large body of studies looking at both the direct and indirect effects of CMC interventions on the acquisition of oral competences. They reveal that CMC produced a moderate positive effect on AL learners' oral proficiency compared to face-to-face communication or no interaction. Furthermore, CMC has a roughly similar effect on pronunciation and at the lexical and syntactic level of oral production. However, it might have a negative impact on fluency and accuracy. It was also found that the effect of CMC on oral proficiency depends on several methodological factors such as task type, outcome measurement, treatment length and assessment task. Major findings include that the benefits of oral practice depend on the nature of the tasks, for instance, the most popular task employed by researchers, opinion-exchange, produced the smallest effects in terms of language development, but it still makes it possible to encounter new people and understand what speaking an AL is really about.

Defining Telecollaboration and Its Scope

The development of telecollaboration projects in language learning has coincided with the expansion of ICT use around the world. Helm (2015: 197) defines telecollaboration as 'the practice of engaging classes of geographically dispersed learners in online intercultural exchange using Internet communication tools for the development of language and/or intercultural competence'. Learners work on a task collaboratively, generally in tandem with a partner speaking a different initial language (IL) and living in a different country. Solidarity and role reversibility are at the basis of the eTandem learning model (O'Rourke, 2007), which was initially seen as two successive monolingual activities. The participants, in turn, construct two roles throughout the conversation exchange depending on which language is spoken: the role of the learner in the AL and of the expert in his or her IL. Tandem learning (e.g. Helmling, 2007) is also based on mutual assistance, learner commitment and learner motivation following the principles of reciprocity and autonomy. The task is carried out via video and audio conferencing and other collaborative tools such as forums, wikis and blogs in a synchronous or asynchronous way. The aim is twofold: (i) to enhance AL performance via interactions with native speakers of the target language and (ii) to contribute to the development of learners' cultural competence and awareness via the cultural negotiations that are necessary to bring the task to a successful completion together. Telecollaboration may involve related languages, as is often the case in European projects (Chazot, 2017; Vlad, 2017), or distant languages such as French and Chinese, for example (Cappellini & Rivens Mompean, 2013; Cappellini & Zhang, 2013; Wang et al., 2013).

However, English is clearly the dominant language for exchanges and is the focus of much of the literature on telecollaboration (Helm, 2015), either because it is the language that learners need to acquire, or because it serves as a lingua franca between speakers of other languages (e.g. Liaw & English, 2017).

Most projects are aimed at intermediate or advanced students either in high school or at university, as Schenker (2017) shows. However, in her own research involving tandems of beginner learners of German in the USA and advanced learners of English in Germany, students' positive attitudes and desire for further telecollaboration projects, as well as their stronger interest in learning German, led to the suggestion that telecollaboration should indeed be integrated into beginner language classes.

O'Dowd (2016) notes the increased use of videoconferencing technology in telecollaborative learning. Videoconferencing studies have revealed increased levels of communication between students. Tandems can lead to positive learning outcomes, including the development of different communication strategies and increases in speaking proficiency. Oral proficiency improvements may in fact be higher than after regular face-to-face classroom communication and learners develop their interactive and pragmatic skills, even though the pressure of the immediate communication situation can result in unsuccessful task completion and fewer instances of negotiation of meaning. The importance of well-designed tasks, network training and carefully selected partners for a videoconferencing project is underlined, but students with less advanced language skills may struggle to understand their partner.

Much research has been dedicated to exploring the unique affordances and differences of text-based and voice-based asynchronous and synchronous CMC. In text-based CMC projects, a lack of oral or visual cues can hinder the flow of communication and trigger phonological problems as, for instance, inwardly the learners are likely to misinterpret the graphemes (see Grosbois, 2006). Studies (e.g. Nishihori, 2011) have shown that CMC can enhance student engagement, especially when using video-chat, and that students do in fact negotiate for meaning and form, making it a potential environment where language learning can take place.

Conclusion

ICT has been shown to offer a wide range of opportunities in terms not only of learning, but also of social encounters. Its effects have been much researched. Clearly, the theoretical choices and practical applications explain the effects, not the technology itself. Our study of various learning environments will confirm these results, but they will also show how important it is to take the context into account, as it is often more complex than initially anticipated.

7 Context

Introduction

The aim of this chapter is to highlight the complexity of defining and analysing context. We will examine the epistemological and ethical problems that are raised, as well as propose a framework of indicators to help shed light on the case studies that follow in Part 2. Hymes (1972: xix–lvii) noted that 'the key to understanding language in context is to start not with language but with context... [and then to] systematically relate the two'. He stressed that knowing what takes place outside the school setting is necessary in order to understand what happens inside. Since then, the importance of the learning context has been debated in second language acquisition (SLA) research with two coexisting positions (Collentine & Freed, 2004), exemplified in the famous Long vs. Firth and Wagner cognitive-social debate (see Seidlhofer, 2003). However, even Long gradually came to reluctantly recognise that a totally cognitive approach to SLA was inadequate: 'researchers recognise that SLA takes place in a social context, of course, and accept that it can be influenced by that context, both micro and macro. However, they also recognise that language learning, like any other learning, is ultimately a matter of change in an individual's internal mental state' (Doughty & Long, 2005: 6). There has been a shift from teaching the code to learning usages of the codes (Blanchet *et al.*, 2008). Consequently, language learning is now generally seen as an extension of, rather than existing independently of, cultures and experiences. As early as 1991, the role of context in language learning was also problematised in two different ways. Galisson (1991) did so in terms of learning environments, while Kramsch (1993) described language as culture in which context played a part. She argued that learners' perceptions of self had to be made conscious and valued in order to highlight cultural differences, and an intercultural situation was conceived as a culture in its own right (see Chapter 5).

Definitions

Context

Context refers to a plurality of things. It consists of all the situational factors that are pertinent to understanding language (and learning) behaviour if we refer to Hymes (1972), but it can also be more practical and refer to the everyday environment of the learners and of the teaching institution. Leplat (2001), for instance, describes (a) *external context*, which includes the physical and social conditions of the activity. It covers various and complex situations and objects, is constrained by time, technology, history, culture and how it is organised. It also depends on a complex interaction of individuals; (b) *internal context*, which is related to the subjects' representations of the external context and the various competing beliefs and values at play in the global activity (individual and group histories, former knowledge and practices, experiences and attitudes, especially to the activity).

To contextualise

To contextualise is an ambiguous verb. Merriam-Webster (http://www.merriam-webster.com) defines it as (a) placing something (such as a word or activity) in a context or (b) thinking about or providing information about the situation in which something happens. In French (Jeannot-Fourcaud *et al.*, 2014), the verb means (a) adapting something to a given context or (b) taking this context into account (studying it and trying to understand it) before starting an activity.

In both languages, as far as this study is concerned, we will select the (b) option. We will also have to determine how we assess the pertinence of a specific aspect of context, how it impacts a situation and also who and why a specific aspect of context is pertinent to (the learners, the teachers, the institution, etc.).

As far as we are concerned, taking the context into account will be directed towards two types of objects: (a) setting up learning environments and practices and (b) monitoring such environments to detect unfavourable effects. Taking the context into account in setting up learning environments implies paying attention to its specific characteristics that reflect a complex and dynamic historical, political, ideological, economic, cultural and educational background. The mere application or adaptation of preconstructed elements from another part of the world (Jeannot-Fourcaud *et al.*, 2014) will not suffice since too superficial an analysis may not be sensitive enough to the fact that its author's point of view is necessarily reflected in any description (Castellotti & Moore, 2008). Such an analysis may result in stereotypical descriptions of the characteristics of the context without revealing its complexity and dynamic nature.

Contexts and situation

The constructs of context and situation are often connected (Blanchet *et al.*, 2008), but situation is more limited in scope. Following Cuq (2004), it refers to:

- The unit of reference in a communicative approach (communication situation) (see Hymes, 1972).
- The unit of reference of didactic analysis (learning situation) describing external data (place, time, etc.) and internal data (mental and physical condition of the learners, their motivation, their history and educational background, their attitudes to languages and language learning, etc.).
- The specific group/classroom situation and how teacher, learners and contents relate.

Context is more inclusive. It goes beyond the learning environment (course materials, lesson or sequence, teacher/learner relationship, classroom, school) and includes the global sociolinguistic, cultural, social, even economic and political, environment while including didactic and pedagogical parameters that reflect the global environment (Porquier & Py, 2004: 58–64).

Interestingly, context-based approaches have also been put forward in other fields of education and go beyond what Cummins (1984) calls context-embedded input/language education, which reflects context as described by Hymes (1972) and Kramsch (1993). Context-based education is an approach to education in science or other disciplines that aims to further the interest of students in science and to connect the concepts studied in national curricula to everyday life (de Putter-Smits *et al.*, 2013). Such programmes aim to facilitate disciplinary development, which traditional concept-based education may hinder by being too abstract (Jeannot-Fourcaud *et al.*, 2014). In context-based approaches, contexts and applications of science are used as the starting point for the development of scientific knowledge as they are closer to the students' experience (de Putter-Smits *et al.*, 2013). It is not the aspect of context we are dealing with in this chapter, but we cannot overlook it as its link with context as described by Hymes (1972) and Kramsch (1993) is obvious and as it may also prove a useful approach in content-based language learning (Content and Language Integrated Learning [CLIL]).

Why Context Should be Taken into Account

Epistemological, social, theoretical and methodological arguments support the need for taking context into account. Ideological arguments are equally important, as highlighted by Freire's (1970) *Pedagogy of the Oppressed* or Bourdieu (1966), who stressed the role of schools in reproducing the values of the dominant groups or maintaining cultural, social and economic inequalities instead of recognising the richness of diversity. Languages and power are related (Bourdieu, 1966) and, beyond the learners' personal comfort, the recognition of their language(s) has enormous democratic and social implications. Studies in the French-speaking sphere of influence (Blanchet *et al.*, 2008) have shown that the personal, local and national sociolinguistic context is often analysed and dealt with in political terms (language policy), but not at the level of classroom language education. This creates contradictory, sometimes conflicting, demands and practices. We can assume that this may be the case in other parts of the world. As far as their education is concerned, there is a need for understanding how speakers of various languages fare in the social, economic and political context of a given community, as shown in Haddad (2008) and Sandberg (2017) for South East Asia, Africa and South America.

We need to be aware of curriculum standards, achievement expectations, programmatic requirements, other policy directives and the various social agencies that serve children. Moreover, it is also wise to remember that schools are nested within their external environment, which includes parents, the community, its economic situation and its values.

At the meso level, Bascia (2014), among others, reminds us that schools are complex, dynamic systems that influence students' academic, affective, social and behavioural learning. A culture of respect and appreciation for diversity within the school can also support parental involvement. School contexts affect the quality and degree of students' learning and potential outcomes, but schools do not have sole responsibility for enabling all these learning outcomes for students. Home and community contexts contribute significantly to students' schooling experiences and their learning outcomes. Deakin Crick *et al.* (2013) note that practices in the classroom and across the school provide vital learning opportunities and developing environments. They mention extracurricular activities, such as clubs and sports, as sites of students' informal learning, where they come in contact and interact with teachers and peers and develop skills that complement their academic work.

At the micro level, the classroom context includes much more than the teacher's instructional practices. The quality of life in the classroom is of great importance to students. Creating an atmosphere in which diversity is respected and individual differences are appreciated contributes to student success and resilience.

A substantive body of research shows how significant progress may result from sometimes minor changes in the context, including teacher training and education. Reviews of this area are provided by Chen and Baker (2010), Kay (2011), Marchive (1997) and Xu (2010). However, Collentine and Freed (2004) put forward arguments that sensitise us to the limitations of all endeavours to 'improve' learning practices, reminding us that in the long run everything depends on the learners. The analyses of these authors may be summarised as follows:

- Kay (2011) explored the influence of the introduction of web-based learning tools (WBLTs) on student attitudes and learning performance. Survey data about attitudes and quasi-experimental data on learning performance were collected from 832 middle and secondary school students. Contexts in which a WBLT is used influence student attitudes and learning performance. However, teacher guidance may provide the necessary scaffolding and focus needed for students who are not yet able to guide their own learning.
- Xu (2010) identified changes in language learners' motivational profile after they experienced a fundamental change from an English as a foreign language (EFL) to an English as a second language (ESL) setting. They seemed to have a stronger desire to integrate with the target language community and appeared to invest more effort in their language learning to enable this integration. They were also more satisfied with the learning outcomes. Immersion programmes are meaningful in developing integrative motivation.
- Chen et al. (2005) also report that in many EFL countries, particularly in some Asian countries, exam measures generally focus more on reading and writing skills instead of listening and speaking skills. When exam measures emphasise more spoken communication and social interactions, the required training will develop rapidly, and success in such an exam will bring socially valued results. However, in Leconte et al. (2018), we also see that testing in some Asian countries has gone against the communicative aspect of language learning.
- Marchive (1997) shows that peer interaction notably changes learning processes leading to more favourable results.
- Collentine and Freed (2004) show that there is no clear-cut superior methodology or instructional technique that facilitates acquisition, even if techniques that emphasise meaningful language use are more commensurate with what psychologists know about how the brain internalises new knowledge. There is a growing suspicion about the inadequacy of a theory of SLA that does not accommodate both the role of cognition (psycholinguistic principle) and general-problem faculties, and the variables defining the learning context.
- Collentine and Freed (2004) also claimed that studies provide no evidence that one context of learning is uniformly superior to another for all students, at all levels of language learning and for all language skills (impact on second language learning of the primary learning contexts available to American students). Contexts foster development very much in relation to who the learners are and

how they respond to the situations. Cultural features may hinder development.
- Collentine and Freed (2004) argue that intercultural sensitivity (e.g. the degree to which a learner is ethnocentric) can have important positive and negative ramifications for the efficacy of a host-family experience abroad, for instance, which in turn affects the extent to which the learner identifies culturally and linguistically with the named culture that the host family represents.

Important insights about the effects of the learning context on SLA have also originated in research on uninstructed learning outside the classroom (see informal learning, Khalil, 2015; Sockett, 2014).

Context Indicators

Context is often described as a dynamic, interactive whole, negotiated by all participants who should agree in their objectives and the various roles they play in it (e.g. Cambra Giné, 2003: 53). Developing the ability to take it into account will be a long and complex process. In spite of appearances, context is not an *a priori* element that participants/researchers must describe. The dynamic nature of context means that it will emerge from the description of the interactive processes that it encompasses, from the understanding of these processes as they are described and from the positions that are taken.

A systemic perspective leads us to postulate that a complex description will be more adapted to understanding the social and human characteristics of learning contexts. Table 7.1 runs the risk of leading the reader to believe that a microscopic analysis will help understand the mechanistic rationality of the context, while they are in fact aimed at sensitising the reader to the complexity of the whole. The more or less stable interplay of all the elements at the various levels is eventually what matters and must be understood in order to see the impact on every individual participant and what can be adapted at each level, for all and every single participant.

In determining context indicators, we will adopt the education system levels as described by Beacco *et al.* (2010) and the Douglas Fir Group (2016):

- international (supra);
- national/regional (macro);
- school (meso);
- class, teaching group or teacher (micro);
- or even individual (nano).

Only macro, meso and micro contexts will be considered here and their associated context indicators, as illustrated in Table 7.1.

Table 7.1 Context indicators

Level	Context indicator
Macro	Social determinations (language and education policies, school and university systems). Implies understanding of the sociolinguistic and sociopolitical context and the status of the various languages and their power relation. Top-down and bottom-up decision-making at the level of the state, the institution, the teaching community, the family and the learner. Organisation of teaching institutions (public, private, commercial), differences in levels of education of the different types of learners, curricular aims, social demands, free or instructed teaching methodologies, teacher training.
Meso	Organisation of teaching institutions (see above). Organisational structures (policies, rules and norms, handling of infractions of norms, infrastructure, facilities, resources, supplies, scheduling). School climate and safety (physical and social-emotional safety, tolerance, discipline policies). Interpersonal relationships (respect for diversity, engagement, social support, school connectedness, shared decision-making, administrative support, community involvement). Nature of professional development (is it systematic and continuous?). Principal's role and leadership in respecting and fostering teacher professionalism, sharing decision-making, articulating a clear and compelling vision (concerning achievement, respect and care) and in modelling and supporting ongoing professional learning and experimentation. Teachers' perception of their role (transmission of knowledge and/or actor in sharing the language/s and cultures). Teaching and learning practices (opportunities for teachers to experiment and learn, support for professional collaboration, instruction and assessment policies, opportunities for students' social, emotional, ethical, intellectual and civic learning). Teacher communities. Teachers' participation in professional learning communities. Teacher–teacher relationships. Teachers' available time for common academic planning. Teachers' individual and collective assumption of responsibility for student learning. Connections between collective and individual dimensions of action. Teachers' use of data to support educational decision-making. Availability of and student participation in extracurricular activities.
Micro	Connections between collective and individual dimensions of action. Learner/s, teacher or tutor. Group (class)/grade or level. Organisation of the space/floor plan. Equipment, technology and problems experienced (minor vs. major). Time (duration of class/course, etc.). Effect of weather conditions on individual learning (heat, etc.). Language/s, discipline/s/, culture/s. Use of other languages (which and what for?). Respective role, status and perception of these language(s). Influence of learners' level of learning and competence on use of the different language(s). Link between learning and students' lives. Variety of teaching methods used. Respect for different learning styles and individual differences. High expectations for all students. Systematic use of formative evaluations. Setting and monitoring of objectives and provision of feedback by teachers. Opportunities for classroom participation. Consideration for social and emotional learning. Positive student–teacher and student–student relationships. Systematic classroom management strategies. Nature and consistency of disciplinary strategies. Lesson plan format (teacher led vs. student based). Collaboration (pairs vs. individual).

Source: Adapted from Bascia (2014).

What is evident from Table 7.1 is the multidimensional nature of the concept as well as the interrelationships and overlap between the different levels and factors. Some indicators apply to all levels:

- daily use of the language(s) which influences how the language(s) can be learnt;
- connection between the learning situation and the social environment;
- homoglot/heteroglot situation;
- links between institutional and natural, guided and informal learning;
- time constraints (daily, permanent, occasional contact with the language(s)).

The various factors that make up the school as an organisation and their influence on classroom teaching and learning have been conceptualised in the literature in a number of ways, but are not well reflected in the list of indicators in Table 7.1. The interactions and relationships between the different factors are complex and indicators often reduce these processes to a single item, which masks this complexity. Failing to attend to the interactivity of various school characteristics can lead to the use of a checklist of items that schools may strive to incorporate with less attention paid to the relevance of those items to their particular milieu (Bascia, 2014).

Instead of visualising three levels, we should imagine a complex and dynamic interplay of networks with people and objects necessarily participating in the activities of more than one network. It is important to remember that every learning situation is a world in itself and that no two language histories will be similar (Cambra Giné, 2003: 3). School context research (Bascia, 2014) has revealed that contextual factors function differently for different members of the school community:

- teachers are more sensitive to classroom-level factors and students to school-level factors such as student–staff relationships;
- students have different expectations concerning their teachers and the relationship they wish to have with them;
- differences are noticeable between schools in the interactions among school-level factors.

Validity of the Construct

The complexity of determining the context should be a reminder that it is a construct whose existence and influence we postulate but cannot actually prove (see social construction of reality, Berger & Luckmann, 1966). We should at least bear in mind that we cannot identify every element nor assess how people are affected by them. Context in itself has no influence. It is a construct often given human attributes and power and is an instance of personification (Blanchet *et al.*, 2008). However, like any construct, it is not endowed with any power, the humans involved actually respond to what we call contextual conditions as they can, and this is what alters the conditions.

Context variations will be constantly noticed. In spite of what has just been mentioned, we may postulate that some features will remain stable while others may change quickly due to decisions or changes at one of the three levels.

Universal Values and Local Contexts

Human beliefs/representations and behaviours are all situated and can only be understood in the contexts where they develop, sometimes paradoxically and chaotically (LeDoux, 2003). What is common to all human beings, with individual specificities, is neurophysiological (LeDoux, 2003). Biological constraints and characteristics, and common points or tendencies will be studied by thoroughly comparing the various situations in their historical, social and human dynamics (Blanchet *et al.*, 2008). Analysts should be cautious of the underlying influence of some constructs seen as universal: the primacy of communication, Western values, superiority of some languages or culture, etc. (Huver, 2015). This is exemplified by the present influence of the Common European Framework of Reference for Languages, which has sometimes been used to justify transfers to other areas in the world based on the supposedly universal value of this instrument without taking the contexts into account. Multilingual language education should be seen as social action reflecting an understanding of local ideologies and fostering personal distantiated educational and human developments.

How to Understand Contexts

Data on school context can be collected through a variety of methods, including focus groups, observational protocols, interviews, town hall discussions and surveys (Bascia, 2014; for descriptions of the various tools, see Dörnyei [2007] for example). Any approach should include students, teachers, staff and parents, and should assess the full range of features that shape student and educator experiences of the school context. This corresponds to what Lewin advocated as early as 1947. Since field research and construction of knowledge adapted to a context implies sharing the work with participants, action research may be conducted, for instance, and has been used in various ways since Lewin (1948). MAG (*Méthode d'analyse en groupe*: group analysis of data; Van Campenhoudt *et al.*, 2009) is an interesting approach for including participants in the analysis of data. This is often practiced in pilot projects in areas where language education is problematic, for example Nepal, Cambodia and Laos, as reported by Haddad (2008) and Sandberg (2017).

Chini (2002) reminds us that most of the information obtained will be beliefs or representations (internal context) that will have to be constantly confronted with the ways the context operates or the people behave (external context). Self-confrontation may prove useful. Understanding representations and discussing them are essential since they will influence learning and teaching practices as well as using these languages in the broader social environment.

When proceeding (see Bascia, 2014):

- At the micro level, data should be collected not only about students and teachers, but also learning and teaching practices. It is important to rethink what information is necessary to collect directly from students and other members of the school community and what information can be collected through passive approaches.
- At the meso level, in addition to traditional tools, the potential of collecting and processing non-traditional sources of data, including administrative records from various sources and social networks, should be examined. This data collection may extend to non-school contextual settings for the student, such as family or out-of-school activity and to postsecondary and adult enrolment in schools, courses and training, as well as sources of informal learning.
- At the macro level, new technology has resulted in an ever-changing landscape for possibilities and costs of data collection. Exploring innovative approaches to survey methods that use newly available technology and possibly involve cooperation of respondents should be considered.

Determining context indicators and their effects can thus be carried out in many ways. One risk is to filter only the elements directly connected to the project that look immediately relevant and accessible. The consequence is a schematic view of the context in which the indicators retained may be selected and sometimes distorted in order to fit the purposes of the project. The context will vary as the project unfolds and needs constant redefinition.

Objectivity of the Analysis

Taking the context into account initially starts with collecting information (based on indicators) in order to determine as many of its features as possible to construct a complete and objective picture. However, context is necessarily a relative construct whose description depends on who selected the features (from which point of view), how they have been selected and how the responses and interactions leading to its description have been analysed, as Castellotti and Moore (2008) remind us.

This implies that whoever is in charge of describing the context (teacher/s, administrator/s or researcher/s) will need to remember that it is epistemologically or ethically difficult to think in terms of neutrality or objectivity (Huver, 2015). Objectivity is not the opposite of subjectivity, nor is it not being neutral when acting or assessing. It is connected to the individuals' values and is part of the data to be taken into account. Basically, it is connected to clearly describing the methodology used to collect and interpret the data and to confronting them to the likely effects of the individuals' subjectivity (Demaizière & Narcy-Combes, 2007). Which is why as many of the people involved in the project (students, parents, teachers and administrators/stakeholders) should participate in analysing the data collected (see MAG in 'How to Understand Contexts'). The initial description should be followed by constant reappraisals of this context.

Not only will the teachers have to be involved in the investigation of context indicators, but they will also need some form of training. Taking the context into account requires (Jeannot-Fourcaud et al., 2014): (a) critical distantiation vis-à-vis contents and teaching methods whose history, mode of construction, initial aims and legitimacy need to be questioned; and (b) an understanding of objectives, their limitations and their potential effectiveness.

Conclusion

The complexity of the task may be a deterrent to action. We agree with García and Kleyn (2016) when we read that institutional support is essential, but we are convinced that some changes at the micro level may often be more successful than top-down reforms and that some very limited changes may be very effective (individual work sheets instead of collective large group activities, for example, Narcy-Combes, 2005). This can be seen in some of the aforementioned cases in Asia (Haddad, 2008; Sandberg, 2017). Irrespective of the various situations, we feel that the answer to the problem is not to adapt methodologies or practices developed elsewhere to a given context, but to start with this context, to work with the participants to understand what is needed and look for ways of responding to the needs in the literature. Context is a variable in language development, a misleading myth would be to believe that some contexts are better than others and that they should be emulated. At best, they might suggest new ways of doing things if these ways are acceptable and legitimate in the new setting.

Part 2
Multilingual Practices in Action

The following chapters are devoted to a systematic review and meta-analysis of qualitative research projects illustrating our theoretical and practical positions and revealing how theory (as described in Chapters 1–6) and practice interact. We will describe the methodologies used, the problems encountered and the ways they have been resolved. We start by explaining the organisation of the study and providing a summary of the presented case studies.

8 Organisation of the Study

Introduction

Part 2 examines different small-scale ('classroom' level), medium-scale (university courses) and large-scale research projects on language learning environments (LLEs; PhDs or institutional projects). They include the development of a Content and Language Integrated Learning (CLIL) teacher training site, a massive open online course (MOOC) and international collaborative language and content courses. The results will be compared with the results of similar research in the literature in order to underline the relevance of a multilingual approach and define what must be taken into account when setting up physical or virtual LLEs and tasks.

There are three ways to read Part 2:

(1) A linear way, starting with the case studies and finishing with a synthetic overview (Chapter 14).
(2) Starting with the overview (Chapter 14) and then going back to whichever of the case studies are of most interest or relevance to the reader to gain further insight.
(3) Reviewing the summary of the case studies as presented in Table 8.1, selecting the ones that are of interest and then exploring the overview (Chapter 14).

Table 8.1 Summary of the case studies

Case No.	Page	Setting/keywords	Country/location
Case 1	74	Elementary, middle and high schools, emergent bilinguals, translanguaging, content-based instruction, co-construction of knowledge	USA – New York
Case 2	78	High school, content-based and task-based instruction (social studies), translanguaging, co-construction of knowledge, social implication	USA – New York
Case 3	78	Elementary school, bilingual class, reading literature, story writing and telling, mixed-ability groups, translanguaging	USA – New Mexico
Case 4	79	Middle school, language of schooling, speakers of different languages, translanguaging, content-based and task-based instruction (mathematics and science), social implication	USA – California
Case 5	82	University, bilingual university, translanguaging, content-based instruction	USA – Puerto Rico
Case 6	85	Bilingual education at primary and secondary levels, benefits of using home languages, content-based instruction	'French-speaking' Africa
Case 7	87	Primary schools, benefits of using home languages when French is the language of schooling, content-based instruction	Sub-Saharan Africa
Case 8	88	University, content and task-based instruction (mathematics), plurilingual education, translanguaging	South Africa
Case 9	89	Adults, young people, informal learning, learning a language via TV (Italian)	Tunisia
Case 10	91	Teacher education, website for subject teachers, content-based instruction (history)	Italy
Case 11	92	Universities and/or high schools, intercomprehension	Europe
Case 12	93	Higher education. Intercomprehension (Romance languages), task-based instruction, large numbers	Europe
Case 13	95	Higher education. Intercomprehension (Romance languages), metareflection	France
Case 14	96	Higher education. Intercomprehension, English vocabulary, content-based instruction (communication services and networks), task-based instruction	France
Case 15	97	Primary and secondary school level, contexts with regional and minority languages, civic and intercultural education	Europe and Quebec
Case 16	100	University and high schools, (collaborative/academic) writing, task and sometimes content-based instruction, translanguaging, use of ICT tools available	Europe and Maghreb
Case 17	103	Primary school level, two-way immersion in officially bilingual city, content and task-based instruction	Switzerland

(continued)

Table 8.1 (Continued)

Case No.	Page	Setting/keywords	Country/location
Case 18	104	University, content (logistics) and task-based instruction, reading task and collaborative writing, plurilingual input and output	France
Case 19	106	University, binational course, content and task-based instruction (applied linguistics), teacher education, co-construction of knowledge, collaborative writing	France and Germany
Case 20	107	University, additional languages, collaborative learning, metareflection, translanguaging	Denmark
Case 21	110	University, plurilingual setting, transmissive practices, translanguaging, power issues	Ukraine
Case 22	111	University, story writing workshop, plurilingual group, social implication	France
Case 23	113	Adult education, migrant population, awareness raising	France
Case 24	114	Open. MOOC, task-based instruction, learners construct their knowledge, plurilingual reflection, no linear approach	France
Case 25	117	University, telecollaboration, task-based instruction, writing	Quebec and Australia
Case 26	118	High schools, telecollaboration, tandem learning, simulations, teacher involvement and preparation	France and Ireland
Case 27	119	University, tandem learning, conversations with a topic	Belgium
Case 28	120	University, distant languages, theme-based discussions	China and France
Case 29	121	University, multilateral telecollaboration preparing university exchanges (Erasmus), task-based instruction	Europe
Case 30	121	University, multilateral intercomprehension programme, Romance languages, scenario and gaming approach	Mexico
Case 31	122	Teacher training, content-based instruction (task design), role of mediation	Poland and Germany/USA
Case 32	123	High school, reflection on the effects of asynchronous communication	USA
Case 33	124	University, specific study of the effects of feedback in eTandems	USA and Japan
Case 34	124	University, specific study of the effects of English as a lingua franca	Taiwan and France
Case 35	124	Adult education, specific study of the development of pragmatic competence, videoconferencing	USA and Germany
Case 36	125	Primary schools, task-based instruction	UK and Portugal
Case 37	125	University, tandem learning, specific study of corrective feedback	France

In the corpus under study, the construct of plurilingualism is found in many definitions and contexts:

- A form of elitist plurilingualism, additive (sum of several rigidly divided languages), selective: international schools, bilingual, double diplomas, etc., depending on what is favoured by the institutions in these contexts. CLIL courses, seen as (bi)plurilingual, represent a privileged choice in multilingual learning environments.
- A social version of plurilingualism, which tends to rely on the language repertoires of pupils to enable them to access academic content in a concern for justice and equity.
- A form of plurilingualism based on an identity ideology, the aim of which is to preserve a cultural heritage.

It is to be noted that even when official language policies seem to promote plurilingualism and use of the diversity of languages that are spoken in the country, they may in fact conduct a policy of linguistic hegemony that excludes those who do not endorse or refuse to comply with the dominant rules (Jonsson, 2017: 27).

A number of multilingual learning environments have been set up on an experimental basis in different contexts that strive to move from a 'double monolingualism norm' towards 'integrated bilingualism' and polylingualism (Jørgensen, 2008: 163). They are often isolated, marginal initiatives that are far from involving large groups. Even in the case of projects initiated by educational authorities, only a minority of the students in a region are concerned with these initiatives. Such environments can be found in multilingual areas, but also seemingly monolingual contexts, generally at primary school level. Most of the proposed environments have a top-down organisation that is imposed by the educational authorities, thus reducing the margin of freedom for researchers and practitioners. However, these experiments are mostly in line with current research on plurilingualism. Due to space limits, sign language had to be left out, although it is an important issue in the literature on multilingualism.

Methods

In our compilation, we have sought to include studies from a variety of sociocultural, educational and international contexts. The review integrates qualitative research from across 37 different contexts in Europe, North America, Africa, the Pacific and, to a much lesser extent, Asia. Some data come from case studies that will be described and commented on, others originate from state-of-the-art research and will be used to complement our general comments. To facilitate understanding of the context, the case studies have been principally organised according to geographical location. Within this overall organisation, Chapters 9, 11 and 13 will, respectively, examine translanguaging, intercomprehension and telecollaboration projects, as well as very specific studies on just one aspect of language development. In Chapter 14, we offer a synthetic overview of what the case studies reveal and consider their implications. We also see how they correlate with studies in other parts of the world.

The wide range of case studies consolidated here necessarily employ many different research methods and data collection techniques. To shed light on them, the current meta-analysis uses the following indicators as presented previously in Chapter 7 (see Table 7.1):

Contextual parameters:

At the macro level:

- geographical setting;
- social/historical situation;
- sociolinguistic and economic situation;
- dominant language in the social environment;
- top-down/bottom-up decision-making.

At the meso level:

- institutional context;
- language of schooling;
- extent of teachers' education and training/professional development;
- type of implemented system: bottom up/top down;
- number of participants;
- set up and implemented by the researcher/the institution/the teachers, etc.;
- learning objectives and tools;
- assessment and evaluation: language development, learning environment and system (by the learners, the educational team);
- measures of success;
- factors enabling or hindering the development of the system;
- consistency with the theoretical stance.

At the micro level:

- student characteristics (age, grade level);
- language level in the various languages in their repertoire;
- languages spoken/known by the students and by their teachers;
- transmissive or constructive approach.

The nature of the sources has made it very difficult to follow a rigorously identical organisation of the 37 cases. In addition, we sometimes faced a mass of information for some cases and a paucity of research for others. Despite these limitations, we have attempted to provide a comprehensive synthesis of plurilingual environments representing varied settings and approaches that contribute a more detailed understanding of the field.

9 North America

Case 1: Translanguaging Practices in New York State Schools

In addition to federal regulations, New York state has attempted to pay more attention to the bilingualism of its students by adopting what is known as the *Bilingual Common Core Initiative* (García & Kleyn, 2016) and its own language standard for emergent bilinguals and assessments. It identifies five levels of progression: entering, emerging, transitioning, expanding and commanding and associated performance indicators. In order to be moved to the expanding and commanding levels, the student must be able to perform the task in the language of the specific standard. New York state recognises the value of translanguaging, but only as a scaffold when core content is taught (García & Kleyn, 2016: 41). The New York State Initiative for Emergent Bilinguals (CUNY-NYSIEB – https://www.cuny-nysieb.org) is a project funded by the New York State Education Department and led by the City University of New York (CUNY) to support schools across the state in the education of their emergent bilingual students.

The three founding faculty members of the programme are Ricardo Otheguy, Ofelia García and Kate Menken from CUNY. The project is student centred and is based on three principles shaped by translanguaging theory (García, 2009):

(1) Bilingual development is neither linear nor static and is context dependent.
(2) Bilingualism is dynamic and not the addition of another language only.
(3) The dynamic processes of teaching and learning of emergent bilinguals need to be supported in the use of their language repertoire.

CUNY-NYSIEB has mainly worked with schools where students have not passed standardised test results, or only partially. They amount to 67 elementary, middle and high schools across the state that have met the following two criteria:

- an above average number of emergent bilingual students;
- students who have not attained the New York state standards in English language arts and maths.

In some schools, the majority of the students were Spanish speakers, in others they were linguistically heterogeneous. Some schools had an English as a second language (ESL) programme, while others had different types of bilingual programmes. Leadership seminars at the university covering the vision and theoretical principles of the programme on dynamic bilingualism, translanguaging and translanguaging practices were offered to principals and other school leaders. The role and support of school principals is key to ensuring buy-in to transforming practices (see Chapter 7). Then, the school set up an emergent bilingual leadership team made up of administrators and teachers from different subject areas. Some schools also included family members and students (see Chapter 7). The seminars involved lectures and collaborative workshops. A faculty–doctoral student team worked on-site with three to four schools for 18 months to support the local leadership teams in planning and integrating translanguaging into their practices by providing professional development (coaching, co-teaching with educators, etc.) (see Chapter 7).

In their book, *Translanguaging with Multilingual Students: Learning from Classroom Moments*, García and Kleyn (2016) present six studies involving elementary, middle and high school settings (for a detailed outline and discussion, see García & Kleyn, 2016):

- The first two studies are English-medium classes with a broad range of multilingual students.
- The next three examine transitional bilingual classrooms with Latino students.
- The final study looks at a dual language bilingual class for Latino students.

A single lesson or series of lessons are described. Lessons were developed collaboratively (teachers and CUNY staff) and integrated translanguaging within the regular curriculum (often mandated by the district). Students' needs were taken into account.

The studies took place in the context of actual classroom settings with teachers and students working within the constraints of educational policies. There were many immigrant students. Different languages were spoken in addition to English among which the most common was Spanish, but a wide variety of languages from all over the world could also be heard. Most students were identified as having lower levels of English proficiency, some were over the conventional school leaving age or had experienced several kinds of problems such as coming from low-income households, having an incomplete/interrupted formal education and suffering from low literacy level in their home languages or having learning disabilities or behavioural problems.

Content included multilingual and multicultural features, culturally relevant reading (e.g. a story written in verse about a young girl who leaves Vietnam after the fall of Saigon and comes to the USA), exploring slavery in the USA through literature and an introduction to key scientific concepts (preselected content).

Lessons were audio-recorded (some were video-recorded) and transcribed to analyse teaching practices, student learning and language use by educators and students (see Requirements for the education/training of teachers in Chapter 3). Data analysis was carried out by teachers and researchers collaboratively (see Chapter 7). Their reflective dialogue was analysed too. Student work was collected and analysed as well as feedback (participation in focus groups or feedback on lessons).

Tools and activities were in the students' language repertoires as well as in English. Students were provided with the opportunity to use multiple languages when collaborating to complete their work.

Cases 2, 3 and 4: A Five-Phase Approach to Translanguaging in Schools

Other studies adopting a similar approach to those presented in Case 1 are provided in García *et al.* (2017). The course design followed a five-phase pattern as summarised below.

- **Phase 1** (*explorar*). This is a phase of co-construction of knowledge (see Chapter 5). The objective is to provide students with the necessary tools and data to understand the object studied (text, concept, disciplinary content, etc.) on the basis of who students were, what they already knew and what languages were present in their repertoire. The tools and the discussion were varied (video clips, galleries of posters and photos related to the subject posted on the walls of the class to stimulate the discussion) and the work was collaborative in the form of brainstorming on what was already known in the group and in the form of discussion (using the languages of the group) of a problem related to the proposed subject matter in the target language.
- **Phase 2** (*evaluar*). Students compared different texts on the subject studied. Their attention was drawn to what was said or not said about the authors' linguistic and stylistic choices, and what was excluded from their text or ignored. Whenever possible, versions of these texts in different languages were provided and learners were asked to compare them. They supplemented these contributions by doing their own research on the subject from websites (captured by

the teacher or personal research) and presented to the group how their findings complemented, contradicted or reinforced what they had found in the textbook or the proposed texts. The task proposed went much further than the ordinary vocabulary and grammar lesson. Learners worked with meaningful content which enabled them not only to build knowledge, but also to become citizens of the country.

- **Phase 3** (*imaginar*). This stage provided learners with the opportunity to transform and take in what they had learned by reinvesting it in a task that made sense to them (writing stories, texts, sketches) and that was adapted to what they could do. Instead of setting unrealistic targets, learning was tailored to the needs of all students so that their individual requirements were effectively catered for and everyone could actually be involved in projects. In this phase, students worked in groups or in partnership to carry out the task for which they could rely on models of what was expected. They could use any language in their repertoire, including for the final production. Students created a product that, although it was a real challenge, they were able to achieve through graded tasks, model available, language to choose from and peer scaffolding.
- **Phase 4** (*presentar*). The finished product was in the target language. Students had to be sensitised to the necessity of adapting the language to the needs of the public, since they had to present their work to an audience. That was the Focus on Form stage (revision of texts, rewriting until the result looks satisfactory) with the help of peers and the teacher. Learners had a template for their presentation providing the start of key phrases in the target language and in their original language. Then, the work was presented to the group, according to the capacities of each learner. Stylistic and language choices were an integral part of the presentation. The metalinguistic capacities of the pupils were thus called upon.
- **Phase 5** (*implementar*). A social action was proposed to extend their work outside the classroom to an enlarged community. For example, learners shared their productions on Facebook, a website, a blog or other social media, considering the choice of the language to use according to the target audience. In the school, students' work was displayed on the walls or in the school resource centre, published in the school magazine or website, and opportunities were found to discuss the work in other classes, with teachers and students. This approach is totally in line with what was seen in Chapters 1–6.

We will now discuss the detail of the three cases.

Case 2: Translanguaging in a Social Studies Class

Case 2 deals with an eleventh-grade social studies class in a New York high school with English as the language of schooling while students speak Spanish at home. The monolingual teacher focuses the content on the introduction to a new genre: public service announcement (PSA). In the students' final task, they had to write their own PSA. The teacher started by showing a video of a model PSA about human trafficking in the USA in English, then in Spanish. Then, she asked the students to discuss the end of the video where a man trips over a woman and says in English (in both videos):

'Sorry, I didn't even see you'.
The woman responds: 'No one ever does'.

The teacher asked: *What did the shift from Spanish to English mean? Why was this done in English?* Students then had to come up with a definition of PSA and discuss the effectiveness of the one they had seen. Texts about PSAs were provided in both English and Spanish and students looked for other PSAs on the web. Discussions and reading were conducted in Spanish and English in different groups. The groups shared their findings and comments in English with the whole class. Next, each group was given a different PSA to analyse, some in English and some in Spanish. The students were asked to discuss their PSA and focus on purpose, message, audience, persuasive language and tactics and effectiveness. A flexible approach was adopted whereby the groups could either (i) discuss in English and write their answers in English or (ii) discuss in English and Spanish and write their answers in English or (iii) discuss in English and Spanish and write their answers in English and Spanish (which involved writing a general idea in English and expanding it in Spanish). A discussion with the whole class followed. Then, the students created their own PSA and presented it to the class. Assessment was made by the group, by peers and then by family (social involvement). Finally, the teacher asked the principal if the PSAs could be posted around the school and the project was explained during the morning announcements. A group of students worked on the announcement they would make the following week.

Case 3: Translanguaging in a Bilingual Classroom in New Mexico

An elementary bilingual class (English–Spanish) in New Mexico with a bilingual teacher took place in a very different context. In New Mexico public schools, about 60,000 students – or about 20% of students in kindergarten through twelfth grade – are designated as English language learners, according to the director of the Public Education Department's Bilingual Multicultural Education Bureau. About 70% of them are

Spanish speakers. In New Mexico, Spanish is a quasi-official language (Romero *et al.*, 2011).

In her dual-language bilingual class, the teacher proposed a bilingual storytelling activity titled '*Cuentame algo: Cuentos de la tierra y del barrio*', featuring stories about the way her students, their families and the local communities relate to their land and traditions. A key learning objective was to enable the students to read literature. With this end in view, she provided Spanish, English and bilingual texts to preview specific textual evidence of the local farming practices in New Mexico (input). She also provided access to YouTube, TED talks and other media sites in Spanish and English to find additional evidence of the topic and made available community resources (bilingual guest speakers, local farming sites, etc.). The students were invited to use the full features of their linguistic repertoires and ask question in whatever language they felt most comfortable. The final task involved them writing their own stories in Spanish first, then in English.

Case 4: Translanguaging in a Science Class

This case is set in the Californian context where Proposition 58 no longer requires English-only education for English learners. A maths and sciences class took place in a Los Angeles middle school with English as the language of schooling. The students speak Cantonese, Mandarin, Spanish, French, Vietnamese, Tagalog, Korean, Mandingo or Fula at home, with a bilingual teacher (English–Mandarin). Proposition 58 is specific to California. It allows schools to utilise multiple programmes, including bilingual education to teach English learners. In bilingual programmes, students learn from teachers who speak both their first languages and English. School districts and county offices of education must ask for annual feedback on English learner programmes from parents and community members.

In this case, an ESL teacher worked with a science teacher. In science, the focus was on genetics and the final task consisted of carrying out and writing up a lab experiment. Students who speak the same home language worked together to build their background knowledge by prewriting and brainstorming on genetics. At this stage, students wrote down what they knew and what they wanted to know using all their own language resources, then shared their ideas in English. They finally wrote up their findings in English. With the maths teacher, students worked on a final project to create bilingual children's books explaining a geometric concept using English as an additional language, as well as culturally relevant examples and connections. Students then had to present their books to elementary school teachers and later to groups of elementary school students with whom they shared a home language. Students were to be assessed on their understanding of the maths content, as well as their creativity and strategic use of both languages. To achieve this end, a variety of readings from newspapers, magazines and websites that connect geometry to the real world, in English, and, when possible, in the students' home language, were provided. Discussions took place in the students' home language to ask questions, make connections and summarise. Subsequently, the students created new geometry world problems using culturally relevant situations and translanguaging.

COMMENTS

In the four cases involving elementary, middle and high schools, languages are used strategically and allocated to particular tasks in advance. As 'bilinguals often use their language features dynamically in order to communicate in effective ways' (Collins & Cioè-Pena, 2016: 125), translanguaging spaces (Wei, 2011) in teacher-led activities were created in the classroom for language fluidity, in order to deepen understanding of both content and language. During group work, the students were free to use whichever language they wanted. In terms of language and content development, input was provided, students constructed their own knowledge, they were creative and there was social implication. The results/benefits of the fluid use of English and another language in the classroom were as follows:

- Students pay better attention in class.
- Better collective understanding of the text.
- Better participation and engagement in learning.
- Students were able to gain critical content knowledge.

The use of multiple media (written, oral, visual, virtual) was shown to increase the comprehension of complex content. The visual and support materials in the learners' initial language (IL) helped students keep up and participate in lessons as they provided multiple points of access to complex content that resulted in better participation and engagement and facilitated the students' ability to work collaboratively in multiple languages.

The students used all their languages when collaborating to complete their work. This:

- Allowed students to shift from a passive to an active role.
- Extended and deepened students' thinking.
- Enabled students to use all their language skills to communicate understanding and find meaning.
- Enabled them to build on each other's knowledge.
- Promoted help between peers (working together to understand the complex text), which they appreciated.
- Encouraged accountability among students for achieving their goals.

As noted by Flores and García (2013: 134), students were empowered to translanguage: 'In collaborative groups, emergent bilinguals feel empowered in what they know, and are therefore more comfortable appropriating English features into their linguistic repertoires'.

These cases confirm that translanguaging is a key element of differentiation as it encourages the participation of all students from diverse language backgrounds and English abilities (García & Kleyn, 2016). The students declared gains in self-confidence and activity. Bilingual students can engage in high-order thinking skills and in the comprehension of complex content texts as translanguaging enables them to 'do more with the English texts than they could have done if they had only used their emerging English' (Seltzer *et al.*, 2016: 146). As a consequence, learning is enhanced. In all the cases, the students engaged deeply in their learning, which promoted participation, the sharing of knowledge, scaffolding and support between peers as well as better interaction between students and with the teacher. This also developed a sense of belonging to the school community. Students experimented with the languages and made connections between cultures, improving their awareness of both their IL and the target language.

We never lose sight of the fact that official objectives and instructions must be taken into account. However, we follow García and Kleyn (2016) and García *et al.* (2017) when they advocate that there should be a difference during the assessment process between the general linguistic performances (the way in which the students mobilise the language to express complex thoughts and make inferences) and the specific language performances (the use of the academic language required by the institution). There should also be a difference between the content and the discourse that is used to account for it, as García and Kleyn (2016) point out: students should not be penalised on their knowledge of content because of their language skills.

Assessment is done jointly and focuses on what the pupils have learnt. The learners themselves, their peers (the group) and their families are involved. The local language policy and the institutional objectives, as well as the measurement tools available, are taken into account. Specifically, in Case 1, holistic assessment showed there was a direct correlation between the way the students used languages during the lesson when they spoke and when they wrote: four of the students used both English and Spanish to complete their English sentence starters about the task to perform. Most started with English but finished with Spanish (same pattern for speaking) and three wrote in English only (same during the lesson). 'Through translanguaging, the natural flow that is part of being bilingual can emerge with the goal of viewing students in a holistic way' (Kleyn & Yau in García & Kleyn, 2016: 115). In another example, most students chose to do a structured cloze poem instead of writing their own poem. This left little room for their own ideas and expressions of emotions, they just had to fill in the blanks. Thus, the activity was not a real-life task and constrained students' production and creativity and was described as 'a missed opportunity' by the authors.

How instruction and translanguaging were analysed and what pedagogic conclusions were proposed will be discussed in Chapter 14 and will be shown to correspond to what was put forward in Part 1.

Case 5: Translanguaging Practices in a Bilingual University in Puerto Rico

We now examine a case of translanguaging in higher education. As Mazak points out (in Mazak & Carroll, 2017), compared to the study of translanguaging in elementary and high schools, this remains largely under-researched in higher education. In their book, *Translanguaging in Higher Education: Beyond Monolingual Ideologies*, the authors present eight case studies, one of which explores a cross-case analysis of three cases of translanguaging practices led by three teachers at a Spanish–English bilingual university in Puerto Rico (the University of Puerto Rico at Mayaguez – UPRM) (for a detailed outline and discussion, see Mazak *et al.* in Mazak and Carroll [2017]). In these cases, students have a range of different language proficiencies and translanguaging is used to develop students' understanding of academic content. In addition, the teachers themselves have different linguistic and cultural backgrounds.

Consideration of the sociohistorical and sociopolitical context of Puerto Rico and its impact on language is key to our understanding of this case. The authors explain how the use of English in classrooms has been contested since the USA implemented English instruction in schools in order to *Americanise* the population, leading to much resistance to English-medium instruction in public schools. The language of everyday communication remains Spanish. However, the role of English in higher education is less controversial as it is ideologically seen as the *language of science* (Mazak *et al.*, 2017: 71). In higher education institutions, there are few explicit policies requiring courses to be taught in English or Spanish. In the UPRM, one such policy does identify Spanish as the language of instruction in most courses with students required to have a working knowledge of English. The individual professor decides the language used in class lectures and in student evaluation activities (Mazak *et al.*, 2017: 72).

In the three Content and Language Integrated Learning (CLIL) courses presented, translanguaging is used to teach content knowledge using all of the students' linguistics resources and to develop their linguistic resources. The fields of study are agriculture (weed science), evolutionary biology and abnormal psychology. The agricultural professor is Puerto Rican (Spanish IL). The psychology professor is a continental US citizen who speaks Spanish. The biology professor is also a continental US citizen with emerging knowledge of Spanish.

The study focuses on the professors' translanguaging practices in these classes and how they were used to create affordances for students to both learn content and develop their academic language in Spanish and English. The authors (Mazak *et al.*, 2017) see their use of translanguaging as intentional, but not always structured or planned. In these cases, translanguaging developed organically, based on students' sociolinguistic, cultural and historical backgrounds. According to the authors: 'translanguaging as a pedagogy is more of an attitude or stance that sees the value of using all of students' linguistic resources and takes steps (some more deliberate than others) to use and develop those resources' (Mazak *et al.*, 2017: 72). The teachers' specific translanguaging practices were identified as follows:

(1) The agricultural professor uses PowerPoint for lectures and disseminates information via Moodle. His academic English is very proficient, but he mostly conducts classes in Spanish. He uses academic materials (articles and diagrams) in English as well as English terminology to favour translanguaging practices (for example: reading texts in English followed by discussion in Spanish).
(2) The biology professor uses a whiteboard and Moodle and adopts a participative and collaborative approach. He conducts classes in English and uses English textbooks. He expects students to have a certain competency in English, but allows them to ask and answer questions in Spanish. The students are actively encouraged to translanguage in class even if it is an English-medium class.
(3) The psychology professor favours group work and discussions. She involves students through presentations – YouTube videos and movies. She feels comfortable giving classes in both languages and actively uses both languages in parallel for terminology, concepts, explanations and reformulations.

'These three professors enacted identities that related to students, strategically positioning themselves as authorities who can successfully apprentice college students in the discourses of their respective disciplines' (Mazak *et al.*, 2017: 87). The authors agree with García and Wei (2014: 94) that teachers who use translanguaging as a pedagogy participate as learners as well, which does not mean that they give up their authority.

COMMENTS

The cases here in a bilingual university in Puerto Rico, while not following a task-based instruction approach, demonstrated how teachers' use of translanguaging facilitated students' construction of content knowledge and access to scientific discourse of a specific field (agriculture, biology and psychology, for example). The teachers strategically used the students' entire linguistic repertoires both to teach content and to further develop students' linguistic repertoires (Mazak *et al.*, 2017: 87). As a result, the students were able to develop both content knowledge and academic English. Depending on the teachers' linguistic and cultural background, translanguaging was used in different ways, but always in ways that benefited all the bilingual students, particularly helping them to engage in academic discourse about their fields and providing them with opportunities to expand their linguistic and meaning-making repertoires, even if the pedagogical approaches seem rather conventional. The cases also showed how important it is for teachers to adopt a stance or openness towards translanguaging for the development of such practices.

10 Africa

Very few projects in Africa, either in Maghreb countries or in sub-Saharan areas, are reported. This is probably due to the exclusively top-down organisation in these countries as well as to the discontinuity between the decisions made at government level and their implementation. However, a few projects show interesting results. These will now be discussed.

Case 6: Promoting National Languages with French at Primary Level

The ELAN (*Ecole et Langues Nationales d'Afrique* – School and National Languages in Africa) project was set up in 2012, after an initial project (LASCOLAF: 2007–2010) had researched the actual needs. ELAN concerns eight countries (Benin, Burkina-Faso, Burundi, Cameroon, Mali, Niger, DR Congo and Senegal) (Maurer, 2016). Four more were meant to join in for the second phase. It is jointly run by *Organisation internationale de la Francophonie* (OIF), *Agence universitaire de la Francophonie* (AUF) and *Conférence des ministres de l'éducation des Etats et gouvernements de la Francophonie* (CONFEMEN).

The objectives of the project are as follows:

(1) To create an international system for the capitalisation and development of expertise (best practice, expertise and training) in the French-speaking world.
(2) To develop bilingual education in African countries.
(3) To empower the educational authorities in order to promote the necessary reforms for the use of African languages alongside French at primary school level.

The project involves the development of adapted learning tools, mainly for reading and writing practice, the design of resources for integrated didactics (i.e. comparative grammar textbooks in four cross-border languages) and the production of guidelines for teacher training. However, implementations vary greatly across countries.

Case 6 (Ouoba, 2016) is an example of a programme set up in Burkina Faso within the framework of the ELAN project. Here, the children learn to calculate, read and write in a language they can all speak, Gulmencema, a local African language from the Oti-Volta region, which is used as a teaching language when the children start school, while French is introduced in parallel. As the languages are supposed to be known, no oral pretest is proposed. From Year 3 on, the method (called Tin Tua from the name of the association that promotes it) is implemented for learning the French language, which is the ultimate goal of the project. As it is difficult to rely on the similarities between Gulmencema and French, this method is based on the differences between the two languages for learning French. Children start with working on their oral skills before moving on to writing in French. As observed, the method is as follows:

- Priority is given to the oral form of the language.
- Language is used as a communication tool.
- Comprehension is combined with production.
- Learners are immersed in the target language system instead of relying on Gulmencema as a tool.

After Year 3, the method prohibits any reference to Gulmencema, to avoid 'unwanted transfer' based on the principle that if instruction was properly made in the first three years, there would be no difficulty transferring the acquisition of knowledge from one language to the other. The material as well as the method used is very similar to those used in audiolingual methods in the past. According to the author quoting Barreteau (1998), learners from schools that followed the method were significantly more successful than learners from schools that did not. It is not obvious how the learners explicitly use their knowledge of their home language, if different from Gulmencema, for learning French.

COMMENTS

The scope of the ELAN project was very ambitious. The very specific and complex sociolinguistic situation of the countries concerned as well as the necessity for developing the standards of education in a part of the world with both a rapidly increasing population and a difficult economic situation is at the root of numerous educational problems. As we saw in Case 6, schools often need the most basic equipment and have to accommodate an increasing number of students. This case exemplifies the difficulty in moving away from a top-down approach and from the monolingual myth even when it is the official objective. However, the impetus that a project such as ELAN has given and the international collaboration that resulted show that beliefs are changing but that practices will evolve slowly. The following case, which was the result of a project that had a more limited scope, is in some ways more convincing.

Case 7: Benefits of Using the Home Languages in Primary Schools

According to Noyau (2016), the options leading to the most disappointing results in the experiments in sub-Saharan Africa are related to proposals for independently juxtaposed content, resources and activities in the initial language (IL) and the additional language (AL). Issues arise when no link is established between the two languages and especially when teachers are not bilingual themselves and teach exclusively in the language they know. To disprove such practice, Noyau (2016) describes experiments in Togo investigating whether using the IL or, on the contrary, excluding it, when learning content could make a difference to knowledge building in the primary school context. Two experiments were carried out in second year and sixth year at a primary school in the rendition of oral narrative and observation sciences (how fire can be produced). The results showed that stories told in the students' IL were richer and better structured. As for their written summaries, they made more comments and focused more on the structural pattern of the story when they were able to reread the story in their IL rather than in French. The dynamic effect of the IL was more strongly felt with the sixth-year than the second-year learners. Rereading the text in their IL favoured a knowledge transforming strategy (the narrative was reconstructed by the child) over a knowledge telling strategy (the narrative is memorised and repeated). Concerning the scientific topic, the experiment showed that when the children were allowed to express their knowledge in their IL, their results for the task in French were significantly better because they were able to structure this complex and challenging action mentally by drawing on their own practical and cultural experience. The simple fact of introducing bilingualism into the class was beneficial to the construction of knowledge. These findings align with other findings in other contexts and notably with what has just been described in the USA (Cases 1–5). Noyau (2016) argues that students should be able to translanguage from the IL to the AL and vice versa. It is essential for learners to be offered the opportunity to develop the necessary metalinguistic awareness required when accessing writing skills. She also argues that quick transitional bilingualism brings only limited benefits (subtractive bilingualism), while bilingualism that continues throughout basic education leads to additive bilingualism that favours academic success and the emergence of individuals mastering their bi/plurilingualism (cf. Maurer, 2011: 48).

COMMENTS

According to Noyau's analysis of the experiments, organising knowledge transfer as in the project *Transferts d'apprentissage à l'école Bilingue* (*Learning Transfer in Bilingual Schools*) (2011–2014 – Burkina, Mali, Niger) is essential to boosting learners in a bi/plurilingual context. This means starting from what the children already know, as it is reassuring for them to feel that they do know something that the school values. To achieve this aim, her experiments show that:

- Curricula and assessment gain by being coherent with a bi/plurilingual approach.
- Adequate textbooks and teaching resources need to be provided.
- Solid teacher training and development are necessary.

Specifically, teachers are still not flexible enough when managing class interactions (offering open-ended questions requiring the learners to think about their answers, leaving them time for reflection, giving them opportunities to be active). Class interactions should involve the following:

- Encouraging learning activities through play and action.
- Devoting more time to writing activities (not just copying) in all areas of learning in the IL and AL, thereby allowing pupils to appropriate writing for meaning.
- Linking the two languages through reformulation.
- Organising the reflective learning of vocabulary by working on the construction of complex words, families of words and lexical fields through language games.
- Encouraging the reformulation of content in the different fields of education to go beyond purely verbal representations of content and to access it through multimodal multisensorial experiences.

This is in line with what was seen in Chapters 1–6. We would add that schools are still not very well equipped and classes are often overcrowded, which makes teaching challenging.

Case 8: Translanguaging in a Mathematics Class in English-Speaking Africa

In the part of Africa where English is dominant, the contexts are not very different from 'French-speaking' Africa. Some researchers are in line with the theoretical framework developed in this book, and, interestingly, some researchers of the ELAN programme draw upon experiments in Anglophone Africa (see Agbefle, 2016).

Mamokgethi Phakeng, a full professor of mathematics education at the University of South Africa, gave a plenary talk at the Drongo Festival, the Netherlands' largest language festival held in Utrecht in September 2015. She explained that although research has shown learners' ILs should be used as a resource to learn mathematics, teachers prefer to teach and learners prefer to learn mathematics in English despite their limited fluency in it. The reason is often utilitarian as they all believe that English makes it easier to access jobs and the international world.

Phakeng also argues in favour of a holistic view of plurilingual learners, different from the sum of two monolinguals, and of language as a resource for learning mathematics. The programme she suggests implementing involves:

- The deliberate, strategic and proactive use of learners' ILs and English together and not in opposition.
- Giving learners interesting and challenging tasks in multiple languages.
- Letting learners perform the task and interacting with one another in the language in which they feel most comfortable.

She shows a case where learners are given real-life tasks in line with their interests and needs in their home language and in English and are organised in home language groups and encouraged to work in the language they choose (see Contexts and situation in Chapter 7). The findings showed that by doing so, the focus shifted from the language to the subject matter: mathematics. The learners engaged in higher cognitive demand mathematics tasks and their participation and interest in mathematics increased.

COMMENTS

This case exemplifies what can be done at university level, but we do not have much information related to the tasks. There is, however, some indication of a move away from a transmissive approach and of improved results in the subject matter, which may be attributed to both the pedagogic stance and the translanguaging practices according to the author. This would confirm what was seen in Part 1 of this book.

Case 9: Informal Learning of Italian by TV Viewers in Tunisia

An unusual case of language development was researched by Boughnim (Boughnim & Narcy-Combes, 2011). Some Tunisian TV viewers acquired proficiency in understanding and speaking Italian simply by watching RAI Uno TV programmes between 1960 and 1990, when the arrival of satellite TV changed the situation. A study was carried out on a sample of 15 such Tunisian viewers. In order to assess their aural comprehension and oral production, they took A2 level tests for the *Certificato di Conoscenza della Lingua Italiana* (CELI, University of Perugia), which complies with the guidelines of the Common European Framework of Reference for Languages (CEFR). All the informants passed the test. Some of them could probably have passed a higher-level test, but that was not feasible at the time.

Fifteen semi-directive interviews were also conducted. Their analysis showed that the Tunisian viewers watched RAI Uno programmes because they had plenty of free time and because television was the only entertainment available. They were attracted by Italian programmes and culture. They started watching Italian TV from an early age (between 3 and 16), and for a long period of time (3 hours per day on average for several years). They mainly watched films and cartoons.

This would seem to prove that a language can be acquired by simple exposure to a medium such as television in some contexts. However, there were favourable elements. What fostered their understanding of a language they did not originally know was:

- Enjoying what they were doing.
- Being able to identify schemata (TV shows in this case) with which they were familiar.
- Inferring meaning by using different semiotic channels (i.e. pictures contributed to valuable comprehensible input).
- Using their plurilingual experience (diglossia in Arabic and knowledge of French) also helped to make the input comprehensible. Viewers stated that they constantly made analogies and comparisons between Italian and French to understand the new language (intercomprehension).
- Using the informal metalinguistic and contrastive capacities that go with plurilingualism (see Chapters 1–6).

COMMENTS

The participants in the study not only described their learning as spontaneous, natural and implicit (Boughnim & Narcy-Combes, 2011), but also described their cognitive efforts to use the resources available (knowledge of other languages, use of pictures) to make sense of the new language. It is important, however, to remember that plurilingual competence is context dependent and that a similar informal experience in a more monolingual context is rather unlikely to happen.

11 European Large-Scale Projects and Intercomprehension Networks

Case 10: A Website for CLIL Teachers in Italian High Schools

In Italy, a political decision requiring the nationwide implementation of Content and Language Integrated Learning (CLIL) reflects a strong political commitment, unique in Europe. All secondary schools must integrate CLIL into their curricula (Hamon & Cervini, 2015). However, the sudden introduction of this policy change left many teachers feeling helpless when faced with the task of teaching their subject in an additional language (AL) of their choice. Consequently, some Italian history teachers had to teach history in French even though they did not feel proficient in the language. This led, in 2015, to the creation of the website *Le français de l'histoire* by an Italian-French multidisciplinary team, with the support of the French Institute in Italy. The site invites teachers to 'play the game of CLIL' and suggests a socio-interactionist and multilingual approach to content and language acquisition. It aims to develop their disciplinary knowledge through the use of two languages and at the same time enhance their discourse and lexical skills by developing their cognitive-academic language proficiency (Cummins, 2007). The free and open website offers methodological tools to support teachers in developing their receptive and productive skills related to the field of history, in identifying situations and tasks related to this discipline as well as specific forms of discourse and useful pedagogical scenarios.

The first entry focuses on the general objectives and invites the reader to reflect on the implications of teaching history in an AL to determine what CLIL really is and consequently what it means to teach history in such a context. Then, it moves on to suggest how intercomprehension (IC) between Italian, English and French can help make sense of the content and how collaborative work and teacher networks to share their experience can ease and enrich the task of preparing a teaching sequence.

The site is divided into three main sections devoted to specific issues on how to teach history in French:

(1) Methodology pertaining to how to comment on written documents; how to state the problem; how to make a presentation and take part in the ensuing discussion; how to write a composition; how to evaluate and self-evaluate learner productions.
(2) Methodological and linguistic support is provided for each of the three high school levels.
(3) Tools are provided for the development of reading/writing and listening/speaking skills through specific advice and links to websites. They can be adapted both to teachers and to learners.

Finally, with the browser, the teachers can find a related webography, elements of discourse for the history teacher, advice on how to find useful resources on the internet and tips on how to learn French with the help of TV5 Monde.

COMMENTS

The tool was introduced to high school teachers, school officials and government representatives on 10 March 2015 in Rome. However, little or no feedback has been obtained so far on the efficiency of the learning device. If we refer to Chapters 1–6, we can see why this site did not reach its ambitious objectives. There was no interaction, no construction of knowledge by the teachers themselves, no practice. An interactive massive open online course (MOOC) might have proved more dynamic (see Case 24).

Case 11: Online Intercomprehension Learning Programme for Romance Languages (Example 1)

In Europe, the Galanet project was the first to implement an online IC learning programme with the aim of facilitating written communication (mainly, although oral communication is also possible) between speakers of Romance languages, i.e. French, Italian, Spanish, Portuguese, Romanian and Catalan.

The Galanet platform (see Agence Universitaire de la Francophonie, 2017) offers an interface inspired by the metaphor of a media centre (with offices, meeting rooms, etc., even featuring a bar to socialise). It is available in various target languages including the languages listed above. Galapro is linked to Galanet and focuses on online teacher training to the key principles of IC programmes so that they can be part of the learning syllabi.

Degache (2018) explores the evolution of telecollaborative practices in an IC scenario in Europe linked with several European projects for

Romance languages IC (Cultura, Galanet, Lingalog, Galapro and Miriadi). The project (Degache, 2018) was set up by a group of researchers and involves volunteer university and sometimes high school students and teachers. The activities are available on a free access learning platform with the aim of developing language and intercultural skills in several Romance languages. The basic assumption is that if organisational circumstances are provided, language development in IC will take place as well as cultural and ethical (mutual acceptance, for instance) competences. A task-based approach is implemented. Approximately 6000 registrations are recorded from 110 institutions in some 20 countries. Tutors are trained through the Galapro platform. Assessment of the programme is carried out through interviews and quantitative and qualitative studies aimed at participants (learners and facilitators) as part of the whole project. However, because of the large number of people involved, it has been difficult to identify what was expected in terms of the final production. Participants found it difficult to come to an agreement on how and when to carry out the work and considered the tasks unevenly distributed.

COMMENTS

One drawback of such a large-scale project is that results cannot be easily assessed and in the case of IC it is made even more complex. The objective is to access content and express it in a language familiar to the learner. Connecting content familiarity and language proficiency is not an easy task for researchers. One can see, however, that care was taken to train the tutors, which is an important asset.

Case 12: Online Intercomprehension Learning Programme for Romance Languages (Example 2)

Masperi and Quintin (2007) propose an example of an IC project that fits within the Galanet programme involving teams of students in diverse Romance countries interacting together. Their task is to co-construct a step-by-step common task which is the preparation and online publication of a press release in four languages. Teamwork stimulates interactions between learners that should consequently foster language receptive and interactive skills. The scenario follows a four-phase development:

- getting to know each other and selecting a theme;
- brainstorming;
- selecting documents for discussion;
- working out and publishing the press release.

Tutors allow students to be relatively autonomous but offer more support as the project develops. Training for tutors is provided (see Agence Universitaire de la Francophonie, 2017) and students have to comply with the Galanet ethics charter to support and regulate the use of the forums and chats.

The researchers investigated whether the aforementioned scenario and set up via the forum contributed to the development of plurilingual IC skills. To that end, they collected a corpus of written messages posted on the forum by the 10 most active students that showed that they were reacting to a message posted by a speaker of a different language from their initial language (IL). They hypothesised that if no improvement could be seen in the practices of the 10 most active students, that would show that the scenario was inadequate and needed to be changed. However, if they did develop better IC skills, more studies would be needed to confirm the results.

The study involved 161 students in 15 teams, coached by 24 tutors. Ninety-one forum threads and 1308 messages were collected, among which 423 messages were retained for the study.

The study of the evolution of plurilingual interactional practices included:

- the language of interactions;
- individual choices;
- results on improvement.

The results from Masperi and Quintin's (2007: 30) study showed that 80% of the messages posted were either written in a common language and monolingual (45.5%) or were in a different language from the students' IL and bilingual (38%). Only 7% were plurilingual and written in an AL. Most interactions were monolingual and involved a common language in Steps 1–3, while more bilingual use could be observed in Step 4, which suggests that tasks and organisation mode play an important role in the choice of languages.

Concerning individual practices, significant disparities were observed. All participants were involved in plurilingual interactions, but only three contributed for the larger part to heteroglossic interactions and four participants accounted for less than 40% of those interactions.

Concerning the development of IC, no evolution of heteroglossic interactions could be observed globally. However, individual results revealed that five participants improved, three stagnated and two fell behind.

The authors conclude that there was no quantitative evolution in the development of IC skills either from one phase to the other, nor inside each phase, so that the scenario had no effect on it. The improvements observed for half of the participants of the study could be explained by the influence of other variables such as individual characteristics, pedagogical support or external contributions. It would be interesting to know why this was the case. One reason may simply be that the course was not long enough to detect any quantitative evolution.

COMMENTS

As in Case 11, an assessment of the results is complex. It would probably be facilitated if a CLIL approach was followed and tasks with precise outcomes were proposed. In Case 16 (Bozhinova et al., 2017), instead of trying to assess if there was progress in a short course, the developmental potential of the course was assessed, including potentially acquisitional sequences (PASs, see Chapter 4). Other indicators were traces of elements taken up from the proposed input in the students' output, and students' engagement in the task (Cook, 2008). In the case of IC, indicators would have to be determined initially.

Case 13: Online Intercomprehension Learning Programme for Romance Languages (Example 3)

Carrasco Perea and Pishva (2007) argue that in order for students to realise how much they can understand when reading related languages, it is necessary firstly to make them aware of their metacognitive and metalinguistic capacities and secondly, to provide opportunities for students to develop new learning strategies. At the then Stendhal University of Grenoble, they experimented with a group of 20 students who had developed theoretical and practical knowledge about IC the previous year. Reflective activities were proposed through which students wrote in the language of their choice about their plurilingual learner-user profile, their intercultural learning experiences and their learning and reading styles. Doing so contributed to raising students' awareness of the accessibility of Romance languages, of the scope of their cognitive capacities and of the need for personal engagement. It remains to be known whether IC actually developed or had the potential to develop, since metalinguistic awareness does not necessarily correlate with language development, but it may with written receptive practices.

COMMENTS

From what was seen in Chapter 5, metalinguistic reflection may help, but it is not directly linked with actual development. Such a short course is likely to be a useful introduction to IC if followed by an actual course in IC.

Case 14: Developing University Students' Academic and Professional Vocabulary through Reading Intercomprehension and ICT

Rodrigues (2012) uses IC for teaching English vocabulary to students taking a university technological degree in communication services and networks (CSN). In this context, students have to be proficient in English and in another language of their choice (Spanish or French). The institution supports the use of ICT for learning languages and allows 118–180 hours for the study of English and 60–122 hours for the study of another language out of an annual allocation of 1800 hours for the whole course. IC is used to help students develop their academic and professional vocabulary in an AL (English, French or Spanish).

The study is based on a 3-month experiment with the collaborative task of creating a wiki in English in one of the students' professional domains. It was supervised by the English teacher and a native speaker of the target language specialised in the field of broadcasting, web design and photography. It was part of the *Vocales Project (Vocabulary in Foreign Language for Communication Services and Networks)*, which involved first-year CSN students at the Allier Technical University in France. It had to meet several criteria:

- A task-based approach as recommended by the Council of Europe (2001) and perfectly adapted to the target audience.
- The use of ICT offering adequate interaction spaces for IC such as Web 2.0, forums and blogs.

The students could use collaborative writing tools such as Etherpad, internet resources and a Facebook account was opened to communicate with tutors.

Information about IC strategies was provided, and the students were encouraged not to limit their investigations to documents in English or French. The activities were not limited to the understanding of written texts. The experiment aimed at encouraging students to develop strategies for IC and to apply them to carry out the task. The project involved 19 students (17 were French, 1 came from Gabon and 1 from China). Teacher intervention was limited to introducing the project, giving information about details of the sessions and of the expected production and finally explaining IC. Tutors received some training about IC with a focus on strategies that work to learn vocabulary. Data were collected through filmed sessions, retrieved Facebook and mail interactions, Etherpad collaborative documents, wikis and pre- and post-questionnaires.

However, the results remained inconclusive. The analysis of the wikis showed that students did not limit themselves to links between their IL and English. They quoted seven other languages, which seems positive. However, the questionnaire results showed that only 48% understood the positive aspects of looking for connections between languages to understand several languages; 42% expressed no opinion. Interestingly, 37% stated that they would not use the strategy again when having to understand a language they did not know well and 47% said that they would rather look up a word in the dictionary (58% stated they used the internet) than use IC strategies to understand languages. When evaluating the project, just under half the students (47%) declared they were satisfied while 42% did not express their opinion.

COMMENTS

Vocabulary as a learning objective may be very restrictive as was the limitation imposed on the students. Learners should be able to choose which strategy is the most effective for them, as seen in Case 16, or perform a task in which using IC is the easiest solution available. Telecollaboration, for instance, might have provided tasks in which the outcome requires going through multilingual documents together within time restraints making it necessary to rely on IC collaboratively.

Case 15: Promoting Regional and Minority Languages through Intercomprehension at Primary and Secondary School Level

Le Besnerais and Cortier (2012) propose an overview of what IC could bring to the language development of primary and secondary school children in bi/plurilingual contexts where various regional and national languages are present in their representations or/and in their language repertoire. The study was carried out in a network of schools in Corsica, Spain, Val d'Aosta, Scotland and Quebec as part of an international project. IC served to help learners to see themselves in the other, and by doing so, to recognise themselves as strangers to the other, and also to learn to know and respect the other language and culture.

Both teachers and learners have experience of languages in contact and of multilingualism at school and outside school. These languages can be official languages that are not widely spoken in the social environment (i.e. French in Val d'Aosta), official languages that are taught at school and spoken in the environment, official regional languages taught and spoken in the environment, regional languages in a diglossic situation, regional languages that are deeply rooted and used locally, minoritised regional languages and minority languages (of immigrant children) at primary and secondary school level.

The regional or minority languages (Catalan, Corsican, Occitan, Scottish, Franco-Provencal) have been integrated in school as part of the curricula with a cultural and linguistic objective. The aim was to foster systematic and natural language variation processing and dispel the very ideological compartmentalisation of languages which causes political tensions.

Project activities were varied and included working on traditional folk tales, legends and fables, tutorials, novels, films, video recordings, blogs, learning platforms, etc. Their implementation was varied too. For example:

- In Canada, starting from the observation of their linguistic and cultural environment and questioning formal and political representations of languages, students worked within the framework of civic education to develop a positive attitude regarding the existing languages and cultures in the country.
- In North Catalonia, a language awareness approach was used to build bridges between students' linguistic and cultural diversity inside and outside school.
- In Val d'Aosta, the institutional (primary/secondary school level) and geosociological (the country where the local variety is spoken and the city where it is not) contexts and two approaches of Franco-Provencal were proposed which highlighted the links between the languages and cultures of French and Italian that are still separated in the curriculum. A competition was organised for the production of pedagogical resources by teachers and learners ending in a big common festival (social implication).
- In South Catalonia, tales were used for their playful intercomprehensive dimension. The online multilingual tutorial *Romance itineraries* was adapted for a course conceived with the objective of offering newcomers to the Catalan school system an opportunity to learn Catalan within a plurilingual perspective. For example, they offer a module to (i) facilitate the identification of languages; (ii) encourage learning two, three or even four Romance languages; and (iii) elicit individual strategies for understanding messages in neighbouring languages.
- In Corsica, tales were chosen as a facilitator of bi/plurilingual education. The focus was on civic and intercultural competences: learning to live with different people, questioning norms and judgments as well as how to read in French, Italian and Corsican.

As there were different contexts and institutions and as the tasks varied accordingly, the results mainly concern attitudes and satisfaction.

COMMENTS

In each of the Cases 10–15, pluralistic approaches were followed (IC, languages awareness, integrated and intercultural approaches). The regional language was used as a bridge or stepping stone to neighbouring, collateral or 'near' languages, related languages existing in the learners' environment as a way to promote better understanding of languages and open up closed communities by establishing sociocultural relations.

An important point to notice in all the participating experiments, besides the systematic promotion of language contact, is the recognition that an approach to language(s) is an individual process.

Resources were available to facilitate familiarity with language variation on the basis of the recognition of shared knowledge of all kinds (lexicon and instructions in the linguistic landscape, lexical transparency, tales, social rituals, etc.). They also contributed to the development of metalinguistic strategies through the identification of translinguistic convergences.

It would also seem that the more successful experiments were those where tasks were well defined. However, there was no assessment of results nor of what learners felt.

12 European Small-Scale Projects

Case 16: An ICT-Supported Translanguaging Approach to Collaborative Writing

The common objective of the following three studies (see Bozhinova *et al.*, 2017) was to support learners' creativity and the development of writing skills corresponding to their field of study, which varied according to the contexts. Because the researchers belonged to European research laboratories, we have included them in Chapter 12. Writing was seen as a translanguaging, recursive, reflexive and socio-collaborative process, triggered by exposure to corpora of online resources and texts featuring the genre to be studied. The course design proposed alternating complex social tasks and form-focused training tasks. Learners were free to collaborate in the language(s) of their choice and to use any online tool available including automatic translators, e.g. Google, Reverso and Babylon, contextual dictionaries, e.g. Linguee and Reverso, and spelling and grammar checkers, e.g. BonPatron and Reverso.

Language development was measured by noting potentially acquisitional sequences (PASs, Chapter 4). Other indicators were traces of elements taken up from the proposed input in the students' output and students' engagement in the task (Cook, 2008). Creativity was measured by taking into account the length of students' productions in relation to the number of issues and themes addressed, their complexity (number of logical operators, number of events and details added and also the observance of discursive and pragmatic rules).

In Bulgaria, the study took place at the American University in Sofia and concerned two groups of 15 B2 (upper-intermediate Common European Framework of Reference [CEFR] level) students participating in a blended learning course of French based on the task-based approach. The participants (eight women and seven men) were of different nationalities: five Bulgarians, two Russians, two Ukrainians, two Kazakhs, one Albanian, one Dutch, one Spanish and one American.

In Tunisia, the study was set at the Institut Supérieur d'Informatique (ISI) in Tunis and involved six third-year students in engineering and three master's-level computer scientists. They used a Moodle platform for the course of French for academic purposes (FAP). FAP focuses on the specific needs and requirements of a targeted audience and formal, discursive, rhetorical and linguistic demands are as important as content (Mangiante & Parpette, 2011). In addition, FAP courses develop methodological skills. The objective of the course was to support students in writing their end-of-study project report or master's dissertation for which they were allowed to use integrated (Word) or online (Cordial, Antidote) spelling checkers, anti-plagiarism software and online translators.

In Morocco, the study concerned a group of 13 students (five girls and eight boys) studying French at a secondary school from January to the end of February, i.e. 5 weeks with 5 hours a week, half of which were devoted to writing a blog. Each student had internet access and a computer at home and 10 computers with internet access were available at the school. The task was writing an article for a blog: starting from a resource text about preserving the use of French in Canada, learners were asked to give their argued-for opinion on the Moroccan situation. They used Framapad, a text editor with which they could publish online collaborative texts.

In each case, the objective was to obtain a complex, socially meaningful, written production (logbooks, testimonials, letters, blog articles, master's theses, etc.) while having all the tools available via information and communications technology (ICT), there was social implication. Synchronous or asynchronous teacher and peer support was available, and step-by-step collaborative work was performed before individual production.

A wide variety of data were collected including learners' productions, video and audio recordings of sessions, student interviews and questionnaires. The data collected in each context enabled the researchers to monitor the experiment and adapt it to the needs that were revealed and to measure the potential for language development.

In Bulgaria, results concerning language development revealed an important qualitative evolution both in terms of language and organisation. Teacher–learners interactions, especially when asynchronous, revealed the presence of corrective feedback and uptake due to the noticing and reflective effect triggered by the resources and the monitoring system. The results also revealed that activation of languages other than French gradually decreased, even though activation of English could still be observed. On the whole, the environment combining digital resources with teacher and peer feedback and follow-up enabled the students to experiment with language and tools and to develop more creative and autonomous writing. Interviews confirmed the usefulness of the tasks, especially social interaction with native writers, and gave details of the way the resources were used and the strategies were developed by students. Students expressed a high level of satisfaction.

In Tunisia, the results showed that the interactions generated PASs and that students were very much engaged in the tasks and programme. In the end, their written productions improved in many ways: they were better organised, they complied better with the genre and discipline standards and the language used was more accurate. However, because disciplinary content was prioritised and time was limited, students complained of cognitive overload which they said is the reason why they sometimes consistently experienced the same problems even after feedback. The methodological aspects and the specific format requirement were acquired for six of nine students. On the whole, students produced more complex texts without totally achieving the expected level of originality, variety and creativity. The use of online tools helped them to become more autonomous and find ways to learn by reflecting on their writing. Tutor feedback raised students' awareness of the existing gap between their written productions and the expected academic standard.

In Morocco, an evolution in students' strategies was observed. Students also developed their metacognitive reflection as regards the relevance of the tools they used. Given that the experiment was limited in time, it was not possible to observe any sustainable language development. However, students' productions were more in line with standard norms due to, in particular, the massive use of the spellchecker Cordial.

Thanks to the blog and the use of the internet, the students moved slowly towards acquiring the necessary skills to write an argumentative text about a chosen subject. As the teacher chose to withdraw while remaining supportive, they discovered a more dynamic way of working in a place that did not look like a traditional classroom. The end-of-course questionnaires revealed that students rated the techno-pedagogic environment positively concerning the evolution of their writing skills and metacognitive reflection. However, some of them resented the fact that the task was too time-consuming. These courses have been maintained with slightly larger groups.

COMMENTS

Teachers relinquished prescriptive and top-down postures and followed the learners along a path that was their own, with the tools available or those they collected themselves, so that the written productions in French were in line with academic standards. The studies had their limitations inherent to these experiments, notably due to the small size of the groups. However, the results show that the frequency of PASs, the input uptakes in the learners' written texts, the metacognitive reflection and the involvement of learners in the experiments make it possible to conclude that the potentiality for development was high. As a consequence, we see that work based on the learners' initial language (IL) and methodological repertoires fosters the development of writing skills and leads to the production of additional language (AL) texts that satisfy academic expectations. The results confirm that learners are developing a flexible control system that allows them to manipulate their own language resources and use editing and writing tools to achieve greater complexity and accuracy in their written texts.

Case 17: Promoting Bilingualism and Biliteracy in a Two-Way Immersion Programme

In two-way immersion programmes, there are two languages of schooling. Students typically receive instruction for subjects such as maths, reading and science in one language of schooling and spend time during art, music and other subjects speaking and learning in the other language of schooling. The Swiss two-way immersion programme *Filière Bilingue* (FiBi) is a choice-based educational alternative in a public school situated on the language border in Biel/Bienne, an officially bilingual city (Buser, 2015). The programme integrates French-speaking and German-speaking students and promotes bilingualism and biliteracy in addition to grade-level academic content achievement. The presence of approximately equal numbers of native speakers of both languages of schooling in the same class provides opportunities for students to communicate with native-speaker peers, creating linguistic and intercultural benefits for both groups.

As immigrant communities continue to grow across the country, the FiBi moved to integrating one-third of French-speaking students, one-third of German-speaking students and one-third of allophone students. The latter are students having neither French nor (Swiss) German as their IL (or ILs). The amount of instructional time is equal in the two languages of schooling at all grade levels (50/50 programme model). These are unifying educational experiences for all students. They start out at the kindergarten level in FiBi, and at least half of the weekly instruction is delivered in the 'partner' language (namely in the other language of schooling, that is either French or German). Offering immigrant students this two-way immersion experience – as opposed to a stand-alone elective language class – sends the message that this school truly sees the value of their native language(s). Promoting inclusivity and equity, this multilingual curriculum includes the two languages of schooling in addition to all the languages of origin of the students of the classes.

Even though the programme started small in 2010 and grew gradually over the years, staff had to build the programming from scratch because it was not something they could simply purchase or copy from 'traditional' (monolingual) schools. A credit-bearing certificate programme (*Certificate of Advanced Studies in Education and Plurilingualism 'CAS Éducation & Plurilinguisme – Bildung & Mehrsprachigkeit'*) was developed at the nearby University of Teacher Education (HEP-BEJUNE) and acknowledged the two-way immersion teachers' surplus load of recent years with a diploma for those educators who were interested in this professional development offering. Nevertheless, teachers of FiBi are still constantly adapting their teaching methods and materials to the needs of this innovative two-way immersion programme.

The linguistic development of FiBi students was documented with various productions (formal and informal) from the very first day of schooling in kindergarten until the end of Grade 2 and some research-based evidence was provided that students reached at least the same linguistic level as students of 'traditional' (supposedly monolingual) classes after the first four years of their schooling with regard to their ability to use the two languages of schooling communicatively.

COMMENTS

Considering the multiple language practices of FiBi students when they interact to acquire new content knowledge, there was a gradual shift from an institutional monolingual approach to each activity to accepting translanguaging whenever the situation made it the easier solution to achieve the learning objective. The very specific situation of Biel/Bienne as an officially and peacefully bilingual city explains that very few other regions in the world have experimented with such an approach, with the early exception of California (Lindholm-Leary, 2001), often for political reasons.

Case 18: Implementing a Plurilingual CLIL Programme in a University in a Monolingual Region of France

This case and Case 19 are direct applications of the epistemological and theoretical stance developed in Part 1. Students following an international master's degree course in logistics at the University of Nantes in western France were assumed to be interested in performing tasks that were close to what they would have to do in their professional life (Starkey-Perret & Narcy-Combes, 2016). This implied using the three or four languages of their repertoire, which gave them a competitive advantage over other students. The 24 students participating in the programme were organised into four groups of six students according to four logistical themes allowing them to use five different languages. French and English were common to all. Spanish, Italian, German and Chinese were ALs unequally shared among them. The students were asked to carry out a press review required by local logistics companies in their area of specialisation. This work was thought to lead to metareflection and reflective exchanges on language and culture. Moreover, as the theme of each press review originated from companies in the region where students do their internship and can hope to find a job, it gave the task the necessary external validity. The project was accompanied by two researchers and regular meetings were planned. Language teachers clarified expectations concerning the languages used and organised support meetings, while logistics teachers supported students to outline and problematise the logistical problem for which the company required an international press review so that they could start collecting articles based on the group's linguistic resources. These articles were intended to make it possible to provide answers to the problem chosen.

The project outcomes were in written form (a report in French and/or English for the company with abstracts in each of the other three languages used in the group) and in oral form (French presentations were made for the contractors and later presentations in English with questions in all the languages used were made before the teaching team). The data collected (through questionnaires at the beginning of the study, interviews at the end and observation of the recorded meetings) showed that even the theoretically best system may not convince learners if they are not prepared to work in it. It was observed that, due to a flaw in the task design, students worked cooperatively (each doing part of the work) rather than collaboratively, which was the expected mode for negotiations to take place. When they actually met, the language used was predominantly French (13/24), or possibly English. The other languages were limited to reading the press. To the question of the perceived usefulness of the multilingual press review compared to the same exercise in French or English, a majority (9) felt that this was a waste of time, two remained neutral and seven gave a positive opinion. This can be explained by the fact that 14 were much more interested in the disciplinary content than in the languages they used. Interestingly, the three Chinese students in the sample (the other 21 were native speakers of French) gave the same answers as the French students, but their reasons, as emerged during the interviews, were anchored in their educational culture with a monolingual vision of learning languages. Their goal was to achieve 'perfect mastery' of the languages they were learning. Nevertheless, the analysis of the interviews and the quality of the final productions of the students make it possible to say that the programme was able to offer a favourable ground for metareflection on the languages they used for some of the students by raising their awareness and also that exposure to an input in different languages may have triggered language acquisition.

COMMENTS

In spite of its objectives, in this context the system did not encourage students to engage in genuine collaborative teamwork, nor to devote time to language development. As in Case 14, telecollaborative work with another European university might have been more effective, as shown in the next example.

Case 19: A Binational Course in Applied Linguistics (France and Germany)

This project (Narcy-Combes & Narcy-Combes, 2014), initiated by Dagmar Abendroth-Timmer from the University of Siegen and Jean-Paul Narcy-Combes and Jose Aguilar from Sorbonne Nouvelle – Paris 3 University, involved 21 master's students, 10 in Paris and 11 in Germany (but nationals of different countries as is often the case in Europe). They worked in tandems (via a teaching platform, videoconferences and exchanges via email or Skype). The content of the master's course (ICT and language learning) was made available in a corpus of 30 articles in French, German, English and Spanish and students had to carry out the following tasks:

- Write three two-page syntheses on three topics related to the course, by selecting the appropriate articles or even by looking up other articles if they felt that was useful.
- Analyse an online language course.
- Write a report on how they had experienced the course and what they had learned.

Each tandem had to negotiate their language of communication (any one) and of production for the syntheses and the course analysis (French or German), and also the choice of articles and working methods, including the frequency of meetings. The experience was rated positively by the students, both in terms of the role of tutors and the contribution to content and language development, as well as in terms of metareflection and the management of cultural differences.

COMMENTS

In both programmes (Cases 18 and 19), which involve university language students, learning is linked to doing a task or several tasks requiring multiple interactions and involving ICT to various degrees. A research programme enables the course tutors to adapt the course to students' needs during its implementation and measure its outcome. Important variables such as the learners, the level of study, the learning content and, most importantly, the voluntary nature of student engagement, may explain why, for example, in the Siegen-Paris project, the students were more involved than in the case of the press review in the International Logistics Master programme in Nantes, France, even though the theoretical underpinnings were largely identical. The Siegen-Paris students had volunteered for the course and due to their field of study they were more directly interested in languages while the logistics students were bound by a contract and had a purely utilitarian view of learning languages. Interactions within the Siegen-Paris project were more 'natural' even though external social validity was present in both cases. This explains the major differences in the results. Moreover, the institution did not allow the same flexibility in the organisation of the system in both cases. The bi-national tandem organisation of the Siegen-Paris project naturally led to negotiations on working languages that could not take place in the case of the international press review.

In Case 18, although the task required by the company was considered valuable, the time constraints and the 'deliverables' to be provided were the actual priorities. As a consequence, interest in the languages themselves was limited compared to student attitudes in Case 19 where curiosity and interest in languages lay at the heart of the programme's success. While the students in Case 19 had agreed to work together to complete the tasks, in Case 18, the students used avoidance strategies and shared the work cooperatively instead of collaborating together. The number of students was also very different, as were the institutional constraints. Contextual parameters are seen to be of the highest influence.

Case 20: Promoting Plurilingualism in a University in Denmark

In Denmark, a parallel language policy has been introduced whereby English is promoted as the international language and Danish as the local language (Daryai-Hansen *et al.*, 2017). This has had a negative impact on the teaching of other languages, particularly in higher education, and prompted the Roskilde University (RUC) in 2012 to offer optional courses (*language profiles*) in French, German and Spanish to all students in bachelor's programmes within the humanities and social sciences. The stated aims of the programme are to 'reinforce [students'] plurilingual and intercultural competences in a second foreign language related to their studies' (Daryai-Hansen *et al.*, 2017: 31) in order to prepare them for an increasingly globalised and plurilingual business context. The students in the programme are explicitly asked to use translanguaging to achieve interactional and social aims (for a more detailed account, see Daryai-Hansen *et al.*, 2017).

At RUC, French, German and Spanish *language profiles* are positioned as academic languages complementing the official academic languages of Danish and English. This is exemplified by the students' translanguaging practices, which include searching for literature in French, German and Spanish as a supplement to literature in Danish and English (linked to project work in Danish and English) and using translanguaging to interact. While emphasis on 'correctness' is still dominant in language learning and teaching, it is replaced with translanguaging here. Students are also asked to reflect on monolingual ideologies and translanguaging and language representations, thus developing metareflection.

The study conducted by Daryai-Hansen *et al.* (2017) concerns the German language profile and focuses on teachers' and students' translanguaging practices and their attitudes towards translanguaging in language teaching and learning. Content analysis was carried out on three data sets: (i) audio recordings of students' and teachers' translanguaging practices; (ii) questionnaires about students' attitudes to translanguaging; and (iii) audio recordings of semi-structured qualitative interviews with teachers.

Students are 'independent' or 'proficient' users of the profile languages (CEFR), i.e. from B1 up to C2 levels. The programme is inspired by the Content and Language Integrated Learning (CLIL) approach and based on collaborative learning. It requires 20 hours/semester (six semester attendance) and its learning objectives are mostly geared towards gaining knowledge and skills in text reading, information searching, communications (oral and written) and reinforcing student autonomy. As mentioned previously, students are encouraged to link this course to their project work; 50% of the bachelor's programme is based on interdisciplinary and problem-oriented academic work in groups. Students can define their own progression and can choose whether to make their presentations in the profile language or in Danish. In order to acquire a language profile certificate, the students have to demonstrate in the evaluation seminar that they have met all the learning objectives. In the final semester, they are required to present and discuss in the profile language. They also reflect on and assess their learning process.

The analysis of data coming from the audio recordings of 17 students in their evaluation seminars revealed the following practices:

- Translanguaging was used at the beginning of the presentations to negotiate the principles of translanguaging.
- The teachers' default translanguaging practice is receptive translanguaging (i.e. they speak German while students use Danish, based on their plurilingual receptive competences). This occurred also in student–student interactions to help them access complex content constructed by their peers. Receptive translanguaging is established as a norm: everybody is allowed to speak German, those who do not understand can ask for help either in German (for more advanced learners) or in Danish.
- In productive practices, translanguaging is mainly used to maintain the communication flow in German with Danish words and sentences used extensively. German words are integrated if the terminology is specific. Students and teachers do not translate titles and quotations but use the original languages. Students also use English words and expressions to express content and to maintain the communication flow.

The evaluation questionnaire, completed by nine students, revealed an overall positive attitude of students towards the university's translanguaging policy. They appreciated the freedom it gave them and declared greater confidence in speaking German, as well as higher motivation to continue learning. However, results also showed that a monolingual German languaging practice is the students' preferred teaching and learning form. The authors acknowledged that 'the students still represent the monolingual paradigm as valid and desirable' (Daryai-Hansen et al., 2017: 43).

Semi-structured, qualitative interviews were carried out with three teachers (45 minutes each). All three teachers said they used both German and Danish in their class. But teachers with German as their first language tended to use German exclusively, while the teacher whose first language was Danish, tended to use Danish primarily. All three teachers emphasised that the primary objective of the class is to enhance students' language skills in German. Two teachers represented Danish as an 'auxiliary language' in this process and English as the lingua franca. Teachers defined translanguaging as a useful tool.

COMMENTS

This case is an interesting instance of translanguaging practices. Students and teachers all agree with translanguaging but still, inwardly, believe that monolingual interaction is the aim. The teachers' main focus was to enhance the students' language competences in German. Through receptive translanguaging practice, they provided input in

German and through productive translanguaging, the students were invited to interact in German. Students used translanguaging to gain and share highly complex academic knowledge. However, in terms of both teachers' and students' representations, Danish and English are represented as auxiliary languages, supposed to pave the way for monolingual language learning. We may wonder whether collaboratively preparing tasks in which the final product (written or oral academic task) is necessarily monolingual (as in Cases 1 or 16, for instance) may not have led to a clearer perception that translanguaging is a fact of life that can also help to achieve satisfactory monolingual performances.

Case 21: Multilingualism in a Ukrainian University

In Ukraine, the status of both Ukrainian and Russian is shifting, and English is slowly emerging as a favoured medium of instruction in higher education programmes. A study (Goodman, 2017) was conducted at the Alfred Nobel University, a private university in the eastern city of Dnipropetrovsk using ethnographic methods. Fieldwork was conducted over the 2010/2011 school year and focused on three groups of students and their teachers:

- A group of 25 students preparing for a joint degree from Alfred Nobel University and the University of Wales.
- A group of 24 third-year students of international economics taking one subject in English.
- A group of nine philologists (majoring in language and literature).

Students in the Welsh programme studied cultural behaviours and attitude. Economics classes were CLIL-type classes and based on content such as marketing and public relations (PR).

The research includes observation of classes taught in English but also, for some subjects taught, in Russian and Ukrainian. Informal conversations were held before or after class with students and teachers. Interviews were conducted with half the students and four of the teachers in spring 2011. The aim of the research was to explore the relative status of Ukrainian, Russian and English at the university and to analyse translanguaging practices in the classroom (for full details of the case, see Goodman, 2017).

Observations and interactions with teachers showed that some teachers see the choice of a language as personal while others choose Russian because of the students' language background and the presence of Russian students. Some selected English because it is the university policy.

However, Russian prevails while English is more used than Ukrainian and in terms of prestige comes first. In the university, students can request their preferred language of instruction.

In every class observed at the university – regardless of the official language of the course – at least one AL was used. In English-medium classes, Russian, not Ukrainian, is the default language supporting the acquisition of English. In Russian-medium classrooms, students often included English words in their PowerPoint presentations, but presented/explained the terms in Russian.

Translanguaging was also observed at university events/conferences, e.g. PowerPoint slides in one language and presentation delivered in another language. University administrators will request speakers to accommodate the audience's preferred language. Thus, a significant level of fluidity among the three languages in interactions could be observed but English remains the prestigious medium opening to the global world.

The researcher's findings suggest that Russian is the predominant language of oral communication in the classrooms, followed by English and then Ukrainian which is threatened. 'The English-only ideology competes with a multilingual reality, and in the context of classroom group work, the multilingual reality prevails' (Goodman, 2017: 63).

However, Ukrainian is the only acceptable language for written assignments (term papers, reports, etc.). So, for classes in Russian, the summative assessment will be in Ukrainian, which is in itself an act of translanguaging. This is linked to social practices and expectations in Ukraine, even if the case of Alfred Nobel University is very specific. English is also emerging as the expected language for written papers, potentially supplanting Ukrainian.

COMMENTS

The situation in this case is very different from what is seen in other cases. Translanguaging seems to be the usual practice that no one questions, but the law is still strict and exams must be taken in the official language of the country. Social status and power relations between the languages are clearly exemplified. The study was a sociolinguistic study. Consequently, the effects on academic writing and content knowledge have not been researched, which leaves many questions unanswered as to whether such practices are favourable or not to knowledge construction.

Case 22: Writing Class for Students from Different Countries

This case and Case 23 feature a situation where immigrants are concerned. Case 22 is about a writing workshop in a department of French as a foreign language (FFL) at a university and concerns a French language course for foreign students (Dompmartin, forthcoming 2018). Case 23 deals with the role of a speaking and writing workshop for the integration of migrants and ethnic minorities (Bretegnier & Audras, forthcoming 2018).

In France, and specifically at university level, the dominating status of standard French has acted as a lid over any attempt at code mixing and has contributed to immigrants feeling insecure even when well integrated into French society. At a French university in Toulouse, researchers offered a group of 15 volunteers participation in a 4-hour weekly writing workshop over 12 weeks, to be repeated on request. Participants came from very different countries, had an upper intermediate level in French (CEFR: B2) and were aged from 18 to 60. The objective was to develop their writing competencies based on the story of their experience of geographical, then linguistic, cultural and identity displacement, thus triggering metalinguistic and meta-experimental reflection. The ILs spoken within the group were taken into account together with French to make learners reflect on the differences they felt between telling a story in their IL versus telling it in their AL beyond the questions of fluency and comfort. Thus, the workshop became the place where a positive beneficial representation of bi/plurilingualism as an accomplishment emerged.

The written text was individual, as each participant had to be given an opportunity of finding a way, a voice of their own. Then the stories were shared within the group. At the end of the semester, a collection of the texts produced was published (social implication). At the same time, a selection of the texts was also proposed via a blog. The final product, as well as the intermediate written productions collected, served as a basis for assessment with learner engagement being the main criterium, which makes theoretical sense (Norton, 2013). How the participants rated the course was not measured explicitly, although their engagement is obvious in the statements they made. Given that it was done with a relatively small group, one can wonder whether it can be easily repeated in different contexts. The conditions for replication were not given.

COMMENTS

This small-scale experiment is in line with what was seen in Part 1 and close to what was done in Case 16. The methodological gains cannot be easily assessed and because of the short duration of such courses the immediate developmental effect cannot be measured accurately. Potential development, however, seems promising.

Case 23: Plurilingual Language Awareness and Self-Recognition

The issue of this experiment is sociolinguistic. The authors (Bretegnier & Audras, forthcoming 2018) believe that the power relationships that stigmatise the immigrants' IL (seen as obstacles and impediments rather than resources) and prioritise French as the one legitimate target standard (seen as a symbol of success and mobility) is a source of social inequalities and marginalisation.

The two researchers set up a two-session programme in a sociocultural centre in a French rural area. Session 1 offered eight sessions of two hours from October 2011 through to March 2012. Session 2 offered seven sessions of two hours from November to December 2012. The programme is part of a special action to support immigrants. It was open to adults benefiting from a programme to help them find a new job, including courses for the upgrading of writing skills in French. For the first session, there were only women in the group (6), all immigrants coming from countries where French is at least partly spoken (Algeria, Mayotte, Morocco, Senegal). Not all had attended school regularly and their level of written French varied. However, all had sufficient knowledge of French to communicate orally. In the second session, four of the women came back, and five men and women who were born and educated in France joined in.

The proposed activities were based on a plurilingual language awareness approach (Candelier, 2003, 2008; Kervran, 2006; Perregaux, 2003) and included pluri/metalinguistic activities, epilinguistic interactions, biographical stories, intercultural activities (meeting someone, introducing oneself) and linguistic activities. They were carried out in many (up to 12) languages, as suggested in Candelier (2003). Germanic languages and Latin were added to the workshop although no one could speak those languages. Interactions were filmed and a thematic analysis of the recordings was carried out.

The results seem to indicate that the work carried out in the workshop may have contributed to the development of linguistic exploration strategies, to the stimulation of the participants curiosity and interest in this exploration, thereby also promoting a process of self-recognition of the participants as capable learners, i.e. legitimate learners but also learners who are interested and happy to learn. They also highlighted learners' plurilingual experiences and skills, thus participating in the process of legitimising languages in general and individuals as speakers and learners in particular. The workshop triggered the clarification and the sharing of experiences, questions and epilinguistic feelings, and opened an area of interpersonal and intercultural recognition. Relations were generated that were more favourable to plurality and linguistic otherness, to feelings of greater linguistic security that were seen as conducive to the acquisition of French as well as to the development of plurilingualism.

Although nothing is said about how the participants rate the course, the small number of volunteer students, the fact that their IL is taken into account and the fact that learners come back for the second session tend to show that the experience was positive for them. However, as in the previous example, the conditions for replication are not mentioned and language development cannot be assessed.

COMMENTS

Cases 22 and 23 are in line with those that pose the question of language learning as political (e.g. Cummins, 1994; García *et al.*, 2017). In this context, as can be seen, they are dependent on the engagement of a few dedicated researchers at a micro level, and the question of replication and of the impact of those experiments remains open.

Case 24: A MOOC that Relies on Plurilingual Reflection

The massive open online course (MOOC) *Paroles de FLE* (November 2015, 2016 and 2017) (Hoppe, forthcoming) aims to meet the needs of learners (CEFR B2) who want to develop their linguistic skills in French, i.e. to understand spoken French better in various situations (e.g. a conversation or a television show), and acquire listening strategies to facilitate understanding of a variety of topics and various accents, voices and rhythms. A placement test is proposed on entry, but among the people who enrolled, there were teachers of French and professionals who needed French for their work.

It is a 6-week course, in which reading listening comprehension methodology and writing and speaking production alternate. The modules are based on authentic and fabricated material followed by learning activities. A complex social task, called 'a challenge', is proposed every week together with a series of activities that enable the students to meet the challenge. At the end of each week, a guiding questionnaire suggests additional activities when needed. Students can either (i) simply watch the videos and complete the learning activities and/or (ii) actively contribute to the exchanges on the spaces provided (i.e. forums) and carry out additional activities.

The course outline is as follows:

- Week 1: The course is introduced and students are asked to sum up an audio document in writing.
- Week 2: Students are asked to scan through written or video documents in order to write a short synthesis.

- Week 3: Students learn how to prioritise essential information, support an argument with facts and debate.
- Week 4: Students learn how to interpret discourse, compare oral and written language to report on facts.
- Week 5: Students learn how to extract information, ideas and opinions to prepare for an oral presentation. They also focus on listening and speaking skills, including understanding accents and rhythms better.
- Week 6: This session is devoted to the synthesis and assessment of what has been done.

Some of the task designs were based on the assumption that the learner's plurilingualism is an asset as a combination of metalinguistic knowledge and strategies that are transferable from one language to another. This contributes to language development through learner reflectivity, adaptability and creativity (as seen in Chapters 1–6). The objective was to create the conditions to favour learner awareness of the advantages that their plurilingual competence is an effective resource for the acquisition of a new language. As a consequence, a plurilingual approach was chosen in order to develop learner metalinguistic and interlinguistic awareness and metacognitive strategies through language comparison, identification of cognates and contrastive analysis to identify linguistic structures. A task based on the intercomprehension of related European languages involved producing a text in French after reading several texts written in different languages to foster deep processing. For example, the task proposed at each session in Week 2 required active collaboration between learners for the translation of four texts in order to produce a condensed text in the target language. The set of micro-tasks proposed for carrying out the main task was based on strategies for understanding written texts and audio-video documents. In the forum interventions, the participants identified that the proposed languages (English, French, Italian, Portuguese, Romanian, Spanish) have common or, on the contrary, very diverse lexical elements and structures. The discussion offered opportunities to develop reflective observation and analysis of linguistic facts and fostered not only the development of the target language, but also that of languages learnt previously. A survey at the end of the task revealed that for those learners 'comparing languages is a way to better understand the language one is learning' (156 respondents out of a total of 197, or 73.2%).

Assessment was carried out at various levels:

- Self-correcting exercises were offered for learning and training tasks.
- The 'challenge' task was peer reviewed and discussion on the forum enabled students to better understand the language problems.

- At the end of the course, an attendance certificate was issued if the students had complied with the course requirements.

The main characteristic of the course was its huge scale: in Session 1, 10,700 participants of 140 different nationalities registered for the course, and 327 obtained an attendance certificate. In Session 2, 12,800 participants of 142 different nationalities registered for the course, and 360 obtained an attendance certificate.

In both sessions, the data confirm that because of the flexible structure of the course, a variety of learning paths were taken that correspond to the specific language needs of the learners. Indeed, it shows that if participants are forced to follow a rigid organisation of the course, they may find it too difficult and voluntarily break free or move towards learning avoidance strategies or develop their own learning ways. Progressions from one activity to another do not seem to follow a well-established curriculum but emerge and modulate according to organising circumstances (Spear & Mocker, 1984) that each participant will create or adapt during the course. They are initially created by the flexibility of the device and even if they remain unpredictable since learning is not preprogrammed (Jessner, 2006), their emergence may be indicative of an appropriation of the pedagogical tools by the learner. The significance that the participants give to the objects they have identified as relevant can be modulated very consistently. If the plurilingual aspect of the course is not its major characteristic, the way it is organised and run corresponds to what theory has told us.

COMMENTS

The plurilingual element in the MOOC was a secondary element but the learners were very sensitive to it. The pedagogic approach was unusual in a MOOC and in line with Part 1, both aspects were rated positively by the learners. However, apart from assessment of the potentiality for development, such a course is too open to allow actual assessment of the development. There is a discrepancy between the large number of enrolments and the small team that run the course, as a result success is a purely individual phenomenon.

13 Telecollaboration

Telecollaborative cases cannot be grouped geographically and do not always correspond to a true plurilingual approach. However, practice reveals that translanguaging occurs whether it is authorised or not. Interestingly, some studies (Cases 32–37) focus on very specific aspects of language development and throw light on micro-events that may open up avenues of reflection on telecollaboration and computer-mediated communication (CMC). Owing to the specificity of telecollaboration, we have chosen to comment on the cases at the end of the chapter.

Case 25: Telecollaboration between Quebec and Australia

Maizonniaux *et al.* (2017) have implemented a telecollaborative project for the development of French as an additional language (AL) for university students in Quebec (French is an AL for these students and is spoken in the country) and Australia (French is an AL). On the Australian side, the researcher is of French origin and specialises in the teaching methodology of reading and (creative) writing in French as a foreign language (FFL) and in Quebec, the researcher is a Quebecer who specialises in teaching French as a second language to newly arrived migrants studying at the University of Quebec in Montreal. The tasks to perform are based on autobiographical literature on the subject of migration and were carried out via a Moodle learning platform over a 7-week period in September and October 2015. In addition to supporting enhanced diversity and to developing new technical and communication skills, one of the aims of the project was to enable the learners to have direct contact with speakers of the target language, whereas they would usually only have indirect contact through authentic documents.

The researchers aimed at finding out whether the telecollaborative project achieved these goals and how it helped participants to speak about themselves by reading and exchanging the proposed autobiographical texts. The data were collected via the Moodle platform and comprised pre- and post-project questionnaires as well as a significant amount of texts produced by the learners. The results were positive concerning the learners' appreciation of the opportunity they had of communicating with their faraway peers and the development of language skills (vocabulary and writing). Learners on both sides were interested in the content of the project and were moved by the subject selected. Tellingly, most of them chose as their final task to write autobiographies about their counterpart rather than themselves. Learners experienced a few technical problems due to the learning platform.

Case 26: Telecollaboration between a French and Irish High School

Guyomard Guihard (2017) set up a Skype telecollaborative exchange between French high school students learning English and Irish learners of French of the same age in an Irish high school over two years (with more or less 20 students in either group). The learners' levels varied from elementary to intermediate (Common European Framework of Reference [CEFR] A2–B1). The conversations took place twice a month and have been made part of the school curriculum on both sides. They typically last 40 minutes: French is the common language for 20 minutes, then they switch to English or vice versa with the initial language (IL) speakers taking turns as experts of their native language. Although Skype allows multichannel (video and audio), plurisemiotic (spoken and written) communication, cameras were not used for the study, which may have reduced the impact of the device. In this project, aiming at the development of students' speaking skills in view of the final exams, interactions were based on social tasks in the form of realistic scenarios involving several skills. Several information exchange tasks related to the general end of secondary school exam programme served as a backdrop for these interactions in which learners focused on both conversational content and linguistic code to understand and make themselves understood.

The topics covered had been studied beforehand by the teachers in charge on both sides. For example, each pair had to choose a global company, describe it and explain the strategies that were implemented to maintain its success on the international scene. The choice of the company was negotiated within each tandem to prevent learners from reading pre-prepared documents, which might have increased phonological nativisation (Grosbois, 2006). The findings pointed to the positive impact of the system: the situation made students active and pro-active. To be able to communicate with their partners, they used any resource at their disposal, including teacher mediation in cases of communication breakdown as well as translanguaging. The study highlighted the anxiety of the less advanced learners who felt overwhelmed by the expert speaker's discourse, which was eased by their partner's attitudes of benevolence and kindness. This helped learners to change their attitudes towards the learning of English or French, triggered their interest in the language and motivation for learning it as well as the pleasure of doing so, all key ingredients for efficient learning (Dörnyei, 2001). After two years, it was noted that the regularity of exposure to the languages facilitated lexical activation and raised learner awareness of the existing gap between what they knew and what they were aiming at knowing in the target language. They were also able to observe that negotiations of meaning helped them to make linguistic readjustments at the phonological, morphosyntactic, lexical and discursive level. They realised that learning a language takes time and investment, that their Irish or French partners also have great difficulty learning the other language and that making errors is part of the ordinary learning process. Technical problems, learner attendance and learner anxiety were found to cause a few problems. Development was measured but as this work is part of a more general course, it is difficult to explain it.

Case 27: Telecollaboration between Speakers of the Two National Languages in Belgium

Another project, led by Marneffe (2017), involves European students of similar ages (18–20) and levels of AL development; however, in a very different context: an applied linguistics bachelor's degree at Katholieke Universiteit Leuven (Antwerp campus) and at Liège University from October 2015 to May 2016. In Belgium, a country that became a federation to try to find a solution to a linguistic conflict, each student has to study either French or Dutch. In the project, speakers of French or Dutch learnt the language of the other community. This telecollaborative project features the same linguistic and cultural objectives and a comparable design as in similar telecollaborative projects.

During the first meetings, students presented Liège or Antwerp where they are studying and prepared their tandem partner's day trip to their city. To do that, they had to decide what activities to do during their partner's stay, which meant inquiring about tastes and preferences concerning cultural or sports activities, meals and available spending money. They were also encouraged to share anecdotes concerning their school life, their holidays and student jobs and finally to discuss controversial issues on the basis of articles they had sought and found. During the first encounters, students communicated in their respective IL (intercomprehension) and gradually introduced interactions following the standard tandem organisation (with occurrences of translanguaging). The necessary tools were provided online concerning academic genres (descriptive, narrative, argumentative), as well as grammatical and lexical support. At the end of each meeting, learners completed a logbook as homework and indicated the date and duration of the conversation (minimum 20 minutes), the subject and genre dealt with, examples of vocabulary learnt and errors corrected, and specified whether they had opportunities to reflect on their own language and culture and the language and culture of their partner.

These logbooks were regularly collected and commented on by the teachers. In the end, although the students' language development appeared to be positive, the researchers questioned the nature of the tasks which seemed isolated and self-sufficient, and not very demanding in terms of collaborative work.

Case 28: Telecollaboration between Learners of Distant Languages

Two projects in the corpus concern distant languages, i.e. Chinese and French. One (28a) is a telecollaboration project between third-year learners of French at the University of Foreign Languages of Dalian in China (CEFR level B1–B2) and master's-level students learning Chinese in the context of international relations and intercultural cooperation studies at the University of Lille 3, or in other contexts (internet-recruited volunteers) in the same area in France (Cappellini & Rivens Mompean, 2013; Cappellini & Zhang, 2013). The second project (28b) presents an eTandem course at institutional level between the Unit of Chinese Studies of the University of Geneva, Switzerland, and the French Department of Hubei University, Wuhan, China. The course is targeted at second-year students (A2–B1 CEFR) from both sides (Wang et al., 2013) and the study covers 3 years of implementation.

While no specific task was assigned to the participants in Case 28a (learners interacted about cultural issues as they chose, as the assumption was that interactions and negotiation of meaning would trigger language acquisition), Case 28b included theme-based asynchronous learning activities on the Moodle platform as well as task-based synchronous oral communication via Skype. Taking into consideration the socio-institutional differences between the two counterparts, one focusing on literacy and cultural knowledge while the other emphasising pragmatic linguistic competences, the course design followed a careful and iterative instructional design procedure so that the eTandem course was gradually integrated into the curriculum of both universities.

In both cases, the objectives were twofold: developing language acquisition and intercultural competence, although the theoretical assumptions at the basis were different. The findings in both projects show that the students benefited both linguistically and culturally from the eTandem exchange. In Case 28a, the authors explicitly stated that the multimodal dimension of videoconferencing, which combines several semiotic resources, enhanced and facilitated communication. They also put forward that because the learners were not bound by the completion of a specific task, there was an increased incidence of negotiations of meaning (most of which concerned lexical clarification) during the interactions. In the second project, they felt concerned by the need to design more contextualised online exchange tasks as well as normalise the course in both universities.

Case 29: Preparing for International Exchanges through Telecollaboration

Jacquier (2017) conducted a 3-year (2011–2014) longitudinal study on a synchronous and asynchronous telecollaborative teaching/learning programme for Polish, Turkish and Finnish in partnership with the State Higher Vocational School in Tarnow (Poland), Galatasaray University (Turkey) and the University of Turku (Finland). All the students were beginners in the target language and were planning to spend a year studying in Turkey, Finland or Poland.

Taking into account research findings in applied linguistics, sociology and social psychology, her research has allowed to:

- Determine a learner profile that is favourable to cultivating cultural intelligence, seen as being able to take part in co-cultural construction as described in Chapter 5 (Puren, 2002).
- Show the determining role of learner communities in the process of cultivating cultural intelligence.
- Develop a model of analysis of interactions that are likely to support the learning process.

The study highlighted that taking into account the partner's linguistic and cultural diversity could be a lever to fostering language learning. That suggests an openness of mind that may explain why learners with versatile tastes are more successful than those whose interests focus on one specific area. However, it also showed that task design is essential to trigger learner engagement.

Case 30: Telecollaboration for Intercomprehension

One well-developed project comprises intercomprehension between four Romance languages (French, Spanish, Italian and Portuguese) at the National Autonomous University of Mexico (UNAM) and involves 16 students, all speaking different Romance ILs in the first round, and 33 Spanish-speaking students learning the above-mentioned languages in the second round. They worked in teams of four with each of the four languages represented. The aim was for learners to develop their understanding of some or all of oral and written messages in the other Romance languages they do not know through their interactions with other learners. The scenario included a game with its rules, challenges, teamwork and distance collaboration. It was a detective game called 'Plurilingual Detectives' whose goal is to find the culprit of a pre-Hispanic codex theft in a museum in Mexico City and determine the circumstances and motive for the robbery. The learners had to perform several tasks, some of which involved lexis while others required longer oral or written productions. The final task was a written one. All the tasks had to be carried out in a limited time and completed over 8–15 days. The course design follows the pattern described in most intercomprehension European programmes (Degache & Garbarino, 2017; Masperi & Quintin, 2007). The findings confirm other findings in telecollaborative and intercomprehension projects about language choice and codeswitching being used at specific moments in a scenario, for example: for encouragement and congratulations, to solve technical problems and misunderstandings and to organise and carry out tasks. Although it has been noted that Spanish- and Portuguese-speaking people find it more difficult to understand Italian, whereas French and Italian speakers have difficulties in understanding Portuguese (especially spoken language), the project showed that relying on teamwork and collaboration with peers facilitated their understanding and contributed to the positive evolution of their representations concerning the comprehension of unknown languages.

Case 31: Telecollaborative Teacher Training Courses

Case 31 concerns teacher training and teacher development more specifically. As in the case of the Siegen-Paris project (Case 19), the two projects described here highlight the effectiveness of telecollaboration in teacher development, especially concerning tasks design, online teaching skills and teacher mediation.

Kurek and Müller-Hartmann (2017) set up a telecollaborative task-based English as a foreign language (EFL) teacher training course in which 25 students from Pädagogische Hochschule in Heidelberg, Germany, and 31 students from Jan Dlugosz University in Czestochowa, Poland, collaborated online in international groups designing and evaluating tasks for prospective telecollaborative learners of English. The teacher trainee students' ages ranged from 20 to 45. English was used as a lingua franca.

The focus of this project was on task design to prepare students for the complexity of the teaching environment that incorporates information and communications technology (ICT) tools and interactions of learners belonging to different sociocultural contexts and which triggers different affordances and requirements. Tasks, therefore, need to be carefully and explicitly designed so as to limit the interpretative scope due to the learners varied cultural backgrounds. In addition, trainee teachers need to be trained to be aware of the underpinning linguistic, cultural, technological and pedagogical implications, which was the aim of the telecollaborative project. Students were placed in a situation in which they were both task designers and evaluators of the participants' products, communications and portfolio reflections. Data analysis based on the participants' productions, interactions and portfolio reflections revealed that the trainees developed awareness of the complex interdependence between technology affordances and teachers' pedagogical choices. At the end of the course, they were aware of the importance of task structure and task sequencing and how they should be taken into account to balance task requirements and the importance of explicit task objectives.

The second project led by Anna Turula (2017) looks at teaching presence online in the context of an action research project involving EFL teacher trainees from the Department of Modern Languages and Literature of the Pedagogical University of Krakow (PUK), Poland, and their international partners from Pädagogische Hochschule, Freiburg (PHF) in Germany and the University of California, Santa Barbara (UCSB), California. This study shows that teaching presence is perceived differently according to the learners' educational culture (EC) (more autonomous, learner-centred EC versus less autonomous, more teacher-led EC). That perception impacts student satisfaction, thus highlighting the importance of context for the (co-)construction of meaning and 'the transformative effect of digital networks in supporting virtual communities that transcend barriers of age and culture' (Turula, 2017).

While the authors insist that good pedagogical support is essential to stimulate learners cognitive and social skills, they also draw attention to the need to keep an open mind regarding how, how much, where and when the teacher should take action or delegate all or part of it to the learners. As telecollaborative projects are complex, dynamic learning environments, teachers embarking on them should carefully plan their presence online. This requires flexibility on the part of the teachers, involving students in the project design so that the more autonomous students can participate and gain motivation, sharing responsibilities between teachers and learners so that more traditional learners can find their way to learner-centred pedagogy. The intercultural similarities and differences as well as the potential situation of misunderstanding should be discussed upstream and general guidelines established. If the aim of intercultural encounters is to broaden the learners' horizon and be conducive to critical distance, it is clear that tasks with a well-defined purpose and focus should be designed in order to challenge routine representations. The authors also advocate mixing online exchanges within class activities to discuss cultural problems and having informal private exchanges.

Case 32: The Benefits of Asynchronous Telecollaboration

Gleason and Suvorov (2011) show that several conclusions can be drawn from the study of language learners' perceptions of Wimba Voice (WV), a web-based voice solution that facilitates vocal instruction, collaboration, coaching and assessment. Although students' overall perceptions of the usefulness of ICT for improving their AL pronunciation and general AL speaking skills, as well as for providing additional feedback opportunities, decreased after using WV-based tasks, their overall eagerness to continue using technology to develop their AL speaking skills improved. Participants reported preferences for using WV to facilitate communication with fellow classmates. Despite the fact that WV was used as a methodological choice for asynchronous oral CMC, where students could focus on their individual speech reflection and planning, many individuals reported that, for them, the strengths of WV lay in its ability to promote interaction among classmates. This preference, despite running counter to the rationale for including asynchronous activities that allow for self-reflection and error diagnosis, may offer teachers and researchers insight into how CMC tasks that focus on improving oral communication skills can be exploited. There are, however, some limitations to this study. Firstly, it used only self-reported data. A second limitation pertained to the late introduction of WV, thus learners were given fewer opportunities to interact with WV activities than if they had begun earlier on.

Case 33: Corrective Feedback in Telecollaboration

Akiyama (2017) considers learner beliefs on corrective feedback (CF) in a 14-week, Skype-based eTandem project between American and Japanese universities. She found that recasts gradually replaced explicit metalinguistic feedback as the students' preferred way for giving and receiving CF as they found it was 'immediate, time-saving, unobtrusive, and easy to provide', and interaction analysis highlighted the uptakes increased when feedback was provided in the learners preferred way. The only participant who went on giving explicit feedback seemed to be positioning himself as a teacher, rather than a partner. This may be explained by the fact that error correction involves questions of identity and face-saving in the relationship.

Case 34: Identity Construction in Telecollaborative Practices

Identity construction is the issue tackled by Liaw and English (2017). The project called 'beyond these walls' was aimed at university students in Taiwan and France who were asked to select, describe, read about and discuss objects of personal significance using English as a lingua franca. It was found that the process raised participants' awareness of one another's identities and shaped the perceptions of their interlocutors as authentic, identifiable individuals with whom interpersonal communication was possible, which is essential in telecollaborative settings.

Case 35: Telecollaboration to Enhance Pragmatic Competence

Cunningham (2017) explores the possibilities of developing pragmatic competence through online exchanges as this skill requires time and regular exposure to situations that can contribute to making adapted pragmalinguistic and sociopragmatic choices. The study focuses on a particularly face-threatening speech act: making requests and on their appropriateness, i.e. are both interpretable and reflecting of social relationships. The telecollaboration involved 17 IL speakers of English from a large, public university located in the US Midwest in web conference interactions with five IL German-speaking professionals. The learners needed to formulate requests with sufficient attention to grammar and surrounding discourse so that the invited expert understood the content of the request and was able to respond accordingly. The results showed that a majority of learners (12/17) demonstrated excellent or good appropriateness. The study highlighted the role of listening (input) to develop pragmatic awareness for the production of appropriate utterances and the need to give students pragmatic guidelines on how to take the floor, organise turn taking and sustain and develop topics (mediation).

Case 36: Bringing Telecollaborative Practices to Primary School Children

Austin *et al.* (2017) show that far from being limited to adult learners at an advanced level of AL proficiency, telecollaborative exchanges are fit for children at primary school level. The study was conducted with two groups of twelve 6- and 7-year-old children from an infant school located in England with a cohort of second language English speakers who have Urdu or Punjabi as their IL and an international school in Portugal whose students are also AL speakers of English but with Portuguese as their IL. They were given a task to trigger interactions. Language and other semiotics (body language, technology and the spatial and temporal dimensions) were used during the communication. What is particularly interesting in this article is the multimodal approach the children used to communicate and how quickly they moved beyond the task assigned by their teachers to engage in personal dialogues and construct meaning by using all the communicative resources at their disposal.

Case 37: Effects of Tandem Practices on Corrective Feedback

Horgues *et al.* (2015) and Manoïlov and Tardieu (2015) collected an English/French tandem corpus as part of the SITAF project (*Spécificités des Interactions verbales dans le cadre de Tandems linguistiques Anglais-Français*), which was launched at Sorbonne Nouvelle – Paris 3 University in France in 2012. Although this type of work is not telecollaborative since participants were in the same location, it is a form of tandem work, and of two-way immersion which could be organised more frequently in European universities (see Case 17). We have chosen to describe it because, in spite of its monolingual stance, it provides insights into how learners can deal with collaborative feedback in such circumstances. Horgues *et al.* (2015) gathered data from face-to-face conversational exchanges held by 21 pairs of undergraduate students (video and audio recorded). Each 'tandem' consisted of an IL English speaker and an IL French speaker. Dialogues were recorded on two occasions separated by a 3-month interval (February–May 2013). Participants were recruited through an online questionnaire on the university website. All participants volunteered freely for the tandem programme and organised their meetings autonomously. They met between two and 23 times with a mean frequency of 12 meetings over the 3-month period. The 21 IL French speakers were all undergraduate students in English studies for the most part. Their proficiency level varied from upper-intermediate to advanced. The 21 IL English speakers were exchange students at the Paris university and represented a range of variants (American, British, Irish and Australian). Research focused on the analysis of AL pronunciation feedback (phonetic CF). The speakers were recorded performing two semi-spontaneous speech tasks: two games eliciting argumentation and storytelling: (i) the Liar Liar game (the IL listener had to identify three lies incorporated by their partner into a personal story) and (ii) the Like Minds game (after discussing a controversial subject, the partners determined their degree of agreement).

As in most tandem situations, the use of French and English was separated with an instructed switch after 30 minutes, which remains a monolingual attitude. The reading task entailed a higher frequency of CF than the spontaneous games activities (learners were more focused on form than communication). It was found that the CF provided by the language partners plays a part in raising the learners' awareness about the difference between their output and target form.

To improve the pedagogical benefits of language tandem programmes, the authors advocate providing tandem partners with some awareness-raising training on the strategies necessary to provide and receive CF effectively. Horgues *et al.* (2015) examine how participants in the study mobilise non-verbal resources (prosody, gestures) in the context of CF. The coding scheme revealed that CF is a highly multimodal activity. Hand gestures, head movements and facial variations were the most frequently used visual resources. The IL speaker's CF provision mobilised hand gestures 66% of the time (44).

Both the IL speaker and the AL learner rely on shared non-verbal resources (e.g. representational hand gestures) to clarify meaning. Multimodality seems to contribute positively to the negotiation of meaning between two tandem partners, thereby facilitating the integration of new AL knowledge particularly for lexical development. Another finding was that participants elaborated idiosyncratic multimodal strategies dedicated to a specific CF stage (request, provision and uptake).

Concerning students' attitudes to providing and receiving CF and to how this differed with teachers' provision of CF, Manoïlov and Tardieu (2015) positioned tandem partners on a continuum from positive (0 to +6) to negative (0 to –6) in terms of their attitudes to giving and receiving CF. The CF received was appreciated by all but two participants. On the other hand, providing CF (correcting one's partner) was associated with more negative attitudes for a third of the students. Students who had a positive perception of CF found the activity of giving CF pleasant, enjoyable and useful.

One of the authors of this book selected 15 recordings from the SITAF corpus to analyse for translanguaging occurrences (75 minutes). Her hypothesis is that students with a more negative attitude to CF will favour the natural flow of communication, which will lead to language fluidity with students accessing their entire linguistic repertoire to understand the content of the message (i.e. more instances of translanguaging). In general, the level of translanguaging was low across all tandem pairs, whether they had a negative or positive attitude to CF, with the exception of one tandem accounting for 63% of all translanguaging occurrences (19 out of a total of 30). The majority of translanguaging occurrences related to discussions about lexical choices. The low occurrence rate can in part be explained by the fact that the majority of the students had followed task instructions given by the research team which were to use French and English separately, but also due to the fact that they were majoring in English. One may then assume that obviously more proficient learners can manage in just one code if necessary, but also that students majoring in a language course at university level in France still have a monolingual attitude.

COMMENTS

Cases 32–37 exemplify the benefits of participating in telecollaboration or tandem projects that can, in the long run, enhance language learning. These benefits include students' increased interest in learning the target language, students' stronger contact with the target culture and perceived cultural knowledge gains, students' raised interest in study abroad and higher motivations levels. There is therefore every reason to support collaborative online language learning.

All the studies that have been considered here have shown that videoconferencing between peers of comparative ages who are IL speakers of one of the languages broadens the scope of the discourse type and lexis available to learners from traditional classroom environments and creates conditions to enhance language learning. This is confirmed by Schenker's (2017) meta-analysis of studies on telecollaboration published between 1990 and 2012, which reveals that weekly communication between intermediate learners who work in pairs or groups may be beneficial for second language acquisition. It shows that videoconferencing, in particular thanks to the multimodality it provides, enables increased levels of communication between students, that voice-chat projects might be most beneficial between 'non-native' speakers and other non-native speakers who do not speak the same first language, especially to develop students' pronunciation skills. Tandems can also lead to positive learning outcomes, including the development of different communication strategies and increases in speaking proficiency. Oral proficiency improvements may in fact be higher after participating in telecollaboration projects than after regular face-to-face classroom communication. Studies investigating the effects of voice-chatting between 'native' and advanced 'non-native' speakers also showed that telecollaboration can help students develop their interactive and pragmatic skills. Even though the pressure of the immediate communication situation can result in unsuccessful task completion and fewer instances of negotiation of meaning, when comparing 'native'/'non-native' communication in voice-chat and text-chat, students generally react favourably to telecollaboration projects through video and/or audio communication and perceive gains in language skills and intercultural competence. The importance of well-designed tasks, network training and carefully selected partners for a videoconferencing project is underlined, but students with less advanced language skills may struggle to understand their partner. A study showed no difference in syntactic complexity in speaking for students who participated in telecollaborative tasks, although the telecollaboration students outperformed the other groups in the amount of language produced in face-to-face conversations.

As far as Case 37 is concerned, from what was seen in Part 1, we are tempted to say that the approach taken by focusing on errors would not be in line with what was written in Part 1 if generalised. The aim of task-based learning is task completion with different levels of achievement and 'errors' are one element that determines these levels. However, in terms of training (see Part 3), the work done may prove beneficial if learners see the point (one of the tandems seems to have been reluctant).

One could also say that telecollaboration or tandem work turns any form of language learning into an actual plurilingual experience and changes the whole attitude to language learning. Brammerts and Calvert (2002) have highlighted some drawbacks of face-to-face oral tandem learning: spoken input is ephemeral and is therefore highly demanding on learner's attention and memory skills. Many tandem participants will naturally focus on content, smooth communication and task completion rather than on form accuracy.

Many authors point to the fact that although the experience is very rewarding, it is also quite time-consuming and technical problems may be a serious hindrance to the development of telecollaboration. Others (Liaw & English, 2017) highlight the dominance of English as a lingua franca. While English seemed to be the desirable language to acquire in most of the projects in this book, it is not the case for projects involving intercomprehension between Romance languages and, though they have not been studied here, between Germanic languages (see Marx, 2012, for example).

14 Learning Languages in Multilingual Contexts: Where are We Now?

Following the description and analyses of various case studies throughout the world, this chapter offers a synthetic overview of their content and complements it with information that was not found in the cases that were selected in order to exemplify our theoretical positions. We have, in particular, turned to meta-analyses from Asia and Latin America to complete our understanding of the problems.

Contexts

Geographical, social/historical, sociolinguistic, economic and institutional contexts

The history of the countries involved reflects either migrations or conquests and dominance. Invasions have been suffered, leading to the symbolic eradication of languages to be replaced by the dominant language as was seen in many of the case studies. Essentially, the dominant language became a desirable value in order to move up the social ladder, prompting many parents to stop transmitting a stigmatising language to their children (and thus relinquishing their identity). A similar situation was, and still is, experienced by immigrants coming to America or Europe. Individuals are well aware that in order to be accepted as part of the community, they need to be able to understand and speak the language of the school, whether it be English, French or German (Hélot & Erfurt, 2016; Maurer, 2010; McIlwraith, 2013; Otwinowska & De Angelis, 2014; Paulsrud *et al.*, 2017). This was evidenced in some of the cases (Cases 1–5, 22, 26). Such situations of migration, conquest and dominance can also be found in other parts of the world (Asia, South America, etc., see Leconte *et al.* [2018] or Canagarajah [2013]).

The sociolinguistic situations echo the historical patchwork. In the French overseas territories and departments for example, as many as 40 different languages can be heard and different varieties of creoles are found and spoken in all of them. However, French is the language spoken by the cultural and social elite, therefore it is desirable, and some parents want the school to promote it and their children to speak it

(Muni Toke, 2016) while others do not, more or less consciously. Such a situation is not unusual, as we have already mentioned (Sandberg, 2017, for instance), much like the 'speak good English' position in Singapore (Gauthier, 1998).

Conversely, in the outer and border regions of metropolitan France, where the local languages were almost completely eradicated at the beginning of the 20th century and where few of the school children speak the 'heritage' language, demand has been constantly growing for bilingual schools. Parents and local language activists have wanted to revive their heritage for identity reasons (Case 15). Consequently, some children find themselves in the odd situation that their own grandparents experienced when they had to learn and speak French at school rather than their own language: they are made to learn a language that nobody speaks at home or in their immediate environment (as seen in Adam & Calvez, 2016 and Coyos, 2016). No precise statistics on this subject were available in the literature we reviewed.

In the USA, a significant proportion of the population has Spanish as their initial language (IL) in states such as Arizona (29.6%), New Mexico (46.3%) (Case 3), Texas (37.6%) and California (37.6%), making it the world's second largest Spanish-speaking country after Mexico (see Burgen, 2015). In New York, only 51% of the population speak English at home, while nearly 15% speak Spanish, followed by 2.8% speakers of Chinese, 1.2% who speak Russian and 1% Italian. At least 16 other languages can be heard to a lesser proportion (see Statistical Atlas, 2015). However, English is the language of schooling and federal and state language education policies prioritise English proficiency attainment for English language learners (ELL), leaving little room for language diversity (see Cases 1–5). In that context also, children need to use a language at school that is neither the language of the home nor that of their environment. English is compulsory to be accepted as a full American citizen. In Canada, where two-thirds of the population are immigrants and multilingualism is pervasive, a balanced bilingualism (English and French) is an asset. As a result, research on plurilingualism has always been evidenced in the country.

In Morocco (Mabrour & Narcy-Combes, forthcoming 2018), the aboriginal Amazigh languages were forced out by the languages of the conquerors, Arabic first, then French (Spanish in the north and south). Standard Arabic and dialectal Arabic have a diglossic relationship. Dialectal Arabic has many local variants. French is still very present in the linguistic landscape and is considered a prestigious language that can open the door to top positions. It has recently been reintroduced as a language of schooling for some disciplines in schools. It is also the language of schooling in scientific and medical universities. English is very desirable in educated circles. Morocco granted the Amazigh language the status of official language alongside Arabic in July 2011. To that effect, the teaching of the Amazigh language was introduced into primary schools. Algeria and Tunisia have very similar language situations (Morsly, 2016). However, the learners' first languages, dialectal Arabic and/or Amazigh, are not officially accepted, though Algeria has followed in the footsteps of their Moroccan neighbour and given Amazigh official status. Even though both languages occur regularly during interactions in the classroom, they are never considered as languages worthy to be used for school education.

Most countries in sub-Saharan Africa (Maurer, 2010) have kept the colonisers' language as an official language as a way of avoiding ethnic conflict. However, given the way partition was made, ignoring ethnic, religious, linguistic and cultural data, major problems could not be avoided. In Djibouti, Mali, Mauritania, Senegal and Tchad, Arabic and French compete for dominance as the languages of schooling. Arabic is the official language in Mauritania, and one of the official languages in Djibouti and Tchad, French being another official language. French is the official language of Senegal and Mali. However, the population speak many different languages and the sociolinguistic situation is extremely complex. The language of the home will differ from the language of the school for most students (Cases 6 and 7), and even the oral variety of French that is spoken by the population differs from the variety taught at school, as seen in Cases 6 and 7 (Maurer, 2010, 2016).

A similar situation is found in countries where English plays a role. English remains one of the official languages in Kenya, Tanzania and Uganda (together with Swahili) where over 60 different languages can be heard. Adopting official languages spoken by only a small part of the population is a means of avoiding ethnic conflict. However, 'speakers of Bantu languages, which are similar in structure to Swahili, generally speak better Swahili providing a distinct advantage in professional circles' (Pereltsvaig, 2011). In that context, South Africa is a unique example as there are 11 carefully chosen official languages representing 99% of the population. By acting in that way, the country has managed to grant recognition to the languages and cultures of its citizens while preventing one language from being dominant over the other and consequently avoiding conflict (Case 8).

The studies we reviewed referring to South Asia and South America report very similar situations. We also noted similar phenomena in Malaysia and Morocco with obvious contextual differences due in particular to recent migrations from India and China that have complexified the language situation.

In Europe, the Polish situation (Otwinowska & De Angelis, 2014), for instance, reflects, among other factors, the way the history of a country impacts language choices and the symbolic value that its people attribute to them. Tellingly, plurilingualism was valued in Poland from the beginning of the 14th century, when Polish and also Lithuanian, French, Italian and Latin were spoken in the country. However, Russian and German became the dominant languages at the time of partition enhancing the symbolic value of Polish which it has retained.

Within the European institutions, no European language officially dominates the others, hence the need to translate the EU directives into all the official languages of the member countries and the development of intercomprehension programmes, but English is the working language (see Chapter 13 for its influence in the telecollaborative cases).

In such complex sociolinguistic situations as have just been described, teachers cannot hope to influence society as a whole and can only change things at the level of their institution at best, or of their students. Even large-scale international programmes cannot rapidly alter the situation (Cases 6 and 7; Fantognon, 2014; Maurer, 2010), as the final results actually depend on the teachers themselves who need adequate training (Narcy-Combes & Xue, forthcoming 2018). Researchers and educationalists can take part in such programmes, but they no longer operate at the level of what we call intervention. We observed that smaller pilot projects that pay attention to the specific needs of the population are more successful, and yet, even if they gain recognition from the state authorities, generalising the new practices remains problematic (e.g. Haddad, 2008; Sandberg, 2017). This is often due to financial reasons and a lack of adequate teacher training facilities and teaching materials.

Huge socioeconomic discrepancies prevail between and inside the countries under study, varying from extreme poverty and total lack of financial, human and material resources to very well-equipped learning environments and highly qualified teachers. Such contextual factors cannot be overlooked (see Chapter 7). Unsurprisingly, in the states of California, New Mexico and New York and in Canada, Germany and Switzerland (Cases 1–5, 17 and 19), learners have no problem accessing computers, TV and video players as well as having the internet at their disposal and working in pleasant, comfortable environments. If it is also the case in most French schools, it is very different in the French overseas territories and departments where living standards are lower and where there is a lack of qualified teachers and teaching materials and where the differences between town and country are noticeable (Hélot & Erfurt, 2016). Material conditions are challenging in sub-Saharan Africa, where schools lack most of the basic equipment that seems so natural in Western countries, and where electric power is not available everywhere (Cases 6 and 7). In Moroccan schools, as there is a two-tier educational system, one for the privileged learners and the other for the rest of the population, only the private system enjoys such facilities and this is far from being rare (see i.e. Leconte *et al.*, 2018; Canagarajah & Ashraf, 2013, for South Asia). Obviously, the socioeconomic discrepancies are reflected in the cases described. Teachers cannot hope to alter the socioeconomic situation and will probably have to try and compensate for the ensuing limitations at their level.

The countries under study have sometimes radically different educational cultures. Most of the countries where French influence is (or was) felt have a very hierarchical organisation (Maurer, 2010), whereas countries where English influence prevails are likely to accept more initiative on the part of their teachers. However, in most countries in all regions of the world, teachers or researchers have to refer to their respective educational authorities and cannot entirely move away from the frameworks and policies they impose (Canagarajah, 2013; García *et al.*, 2017; Hélot & Erfurt, 2016; Leconte *et al.*, 2018; Mazak & Caroll, 2017; Otwinowska & De Angelis, 2014; Paulsrud *et al.*, 2017).

Our selection of studies covers all stages from primary school to university level. Unsurprisingly, the schools that are subject to government supervision and decisions are not as free as other schools and universities to experiment with new systems, but even in such schools, teachers have been able to adapt, and teams of teachers and researchers can be even more successful.

Countries where French plays a role

In these countries (mainland France and French territories, North Africa, so-called francophone sub-Saharan Africa), different contexts can be seen highlighting differences between primary, secondary and higher education; rural, semi-rural and urban areas; rich and poor areas.

In mainland France, one must clearly distinguish between:

- the outer and border regions: the languages of origin (e.g. Alsatian, Basque, Breton and Flemish) are no longer spoken there by children and teenagers. However, an attempt at reviving them is made in kindergarten and primary schools at the associations' and local educational authorities' (*Rectorats*) instigation following the Bologna Process (1999) (Hélot & Erfurt, 2016). Children (and their parents) gradually give up learning these languages as they get older in favour of more *useful* and prestigious languages.
- International Sections (IS) were implemented in 1981 and concern 16 different languages and partnerships with 19 countries (Hélot & Erfurt, 2016). The students of all levels of education belong to an international elite and have very comfortable socioeconomic backgrounds. They must be at least bilingual when they register for the course. Content should be taught by a native speaker of the language of instruction, but it is not always the case (Hélot & Erfurt, 2016).
- Bilingual Sections (BS) concern secondary education only and were implemented in 1992. There are two categories: BS for European languages (Dutch, English, German, Italian, Portuguese and Spanish, with the addition of Russian) and BS for oriental languages (Arabic, Chinese, Japanese and Vietnamese) (Hélot & Erfurt, 2016).

- Immigrants' languages are subjected to specific programmes to cater for the language needs of immigrant populations at all levels, including adults, with mixed results (Hélot & Erfurt, 2016) (Cases 22 and 23).

In French overseas departments and territories, heritage languages (creoles and original first languages) are only taken into consideration at kindergarten and primary school level. As French is the language of schooling and social status, children drop their heritage language studies at secondary school level and quickly forget what they have learnt (Hélot & Erfurt, 2016).

In sub-Saharan Africa, ILs or national languages are not at all tools for social success or mobility, or only to a very limited extent. Therefore, French is the language of schooling in Mauritania (Candalot, 2005), in Djibouti, Mali, Senegal and Tchad (Maurer, 2010). However, successful attempts have been made to implement bilingual learning and teaching at primary school level as we have seen (Maurer, 2011, 2016) (see Cases 6 and 7).

In North Africa, French is the indisputable language of schooling at university level for the study of scientific subjects. However, Standard Arabic is the language of schooling prior to that, thus accounting for a very high failure rate in the first year of university (Cortier *et al.*, 2013). As a result, French was reintroduced at primary school level in 2016 in Morocco to tackle this problem. In Algeria, resentment against the former coloniser prevents authorities from taking such steps, while in Tunisia the use of French in schooling has never been questioned (Mabrour & Narcy-Combes, forthcoming 2018).

The language situation is very similar in countries where Spanish and Portuguese play a part due to a colonial period (e.g. Africa and South America with contextual variations). The situation is made more complex, in particular at the level of higher education, by the global role of English which is a strong competitor for the former colonial languages (see Boukri-Friekh, 2011, for instance). This is very different from what can be seen in other parts of the world where English actually plays a dominant role (e.g. Canagarajah & Ashraf, 2013; Leconte *et al.*, 2018, for South East Asia).

Countries where English plays a role

Support for language learning has become an important rational argument since various sociolinguistic studies (Genesee, 1987; Siguán & MacKay, 1986) showed that the substitution of the language of origin with the language of the host country might have negative consequences, in particular by confining multilingual pupils to semi-linguistic or subtractive bilingualism. However, several countries, in particular the USA, limit their investment in the teaching of languages of origin to a one-size-fits-all dimension (Cummins, 1984).

Canada is a federal state where exclusive responsibility for education rests with the provinces, which makes it difficult to generalise about curriculum or learning outcomes (see La politique des langues officielles du gouvernement fédéral, 2017). However, the decisions concerning which language is to be used in social life and in education are shared between the federal government and the provinces. Thus, in 1988, a law was passed to promote French–English bilingualism at all levels in society. Since then, English and French have been taught and used in the educational system, and considerable efforts have been made to develop equality between the two languages. In a country where 42% of the population has an immigrant background, three provinces have developed dynamic plurilingual programmes: Ontario, Alberta and Quebec (McAndrew & Ciceri, 2003). Programmes that focus on the objective of maintaining languages and cultures of origin have been developed generally in response to the mobilisation of the minority groups themselves (i.e. Ukrainian in Ontario) rather than for pedagogical reasons or a request from school stakeholders. However, the teaching of languages of origin has increasingly been defined for the last 10 years as a measure of intercultural enrichment. While this goal is highly valued today, it should be noted that the recent context has also made economic competitiveness emerge as an important argument for advocates of such education (Cummins, 2005).

In the USA, over the last several decades, spaces for bilingualism have shrunk and bilingual children and teachers are blamed for their students not performing at *appropriate* levels in English (Kumashiro, 2012). The No Child Left Behind (NCLB) law of 2002 requires states to test students in Grades 3–8 each year and to assess the school and the teachers' performance based on these test scores. It also requires them to assess the English proficiency of ELLs annually and monitor their progress. Common Core State Standards (CCSS) were developed in English language, arts and literacy and maths and have been adopted by 42 states. Little attention is given to bilingualism in the CCSS documents. The standards do not mandate a specific curriculum, pedagogical approach or required materials. They apply to all students regardless of their English development. In 2015, President Obama introduced the 'Every Student Succeeds Act' to replace the NCLB in order to give more flexibility to states on how to test students and on whether to adopt the CCSS. The emphasis across the USA is to get students to perform at proficient levels in English and to show what they can do in other subjects usually in English, without regard to the language diversity of the nation (see Cases 1–5 that testify to a different position).

In sub-Saharan, so-called *English-speaking* Africa, although efforts have been made to develop language learning programmes at all levels in the educational system, the same problems as the ones identified in *French-speaking* countries prevail. The mastery of English is the gateway to top-paying positions and parents resent the use of African languages at school for fear they would impair their children's prospects. Besides, there is often a real lack of teaching material in African languages and qualified teachers (see Case 8).

We have already highlighted a number of similar problems in South East Asia (Canagarajah & Ashraf, 2013; Leconte *et al.*, 2018) and mentioned Sandberg's (2017) plea for sensitising parents to the difference between English as an additional language (AL) and English as the language of schooling, if it is not the child's IL.

European trends

Promoting the languages of each of the member countries was a key issue in Europe as early as 1992 with the European Charter for Regional or Minority Languages (see Council of Europe, 1992). Since then, the pledge has been renewed several times (e.g. the European Parliament resolution of October 2001 on linguistic diversity) and many large-scale intercomprehension projects have been supported (see Cases 11–15). At the same time, double degrees were created from end of secondary school degrees to doctoral degrees (Case 19).

Countries where pluri-multilingualism has been the rule for some time and is still thriving, such as Switzerland (Case 17) and the multilingual Italian autonomous provinces of Alto Adige/South-Tyrol and Val d'Aosta, serve as laboratories for Europe with the aim of developing multilingual education in the area (Gajo, 2003). However, the context is both so complex and specific that the findings cannot possibly be generalised without precautions.

The languages spoken by migrant populations are treated differently, as they are very seldom considered desirable languages to be acquired by the host populations. Immigrants are always expected to be able to master the host country language (Case 22). The better they can use the language, the better integrated they are. In Germany, the MIsprache project was implemented in order to integrate the immigrant population (adults and children mostly of Turkish, Polish and Italian origin) into German society. The German language is seen as the unifier. When languages of origin are taught, what the authorities have in mind is to help to facilitate their recognition on returning to the home country (Otwinowska & De Angelis, 2014).

In Poland, where no less than 12 different languages beside Polish can be heard for 2% of the population, Polish is compulsory at school, but allowances are made for other languages (Otwinowska & De Angelis, 2014). The Ukrainian situation (Case 21) is a particularly complex one.

Teacher Education and Training

When the focus is on plurilingual education and teacher training, the situation varies considerably from a given context to another.

In Switzerland, in-service training in English and bilingual didactics are compulsory (Otwinowska & De Angelis, 2014). However, it is the only instance in which proper teacher education is mentioned. In France, most teachers rely on their pre-service training, which results in teachers seeing bilingualism as the juxtaposition of two monolingualisms. In a few examples, special training in bilingual pedagogy has been provided, whether in-service (Guadeloupe, Guyana) or pre-service (Aquitaine, Languedoc-Roussillon and Midi-Pyrénées) or both (Basque region). In most cases though, no specific training at all is provided and teachers feel helpless even when they embrace the notion of bilingual teaching (Hélot & Erfurt, 2016).

In the USA, where teachers are more self-reliant, enjoy greater autonomy and have easy access to the documentation they need, self-study is the rule. However, when dual language education programmes are implemented, the lack of adequately trained teachers is a general complaint, although in-service training is widely provided in the form of summer courses, workshops, seminars and conferences as well as webinars and online programmes (US Department of Education, 2015).

In Morocco, top-down training sessions are provided nationwide when needed. However, the gap between what is advocated in terms of plurilingual education and what teachers are actually able to do can still be felt. Besides, the teaching conditions vary greatly whether the school is set in a rural, semi-rural or urban area, rural school being the poorest (Mabrour & Narcy-Combes, forthcoming 2018).

In French-speaking, sub-Saharan Africa, one of the major problems is the fact that teachers are under-qualified with a majority of them having a secondary school diploma at best and holding precarious low-skilled and low-paid jobs. Thus, even though steps have been taken to provide pre-service and in-service teacher training (Maurer, 2010), the situation remains problematic.

As has already been mentioned, similar problems are evidenced in South East Asia. We suggest that OEP could be one way of complementing what state institutions provide (see www.TESS-India.edu.in).

The Consequences of So Many Different Situations and Positions

What emerges from the findings above is the polysemy of the constructs of multi/plurilingualism, as multiple meanings, from very positive to quite negative, are associated with the terms depending on the context. In the USA, the notion of 'emergent bilinguals' for children whose home language is different from the language of schooling has been proposed (García et al., 2008) to replace the institutional term of 'English language learners' or worse 'limited English proficient students', which shows that the discussion on bi/multi/plurilingualism is ideological and political in essence.

From what the case studies revealed, let us try and define what is it to be bi/multi/plurilingual.

Depending on the context and the people involved, it may mean:

- 'Knowing' and 'knowing how to use' one or two prestigious European languages (English, French, German, Spanish) and being recognised as part of an equally prestigious elite (European and international sections of high schools) (Hélot & Erfurt, 2016).
- Being able to understand interlocutors belonging to the same linguistic family without necessarily speaking that language (intercomprehension programmes).
- Learning a lingua franca such as English.
- Living in an environment where two or more languages coexist (Canada, Catalonia, South Tyrol, Switzerland, India, Pakistan, Singapore, etc.).
- Having another (less prestigious) language as an IL than that of the host country and needing help to learn it to be able to become 'one of them' and have access to an education (the case of immigrants).
- Having two or more partially accepted varieties of local languages in one's repertoire and being educated in a different language in one's own country (Standard Arabic and French in Mahgreb, and French in French-speaking Africa).
- Being monolingual in one prestigious language and having a so-called heritage language learnt for ideological reasons (French border areas [Hélot & Erfurt, 2016]; Hungarians learning Hungarian in Austria, or Poles learning Lithuanian [Otwinowska & De Angelis, 2014]).

Clearly, these different situations do not quite correspond to what seems preferable and they will trigger different cognitive, affective, identity and social consequences and implications on the learning environments. However, along with García *et al.* (2017), we think that it is imperative to ensure that educationalists see the plurilingualism of students as a resource, never as a deficit, and plurilingualism as a dynamic and complex process and not as linear and unidirectional. This can be done at the micro level as studies show that it is the most effective route to individual 'success' (Haddad, 2008; Leconte *et al.*, 2018; Sandberg, 2017).

Implemented Learning Systems

Initiative

In most of the cases under study, the learning system was set up and implemented either by the institution or by the researcher(s).

- In French primary and secondary schools, nothing can be done officially without the agreement of the educational authorities, so projects (e.g. teaching creole and in creole at primary school level) are

either initiated by the educational authorities or by an approved team of researchers (Hélot & Erfurt, 2016).
- Intercomprehension projects in Europe (Cases 11–15) are official European projects and must be peer approved.
- In Canada, immersion programmes are part of the educational policy of the country.
- In North Africa as well as in sub-Saharan Africa, education is in the hands of the governments and decisions must be applied nationwide. Despite this, researchers do research the field and propose recommendations (Bensfia *et al.*, 2013; Maurer, 2010; Noyau, 2016), and large-scale multinational projects also exist (e.g. ELAN, Cases 6 and 7).
- Non-governmental organisations (NGOs), UNESCO and other international institutions also implement, run and assess multilingual language projects. Many of them combine top-down and bottom-up organisations (e.g. Haddad, 2008; Sandberg, 2017).

However, teacher initiatives (with the support of at least one researcher) can be noted in regions such as Corsica (France) (Case 15 and Di Meglio & Cortier, 2016), or countries such as Switzerland (Brohy *et al.*, 2014) where the implemented projects were based on the voluntary involvement of students and teachers, as well as in South Tyrol (Italy), where the request was initiated by parents who addressed the local authorities, which resulted in an agreement between the municipality and the local education authority.

Similarly, California, New Mexico and New York (Cases 1–5) show that the initiative may come from the teachers, with the help of a team of researchers, as teachers are granted some leeway providing the learners perform satisfactorily in the national exams. Cases 1–5 were implemented in the form of an action research programme involving the stakeholders in the community: children, parents, educators, researchers and educational authorities. Sandberg (2017) in particular gives instances of small or medium-sized pilot projects in South Asian countries that have more convincing results than many large-scale programmes and that have nevertheless influenced the states to alter their language education policies.

As far as language learning environments (LLEs) are concerned, teachers always have a way of acting at the micro level if they are sufficiently informed and motivated.

Learning goals and tools

Two major approaches dominate the way institutions implement their idea of plurilingual learning and teaching: Content and Language Integrated Learning (CLIL) and target language learning (TLL).

CLIL or content-based instruction

As we saw in Cases 10 and 17–19, the approach benefited from the support of the EU as early as 1995 (European Council, 1995). We would tend to identify as a sub-type or variant of CLIL the situations in which immigrants find themselves when they attend a school where the language of schooling differs from their home language. Content-based instruction (CBI) is not very different from CLIL in practice. In that situation, they are expected to acquire content knowledge through an AL they do not necessarily master to a sufficient degree to develop their understanding of academic content. We saw in Chapter 3 that results do not always correspond to what was expected for reasons that should be taken on board when implementing learning environments.

Bilingual programmes have been developed, notably in the USA (García *et al.*, 2017; García & Kleyn, 2016; Paulsrud *et al.*, 2017) based on the concept of translanguaging (García, 2009; Williams, 1994), which moves away from a strict separation of languages (Cases 1–5, 17). Such case-specific examples are to be encountered in two French regions (Corsica and Midi Pyrénées, see Hélot & Erfurt, 2016), Italy (South Tyrol) and Switzerland (Otwinowska & De Angelis, 2014: Case 17), Sweden and Belgium (Paulsrud *et al.*, 2017). The cases in our corpus show that most of the problems raised by CLIL or CBI can be overcome.

Bilingual programmes in Val d'Aosta (Cavalli, 2005), two-way immersion programmes or primary classes in Southern Asia, for instance (e.g. Canagarajah & Ashraf, 2013; Haddad, 2008; or Sandberg, 2017) are examples of bilingual or multilingual CBI with a more or less official status.

Our research and data from other sources (e.g. Canagarajah & Ashraf, 2013; Haddad, 2008; Sandberg, 2017) show that practices can change at the micro level even in very traditional settings and Case 10 (history in Italy) clearly underscores the fact that top-down decisions are often too hasty and do not pay attention to the actual needs of students and teachers.

Target language learning

TLL refers to courses focusing on the language to be learnt, in parallel to the mainstream curriculum, whether it is a minority, local or heritage language. This organisation may also concern the language of the host country taught to immigrants. The main problem lies with the fact that the languages are taught separately, in isolation, and more often than not, in a teacher-centred way (Hélot & Erfurt, 2016).

It should be noted that concerning Morocco, and indeed most North and South African countries as well as South Asian countries (Malaysia, for instance), there is a combination of the two approaches. French or English is taught as a subject in itself, while subjects (especially scientific subjects) are taught in French or English, according to who the former coloniser was (Bensfia *et al.*, 2013; Cortier *et al.*, 2017; Maurer, 2010; McIlwraith, 2013; Leconte *et al.*, 2018).

As far as an AL2 is concerned, especially in the case of French coming after English (or vice versa), as they are seen and felt as typologically close, the use of the other language often has a facilitating role in classes (metalanguage, explanations) and reduces language anxiety (e.g. Bailly *et al.*, 2009; Bozhinova, 2018; Cuet, 2011; Hopkins, 2014; Leconte *et al.*, 2018). The instrumental role is prevalent in practices (see Chapter 2). However, research results show that French or English can be a supplier language (see Chapter 2) when learning the other language (Souliou, 2014; Wehbe, 2017), but this is not generally exploited. Canagarajah and Ashraf (2013) rightly suggest that plurilingualism should go with strategy awareness. Few cases similar to Hopkins (2014) in Hong Kong actually have tasks combining the two languages (see Case 18 too). Interestingly, similar studies for French and German, which are not typologically close, are described in Robert (2016). Nevertheless, it is still an aspect of AL learning that should be investigated more deeply in connection with intercomprehension.

Some interesting and more or less formal cases found in the literature have features combining two- or three-way immersion, informal learning and metareflection (e.g. Gorter, 2013 or www.TESS-India.edu.in). Both suggest using all the resources available in the everyday environment. Canagarajah and Ashraf (2013) describe Indian textbooks in which technical or scientific terms are introduced in English when they are not known in the local languages and show that the mixing of languages can be found in materials used to teach English.

Task-based language learning and learning materials

Teachers in the selected examples (most cases) tend to follow a form of task-based approach as they try to involve their learners in a creative project that combines content and language and maintain their interest. It is also the case for example of the 'orero project in Tahiti where an ancestral practice (storytelling to an audience) has been revitalised (Paia & Vernaudon, 2016), or the *Cuentame Algo* experience in New Mexico, where children and parents tell about their experience. Learning through stories, songs and poems, or theatre based on local folklore is used at primary school level in Corsica (see practices described in Case 15). Such practices are also described in our South Asian references (Haddad, 2008; Sandberg, 2017).

In most parts of the world, there is still a very serious shortage of basic resources and teaching devices. However, one may think that, in the digital age, teachers can be proactive and creative, or invert the pedagogy and let the students collect the documents and create the task (Cases 1 and 19). Indeed, there are examples that when material is scarce, the best solution is to produce it. Apart from the cases we have described, we saw that in the Basque country, teachers have produced their own specific teaching materials (Coyos, 2016). In a similar effort, in another French region (Aquitaine, Midi-Pyrenees and Languedoc-Roussillon), materials were produced in the form of Romance language intercomprehension textbooks (Case 11 and Escudé, 2016). However, an experience in Morocco, where a textbook was produced in order to facilitate access to French for academic purposes (FAP) at university level, ended in failure as nobody used it. Haddad (2008) and Sandberg (2017), among others, also describe instances where learners actually went and found documents and data that they would use to learn the languages spoken in the area. In the USA, the teachers in Case 1 used available resources in their immediate environment to fulfil their purposes starting with the internet and letting the learners construct their knowledge. This tends to demonstrate that top-down directives and funding are no substitutes to teacher development, creativity and involvement. Adequate reflection on tasks also seems to be one of the keys to change.

Assessment and Evaluation

We have long advocated that research in language development should assess what development took place in a given experiment (Narcy-Combes, 2005). We are now going to turn to how language development is assessed and to how learners, the educational team and the institutional authorities assess the learning environment and system. In the multilingual programmes we have collected, assessment and evaluation seem to be the stumbling block, they are frequently left out or incomplete.

When a CLIL programme is implemented in the countries studied (Case 21), learners' knowledge of the subjects they studied is assessed exclusively in the target language (in Ireland, Hungary and Austria, learners may choose whether they want content to be assessed in the CLIL language or in the mainstream language) (for details see Eurydice, 2005). In the other instances, assessment is carried out through national testing (Maghreb countries, US states, Europe, Asia) or not at all (Guadeloupe, Guyana, Mayotte and Tahiti, e.g. see Hélot & Erfurt, 2016).

However, when a research project has been implemented and endorsed by a government authority, assessment and evaluation are more likely to be part of the programme. Even then, learning outcomes are seldom directly measured (no comparison of test scores and statistics).

Success is generally measured through students' engagement and classroom participation, better comprehension of academic content reflected in students' interest, results in academic exams (the experiment is successful if the students obtain equivalent or better results at exams than those obtained by the mainstream population) (García *et al.*, 2017; Hélot & Erfurt, 2016; Mazak & Carroll, 2017; Otwinowska & De Angelis, 2014). Evaluation should not be mistaken with certification or with some form of large-scale testing, which often run counter to what this book aims to foster, which is personal language development.

Factors Enabling or Inhibiting the Development of a Bi/Plurilingual Programme

The facilitating factors can be linked to place and people, identity, circumstances, structure, policy and pedagogy. Countries or regions that have a long tradition of plurilingualism in Europe, such as the Italian South Tyrol and Switzerland, tend to implement bilingual programmes more easily and teachers and learners tend to feel more comfortable when dealing with more than one language in the classroom (Case 17). It is also the case in border regions where the language of the neighbour has been part of the linguistic landscape for decades, such as Alsace (Hélot & Erfurt, 2016) or the northern part of Sweden (Paulsrud *et al.*, 2017). However, geography and plurilingualism are not sufficient, as exemplified in the Maghreb countries and sub-Saharan Africa which are plurilingual areas but find it hard to attain an acceptable standard in the language of the school and implement programmes that can permit it (Maurer, 2010; McIlwraith, 2013). Southern Asian countries are in a very similar position (Canagarajah & Ashraf, 2013; Leconte *et al.*, 2018).

Identity factors facilitate the implementation of bi/plurilingual programmes in areas where people are proud of their identity and of their inherited language and culture. For instance, in French Polynesia and New Caledonia, Corsica and Brittany, militant activists on the part of parents' associations, cultural activists and researchers work efficiently to have the necessary structures in place in order to ensure the children can learn the regional language (for more details see: Adam & Calvez, 2016; Di Meglio & Cortier, 2016; Fillol & Colombel, 2016; Paia & Vernaudon, 2016).

The corpus shows that the sustainability and success of the implemented plurilingual programmes are based on bottom-up micro initiatives involving dedicated teams of teachers and researchers that collaborate and benefit from the support and commitment of the school authorities and this is corroborated by reports such as Haddad (2008) and Sandberg (2017) for Asia, Africa and South America. The students' active participation corresponds to the teachers' creativity and engagement (García *et al.*, 2017; Hélot & Erfurt, 2016; Mazak & Carroll, 2017).

More importantly, the participants' attitude towards bi/plurilingualism is a key factor in the success or failure of such programmes. When teachers and school administrators become aware that taking into account and encouraging the use of the immigrants' IL may have dramatically positive social and cognitive consequences, they move towards considering bi/plurilingualism as an asset favouring openness rather than a drawback. In such environments, learners translanguage freely and compare languages when needed (García *et al.*, 2017; García & Kleyn, 2016; Mazak & Carroll, 2017). This is demonstrated in most of our cases and in reports such as Haddad (2008) and Sandberg (2017) for Asia, Africa and South America. Other facilitating factors will obviously be institutional support and funding and living and working in a plurilingual environment.

The hindering factors are linked to ideology and representations of what a language represents in terms of social achievement and power and, consequently, to nation-state restrictive policies. As mentioned above, in the USA, even though there is no official language, English is still the dominant language in the country and English proficiency attainment is key to government policy of integrating immigrants into US society. Home languages are perceived negatively, a perception which is exacerbated by the current political climate. Those perceptions are not limited to the USA and can also be observed in any of the contexts that constitute the corpus of this study. For example, in France, French is the official language and the language of schooling (Hélot & Erfurt, 2016). In schools, mastery of this language is highly valued and little attention is paid to the other languages that the learners speak. In Germany, a deficit-oriented language perception prevails. German is seen as the great unifier. Persons belonging to groups of foreign origin and the languages they speak are marginalised and undervalued (Leichsering, 2014). In Sweden also, Swedish is considered the main language, i.e. the common language in society that everyone must be able to access and can be used in all sectors of society (Ministry of Culture, 2009 in Rosen, 2017). It is also the case in the Maghreb countries where a good command of French is the only way to succeed at university and to get a top-paying job (Bensfia *et al.*, 2013). Teachers for their part hold beliefs on what the language(s) of the school should be like (see mastery orientation, Chapter 5) as shown in the LASCOLAF report (Maurer, 2011). The language ideology that is diffused by the nation state is then one of the major hindering factors to the implementation of bi/plurilingual programmes. Our reports for Southern Asia, Africa and South America do not contradict these phenomena, but show ways of overcoming them locally.

People often have beliefs about their original language which do not help in the implementation of bi/plurilingual programmes. Even when a nation state, be it the USA or European countries, claims a bi/plurilingual policy, it reflects a monolingual bias most of the time (or a bilingual bias as in some Asian countries). Languages are separated in the school syllabi and little space is provided for the emergence of multilingual meaning making (Hélot & Erfurt, 2016; Rosen, 2017). Teachers work on the basis of the 'one teacher = one language' principle.

Other constraints are related to the political and economic situation. The lack of continuity between political will or decisions and their operational implementations, the lack of political and institutional continuity (for example, the important turnover among chief education officers in the French overseas territories), overcrowded classrooms, insufficiently trained or untrained teachers and the lack of adapted teaching material and resources impact negatively on the sustainability of any learning programme.

Setting up large- or small-scale projects will have to take all this into account and find ways of overcoming the resulting tensions that learners and teachers may feel. This will sometimes be easier at the micro level than at the macro level as shown in the 37 cases.

Consistency with the Theoretical Data

As mentioned above, top-down, teacher-centred, discipline-based projects cannot be adapted to learners' needs and they seem to prevail in most of the countries under French influence, including mainland France. Approaches that prioritise a strict standard form of the target language and rote learning as is the case in sub-Saharan countries (Maurer, 2011: 16–17; Noyau, 2016) make matters even more difficult. A compartmentalised, juxtaposed vision of languages, elitist, unequal and selective approaches, a lack of recognition of learners' IL, reduced teaching hours, an absence of opportunities for language use outside school are points of substance that go against the theoretical data concerning the link between the language of schooling and learner development. More often than not, the learning outcome is not measured, which is a problem when it comes to evaluating the validity of a learning programme.

What was seen in Chapter 7 has been confirmed. This study clearly highlights the complexity of determining the effects of the context. There is no universal way of doing so as the interplay of all the elements and human action is neither predictable, nor static and certainly not predetermined. As we have noticed, in a number of cases, either in a micro context or in a meso context, as in the case of projects that concern more than one isolated experience, teachers and researchers have successfully been experimenting with bi/plurilingual programmes with the support of educational authorities in contexts that did not seem propitious. Some cases show that apparently non-ambitious, isolated, efforts can make a significant impact in:

- adapting practices and learning environments to what is now understood of learning and of the plurilingual language development of individuals;
- paying attention to who the learners are and to how they learn;

- making sure that learners are active in collaborative construction of knowledge while offering the necessary mediation;
- triggering learners' intention to actually do things that are socially meaningful.

As researchers and practitioners, we have come to think that a ripple effect from a small-scale experience is just as likely to be successful as an ambitious top-down project. The combination of the two may prove worthwhile or as exemplified in Case 1 or as was attempted in Picardie (France) in the 1990s (Narcy & Biesse, 2003): local initiatives were supported by a top-down regional programme which provided financial and theoretical support. Our position is confirmed by the similar ripple effect that resulted from the Cambodian and Nepalese projects described by Sandberg (2017), for instance.

15 When Theory and Practice Meet

What we have seen so far enables us to make a checklist of what has to be taken into account when organising language learning environments (LLEs) and designing tasks. As mentioned in the introduction to the book, the various constructs can be seen as crystals in a kaleidoscope, each tilt giving a specific organisation (like a theoretical paradigm). In Table 15.1, the crystals have been reorganised independently from their theoretical source.

The number of elements that have been retained should not deter teachers. It is not possible to control every aspect to everybody's total satisfaction, but airplane pilots go through longer checklists... Complex systems require teamwork, which helps to redistribute the workload while making sure that all the items are taken on board. In the various case studies that we have presented, we see clearly how complex it can be to take all the crystals on board. Some teams have been more successful than others – contextual elements clearly explain why (teacher education and connection with research, technological facilities, close-knit teams, etc.). All of them, because they tried to take who the learners were into account and to empower them, triggered a development that is likely to have long-lasting consequences and which longitudinal studies should investigate. In line with Turnbull (2016), our research for this book has shown us that there are no convincing arguments to justify a difference between multilingual language classes and so-called monolingual classes, as learners in both settings are emergent bilinguals. As a consequence, what will now be presented is just as relevant for so-called 'monolingual' settings as for multilingual classes.

148 Part 2: Multilingual Practices in Action

Table 15.1 Checklist for organising LLEs and designing tasks

Dimensions	Key factors to be considered: The crystals
General nature of learning	• **Influence of culture and discourse.** Cognitive development is necessarily cultural (Troadec, 2007) and discourse based (Gavins, 2007) and knowledge has been described as resulting from a social construction (Berger & Luckmann, 1966). • **Emotions and learning.** Emotions play a determining role in learning. • **Importance of action.** Learning is performing (see Fisher, 2012). Action and thought and/or action and discourse cannot be separated (Schurmans, 2001). • **Co-construction of knowledge.** It results from flexible, collaborative, situated and distributed co-construction (Hutchins, 1995; Vygotsky, 1962). This construction is both an individual and a situated and social phenomenon. • **Distantiation and reflection.** Any form of complex learning requires distantiation and reflection, which will be facilitated by mediation. • **Observation.** People acquire behaviours through their observation of others. To imitate a behaviour, the person must have some motivating factor (a personal intention). • **Expectations.** Expectations need to be destabilised (de Bot & Jaensch, 2015) if learners need to alter their habitus (Bourdieu, 1980) and to engage in the process of learning (accommodation after initial assimilation) (Piaget, 1970). • **Consciousness of what an activity is.** Becoming conscious of an activity is the result of the interaction between individuals and their environment. It emerges from the pooling of their interpretations and justifies collaborative learning (Gibbs, 1999–2000). • **Collaboration.** Problem-solving, meaning and form negotiation can be more effective in collaborative tasks than in traditional classroom interactions (Pica et al., 2006). • **Negative and positive reinforcement.** The former discourages the continuation of the modelled activity, whereas the latter fosters motivation.
Nature of language	• **Language as a triadic entity.** The faculty of language, speech or discourse and linguistic descriptions are indissociable elements of one whole and one cannot be mistaken for the other. • **Language and context.** Language is an embodied and situated activity.
Language processing	• **Practice and automaticity.** Meaningful interactive practice will ensure automaticity of processing language in real-world interaction. • **Realistic practice.** Realistic practice settings will help retrieve the data and skills in similar situations. • **Instances (chunks).** Language development may result from exposure to instances rather than to single words (formulaicity). • **Situations and language.** Connections between situations of use and linguistic features should be developed until the presence of one situational or linguistic element will activate the other(s). • **Cues and language learning.** Each language gives cues that signal specific functions and learners must be sensitised to the relative importance of the different cues appropriate in their various additional languages (ALs).
Content	• **Familiarity with domain.** Learners learn best the discourse of the domains with which they are familiar. • **Plurilingual collaboration.** Plurilingual syllabi in collaboration with all forms of plurilingual or 'native' speakers or advanced learners would make interaction more fruitful and facilitate access to content.
Language/culture biography and its consequences	• **All languages are valuable.** It is important in a plurilingual group to be sensitive to language status, to value all languages and to highlight the benefits of all forms of plurilingualism. • **Learners' biography.** It is useful to know some of the learners' history and which languages they know. • **Translanguaging.** This way of processing language is inevitable (unconsciously or consciously). It is how humans process languages.

Table 15.1 (*Continued*)

Dimensions	Key factors to be considered: The crystals
Interaction and learning processes	• **Interaction and reflection.** Meaningful interaction will trigger learning processes and distantiation. Some form of intrapersonal cognitive work may prove useful (training tasks). • **Metalinguistic awareness.** Some form of metalinguistic awareness and of contrastive analysis can play a useful role and can be integrated in the tasks. • **Connection with the real world.** Computer-mediated communication (CMC) learning environments are now directly connected to the real world and learners may 'meet' real users of the language and specialists of the disciplinary content they learn.
Mediation/ teachers/tutors	• **Social mediation.** This is mediation by others in social interaction, e.g. mediation through experts and/or peers. Language, but also portfolios, tasks and technology are forms of mediation. • **Self-mediation.** This is mediation by the self through private speech and introspection. • **Autonomy and isolation.** When learners are isolated, their apparent autonomy is not an advantage as they must do without mediation and evaluation is more problematic. • **'Nativisation' (or assimilation).** This reinforces the need for mediation. • **Plurilingual teachers.** Teacher teams should be plurilingual and pluridisciplinary (see adjunct Content and Language Integrated Learning [CLIL] in Chapter 3). • **Context and learning environments.** The organisation of all learning environments is context dependent (ideologies, cultural habits, expectations, needs and, of course, means will be taken into account) and learners coming from other contexts may find it difficult to adapt.
Processes in language learning	• **Assimilation and accommodation.** Also named nativisation and denativisation, they are key processes in language learning (made complex in plurilingual circumstances). • **Parallel processing.** Linear or serial processing is now seen as a less productive hypothesis than parallel processing. • **Role of a 'monitor'.** Explicit collaborative work, supplemented by micro-tasks may facilitate language management and the use of compensation strategies and set up what some would call a 'monitor'. • **Corrective feedback.** It may be beneficial if the learner's face is saved during meaningful interaction. • **Noticing.** It is a decisive phenomenon in language development; noticing the gap is noticing interlingual or intralingual meaningful differences, and tasks should trigger it unobtrusively by focusing on the necessity of noticing to achieve the task. Noticing is facilitated by input enhancement or flooding, or collaborative interaction. • **Depth of processing.** It is what allows adequate form-meaning links (tasks should be meaningful). • **Accuracy and fluency.** Both require the integration of meaningful activities with form-focused activities, particularly those requiring output. • **Input requires frequency, quantity of exposure and salience.** Focusing on form, noticing and restructuring of ALs are driven by the frequency and importance of the features in the learning situation, or through explicit reflection, if followed by meaningful practice. • **Input should come first and output later.** If collaboration between learners is not possible, work on input/uptake should precede output, which should not be required too quickly. • **Comprehensible output.** It leads to development in meaningful interaction. • **Learnability.** The learnability or the teachability of what is proposed should be questioned beforehand. • **Translation and translanguaging.** They have a facilitating role in particular in reading and writing situations, learners will need to reflect on what is effective.

(*Continued*)

Table 15.1 (*Continued*)

Dimensions	Key factors to be considered: The crystals
Practice	• **Practice, rehearsal and rote learning.** They should not be discarded but integrated into meaningful activities.
Feedback	• **Recast.** Only systematic and explicit recasts will help. Feedback may take the form of positive advice to perform tasks that help restructure the AL. • **Language of feedback.** Metalinguistic and metacognitive information must be given in an accessible language in the course of actual practice.
Culture	• **Attitudes.** They imply relativisation of self and value given to others, suspension of belief in own and disbelief in other's behaviours, beliefs and values. • **Empathy.** Knowledge of one another's behaviours, beliefs and values and of how each is seen by the other requires comparative methods and specific skills. What is required is the ability to: (i) interpret and relate 'documents'/'texts' based on existing knowledge and attitudes; (ii) discover (in own time or in interaction) new behaviours, beliefs and values; and (iii) interact in real time based on other preconditions and skills. The responsibility of the teacher will be to develop 'critical cultural awareness' by acting co-culturally and acquiring adequate intercultural competence.

Part 3
Designing Contextualised Language Learning Environments in a Plurilingual Perspective

In this part, we will define a flexible and adaptive framework for taking into account the crystals we have described and the effects of the contextual, cultural and/or individual variations. We aim to provide a practical, yet theory-driven guide to setting up learning environments and designing tasks. As we have concluded at the end of Part 2, we strongly support the position that any language course is a plurilingual experience and should be treated as such.

16 Multilingual Language Learning and ICT

The combined consequences of the review of the literature leads us to favour blended learning environment(s) combining face-to-face activities and group, collaborative or autonomous online work whenever possible. However, the use of digital technology as a support for each of these different moments will be a function of contextual resources and constraints.

Resorting to information and communications technology (ICT) and computer-mediated communication (CMC) should be tightly integrated into course and task development upstream. ICT helps to change learning conditions to adapt to the varying origins and needs of learners. In large courses (e.g. Andronova, 2016; McAllister *et al.*, 2012), students can be divided into small work groups who (tele)collaborate and produce either group assignments or part collective and part personal assignments, and have regular meetings with tutors. The collaboration will make it possible to highlight likely content, discourse/language or cultural problems and sensitise each learner to whether he or she does or does not need the mediation of the tutor to overcome his or her difficulties. In multicultural settings, this can be a way of organising learners with different initial languages in an adequate way that will facilitate collaboration. Resource centres can be made available to help students who need some support both in terms of content and/or of discourse/language (see Brudermann, 2010). Such resource centres can be shelves with documents available in different languages and scripts to facilitate retrieval of the necessary information. If tasks are published on a blog (they can also be posted on a physical board), some controversial ones may raise debate among students. This will have to be mediated by the course tutor. Indeed, peer and/or tutor mediation can become a real challenge when ethical values (plagiarism, for instance) and cultural values (contributions reflecting either the learner's habitus or stereotypical views) are concerned or when pragmatic difficulties arise, especially when the community is culturally diverse (see also Lamy & Hampel, 2007). Teachers will need to be trained to ensure that the co-construction of culture (Chapter 5) runs smoothly as CMC learning environments are directly connected to the real world and learners may 'meet' real users of the language and specialists of the disciplinary content they learn, which can prove complex at times. Table 16.1 outlines how ICT tools can be used jointly depending on the objectives of the course. Special attention will be paid to assessment and reflectivity.

These environments and tools can either complement or replace physical environments and tools and may be used by people with an intermediate practical competence in ICT. Digital tools also allow document sharing and synchronous or asynchronous written or oral exchanges. Creating virtual learning environments (VLEs) or websites makes it possible to organise small-size adaptable systems at a reduced cost and to handle both collaborative practices and the complexity and nonlinearity of individual learning. Powerful content management systems (CMS) (WordPress, Wix, Google Sites) or learning management systems (LMS) (Moodle, Edmodo) are now available at low or no cost and to people with low digital competence.

If computers are not available and/or the internet is not accessible, traditional tools can be used. What matters is not the tools, but the way the work is organised, as we saw in the biology class in Morocco (see Chapter 3).

Table 16.1 Essential tools, systems and tasks

Tools, systems or tasks	Affordances and constraints
Virtual learning environments and (virtual) resource centres	Platforms may have different technical capacities, which will influence how VLEs or resource centres operate.
Forums	They provide asynchronous communication and are low-technology tools. The threaded written discussions leave time for preparation and rehearsal (which can be useful). Discussions should be included in the curriculum with specific instructions or required by the task. They can be multilingual (relying on intercomprehension). Monitoring is relatively easy to carry out in order to increase potential outcomes that are still limited (Lamy & Hampel, 2007). They facilitate constructed disciplinary exchanges. They should be supplemented with oral exchanges.
Chats	They provide synchronous communication in the form of written discourse that is often described as similar to oral discourse. This is partly validated, but written output results from different processes than oral output and the effects of the written mode have been shown to affect the phonological nativisation of the words acquired in such interaction (Grosbois, 2006). Compensatory tasks should overcome these effects. Task instructions will enhance negotiation of meaning by reducing topic or form avoidance. Obviously, multilingual practices are possible (intercomprehension and translanguaging is often resorted to).
Webquests	They can provide useful individual and collaborative work (Catroux, 2006). Careful planning and instructions can lead to positive uptake. Webquests can also be used as tasks that do not require output: the task in this case is to sort out the information gathered. A webquest is a search for (multilingual) information on the internet that the teacher can preselect or not. The active, autonomous, co-construction of knowledge resulting from a webquest will prove useful to replace transmissive teaching.

Table 16.1 (*Continued*)

Tools, systems or tasks	Affordances and constraints
Telecollaboration/ tandem learning	Tandem learning or group telecollaboration combines the characteristics of chatting, webquests, etc., between speakers of generally different languages (alternate monolingual practice in general). Commentaries concerning phonological problems applying to chats apply here if it is text based. Precise task instructions negotiated with learners will lead to better results (problem-based tasks, social outcomes, etc.) and compensatory tasks can help. Intercomprehension, the learning of two languages and translanguaging may result from such work. Instructions, themes, supports and tasks must be carefully chosen according to the curriculum, learner levels and individual characteristics. A specific outcome is preferable to avoid simulations or exchanges where difficulties may be avoided. Post-task feedback is possible.
Multi-user object-oriented environments (MOOs) and virtual worlds	They have a complex architecture and provide a motivating spatial metaphor and graphical-cum-textual possibilities. Research results (Aimard, 2005) show that acquisition is limited if no defined instructions as to roles and actions are provided, but this can easily be overcome. Sound-based interaction will be more beneficial and may lead to multilingual exchanges or intercomprehension. Empirical data show that development remains limited when instructions are not clearly defined and if individual roles and actions are not clearly specified.
Videoconferencing	Apart from complex planning requirements, it offers a number of positive options. The sessions can be integrated within a wider pedagogical framework (Lamy & Hampel, 2007: 139) and they can be prepared and exploited by other tasks, which gives them a structuring and motivating role. Instructions as to themes, materials and activities should be carefully devised in relation to the curriculum, learner level and individual characteristics. Correction and feedback are not appropriate during videoconferencing, but the exchanges can be recorded and used for post-session feedback. Intercomprehension may be developed and translanguaging may be resorted to.
Blogs	They require learner training and integration with other activities. They lead to the collaborative construction of knowledge. Creative and reflective benefits may result from such work. Unobtrusive instructions might lead to more acquisition. They allow co-construction of knowledge and enhance creativity and reflectivity. A multilingual approach and translanguaging may be beneficial, especially in the work leading to the production. Non-directive instructions will facilitate language development. Blogs are a way of giving social legitimacy to the tasks.
Wikis/collaborative document writing tools (cf. Google Docs)	They are collaborative websites that comprise the perpetual collective work of many authors. They resemble blogs, but in wikis anyone can interfere with the content that has been placed on the site. Both blogs and wikis require technical support for teachers and learners alike. Careful attention will be paid to the instructions, and feedback will be complex to handle. As in blogs, a multilingual approach and translanguaging may be beneficial, especially in the work leading to the production. Blogs and wikis increase the role of learners as course designers and organisers. They make the role of the tutor more complex in his or her assessment of the knowledge created. They develop the social aspect of the tasks.

(*Continued*)

Table 16.1 (*Continued*)

Tools, systems or tasks	Affordances and constraints
Mobile devices	Mobile devices have long been used (e.g. Walkman, see Narcy-Combes, 2005), but electronic devices certainly provide more scope and flexibility. Instructions and feedback will also be more complex to provide. Incidental acquisition is very likely to be high; means of overcoming the unperceived effects of nativisation can be suggested after feedback sessions, which can include discussion on the best ways of using these devices. Instructions and feedback will be more complex to organise due to technical limitations. Mobile telephones prove to have a very useful role in many regions of the world (see i.e. Kukulska-Hulme and Bull [2009] for language learning specifically; Valk *et al.* [2010], Vosloo and West [2012] or Kukulska-Hulme and Bull [2009] for Asia, Burston [2015] for Africa).
Digital whiteboard	They are worthwhile for collective or metareflective activities. Research results show they may often reinforce teacher centredness (Villemonteix, 2016; Whyte, 2015).
MOOCs/small private online courses (SPOCs)	Tasks will adapt to how multilingual the audience is and instructions should be accessible. MOOCs should preferably be constructivist and not instructivist.
Games	Games help and encourage many learners to sustain their interest and work. Games also help the teacher to create contexts in which the language is useful and meaningful. The learners want to take part, and in order to do so they must understand what others are saying or have written. They must also speak or write in order to express their own point of view or give information. Games provide one way of helping learners to *experience* language rather than merely *study* it.
Other online tools such as dictionaries, translators, spell checks, word processors, concordances, etc.	Their affordances and the problems they pose and how to overcome them have been described (Chapter 6). Multilingual practices have been shown to facilitate reception and production (Chapters 3 and 6).

17 Designing Courses and Tasks in a Multilingual Perspective

We advocate language learning environments (LLEs) that can cater to teacher- or learner-designed (social/macro) tasks with fluid content on the one hand and can work with information and communications technology (ICT) support and monitoring when the need arises on the other hand. What we describe will require further research or reflection from the users in order to be implemented to its fullest capacities. It will be effective only if 'freedom to learn' and learner reflectivity and responsibility go hand in hand with respect for who the learners are, where they come from and where they would like to go. A compromise is necessary between institutional demands and the learners' personal objectives, which will imply careful study of contextual constraints.

Our course engineering approach comes down to two main phases:

- **The investigation phase** made up of the analysis and design steps in terms of context, language learning requirements and pedagogical engineering leading to the final specifications.
- **The implementation phase** made up of the actual implementation, the course itself and the assessment steps.

Towards a New Approach

In line with the Douglas Fir Group (2016), we think that learning should be less based on performances and more co-constructed with participants. Rather than proposing very structured learning environments and tasks, we will rely on *organising circumstances* (Spear & Mocker, 1984), letting what happens shape the course. Our approach goes with a political and ethical engagement (Médioni & Narcy-Combes, 2016; Narcy-Combes, 2005) which is justified by the conclusion to the case studies (Chapter 14). As was seen in Parts 1 and 2, learning environments and situations have individual, social and relational implications. Languages, cultures and contents cannot be dissociated, and contexts and institutions must be taken into account. Educational engineering will not give all the answers on its own.

The growing evidence for language as an individually determined emergent and dynamic system (Lowie, 2017) changes our view of the transmissive teacher. We saw that language emerges from exposure, use and intentionality, teacher explanations and descriptions may not be the optimal learning strategy. Focusing on grammar issues may be useful, but it will be hard to determine what input, practice and information the individual learner benefits from. If languages can be learned, but not taught, teaching will be redefined as providing the individually determined and changing optimal conditions for learning to take place.

If variability is part of the learning process, and it should be acknowledged, then learning environments should be organised so as to make it possible (Lowie, 2017). What was called 'fossilisation' is the result of an attractor state; getting the learner out of it may require a strong perturbation (obstacle) that leads to the reorganisation of one or more subsystems and that may result in increased variability to signal learning. The most appropriate obstacle can be any form of socially legitimate input, or necessary output, but is again individually determined. Specific tasks will ensure that it is so.

Concerning assessment, Lowie (2017) reminds us that measuring at one point in time may not be representative of what the learner can optimally do in the language, especially when the focus of the assessment is on only one aspect of language use. A representative analysis of language development can only be based on a multidimensional assessment at different moments in time. Thus, continuous assessment should be the norm.

The knowledge distributed among humans (Hutchins, 1995) must be dissociated from the individual internal processes that manage it. From our point of view, language circulates among humans in material forms (including sounds). It is used in the form of context-dependent, content-carrying discourse. Competence is a social construct that has been reconstructed *a posteriori*. It is not, and cannot be, assessed directly. Only oral or written performances can. They are not objective indicators as they will be modified by external (setting, etc.) or internal (stress, anxiety, other emotions) context-dependent variables.

We postulate that, since content in a given cultural environment is what triggers the recourse to language, it is probably wiser to determine the various social encounters and tasks that the learners will have to face and to study/record/collect data corresponding to the expected language situations in order to provide the initial input for the learners. The learners' ensuing language-based or sociocultural needs will be determined from the initial work provided by social tasks or tasks designed as realistic replicas of these social situations. Learners need socially situated tasks (see Chapter 7) that enable them to see the regularities of linguistic and discourse structures which they need to react, then act in new situations.

The objective is the gradual emergence of (re)acting intentionally in meaningful interactions in a way that corresponds to individual and institutional expectations. Solving the problems generated by the tasks should trigger the development and stabilisation of processes that will modify the learners' affective, cognitive and linguistic system(s) (see Part 1).

We will then describe environments proposing 'actions' that will raise learners' intention. They will need to be implemented, ordered and followed while being aware that progression, continuity and predictability will not be shared.

Curriculum as Interaction

Curriculum development is the systematic planning of what is to be taught and learned in institutions (courses and programmes). In many countries, these curricula can be found in official documents and made mandatory by departments of education. Teachers then decide how this should be carried out and distinctions have to be made between the official or planned curriculum from the *de facto* curriculum, the way in which what is actually learned is organised.

Extensive work on curriculum development has been carried out in the past 30 years (Grenfell, 2000). Let us say that curricula can be seen as guidelines for the organisation of courses (such as the list of social situations and expected language outcomes), but not necessarily as inventories to be scrupulously followed, in the same way as syllabi. Misconstruing the role of curricula and syllabi may result in the mere rote learning of set phrases and grammar exercises.

The Common European Framework of Reference (CEFR) levels of achievement describe what a learner is supposed to be able to do in reading, listening, speaking, writing and interaction at each level. These descriptions were based on experience and cannot claim to be the faithful results of thorough research into interlingual development. Such research, which led to useful results (e.g. Ellis, 1994), should be encouraged in order to bridge the gap between theory and institutional practice.

Descriptions of levels and attainments, like curricula, are guidelines, and with van Lier (1996) and other authors (e.g. Beacco, 2000), we will endeavour to show that a curriculum can be seen as interaction with the real world. As a consequence, the curricula can also be experienced as interaction and learners can, when the context allows, become their own course and task designers (White, 2003: 156–157). As a way of increasing learner involvement, the content does not have to be predefined but can be selected and negotiated through the course as language and content learning and language use are intimately linked. The shift is reflected in the design of the materials, the roles envisaged for teachers and learners and the formation of learning networks. Leaving materials open encourages and shows learners how to access and use resources in their personal context, to carry their learning into the community and to develop strategies for taking greater responsibility for their learning (White, 2003). However, mediation must play its part in order to ensure that nothing is overlooked. García and her colleagues (Cases 1–5) and our own Paris-Siegen project (Case 19) show that if contextual constraints make it difficult for learners to collect the material and organise the tasks, data banks can be made available and students asked to construct the course (tasks) from the documents that have been made available. Mixed solutions can be implemented.

Content and Language Integrated Learning (CLIL)/ Bilingual Education in Curricular Development

As seen above, the emphasis on content, which is of paramount importance, can be found in immersion programmes and bilingual education in North America and in CLIL programmes in Europe. The curriculum that such courses refer to is designed by the specialists of the discipline taught. Such courses cannot prepare learners for other situational contexts in any direct way. CLIL classrooms provide a familiarity for dealing with particular situations. Participation with '(non-)native speakers' helps develop topic knowledge and participation in educational discourse, increases learner capacity to understand the linguistic code, but parallel to the disciplinary curriculum, interactions within the course should help to implement an additional language (AL) curriculum specific to each learner. Computer-mediated communication (CMC)-supported multinational courses (Case 19) prove to be very effective. Since familiarity with content facilitates language development (Bygate *et al.*, 2001), an appealing and/or legitimate content is likely to lead to more fruitful interactions among learners with different contextual backgrounds but similar professional or other interests.

We follow García *et al.* (2017: 268) in stating that: '[in] teaching additional language learners content, teachers need to have deep understandings about the language system in which they are teaching. They also need to be thoroughly familiar with pedagogical practices surrounding bilingualism and the development of bilingualism'. They need to understand, for example, the important role that the initial language has on the development of the AL, and of the interdependence of both languages (Cummins, 1979). And beyond psycholinguistic understandings, these teachers need to know how to build on their students' initial language and literacy to develop literacy in the target language. As researchers, this is what we advocated in *le français de l'histoire* (Case 10).

Types of Language

The objective of language learning and teaching is no longer to offer linguistic models, but to suggest or offer situations requiring actual use of the language(s) to be learnt, so that interaction triggers learning processes and reveals individual learning needs.

Due to the influence of contextual variables, it is easier to define what a specific variant of an AL is than to define 'general language' and codemeshing makes this even more complex (Canagarajah & Ashraf, 2013). The approach we advocate will thus sensitise learners to variations. Input must then conform to actual usage (including specific variants such as *webspeak* Chapelle [2003], or the language of texting) as required by the course and by what learners can access. Bozhinova *et al.* (2017) show that learners become aware of when norms must be followed and when more flexibility is acceptable. Understanding the role and values of norms seems more effective than pure prescription. Formative evaluation should sensitise learners to that.

Social situations, real-world activities, curriculum as interaction, CLIL-type or content-based courses and sensitisation to variations are keywords for us. Our emphasis is on interaction, doing and realism.

Implications for Learning Activities

Studying language as a construct in a systemic approach led us to think that the *actional approach* of the Council of Europe (2001) and task-based language teaching (TBLT) (e.g. Bygate *et al.*, 2001; Ellis, 2003; Willis & Willis, 2007) could answer some of the questions that came up, since both seem to provide solutions that take into account the sometimes conflicting theoretical demands we have studied (we consider TBLT as an extension of project-based and problem-solving pedagogy, see Chapter 6 and Bertin *et al.*, 2010).

TBLT and learning is already well grounded in language education (Bertin *et al.*, 2010). The role of tasks and task design has also always been an important issue when designing telecollaborative learning environments. O'Dowd and Ritter (2006: 631) found that 'in the end of term feedback, all the negative comments made by the ... group in reference to the project were in some way related to aspects of task design. Students complained that the teachers' choice of topics hindered the development of group relationships and learners expected the correction of linguistic mistakes'.

Task design in blended learning environments is complex and 'teachers frequently transfer tasks used in face-to-face settings to online environments without adapting them to new settings' (Hampel, 2006: 106). The task factors that are recognised as being crucial for telecollaborative contexts are the balance between task support and task demand achieved mainly through clear task structure and adequate technology support (see Chapter 13).

Social Situations

Social situations listed in the curriculum will be converted into tasks, or attempts will be made to actually create them (Ellis, 2003) in activities that are socially meaningful for the learners and based on content that seems relevant and legitimate to the learners. The difficulties the learners will encounter on their way to succeeding in the tasks will help them to become aware of what has to be noticed and practiced in order to reach their objectives. They will also legitimise the training work (micro tasks). As living in society implies becoming familiar with the ways social activities are performed and with the tools used by members of that society, learning cannot be restricted to the classroom, learners have to encounter real people in all their moral and social complexities.

We propose an approach based on tasks, projects and problem-solving activities and favour actual social tasks in accordance with the findings of informal learning (see Chapter 6). The aim is to combine the benefits of formal and informal learning, as demonstrated by a small-scale experiment at high school level in Morocco found in Khalil (2015). The teacher/tutor will be a mediator and scaffolding is provided by peers or other people (Gibbons, 2002). Social tasks stimulate engagement/investment (Springer, 2009) and language development will be sustained by training tasks when the necessity arises and when interaction is not sufficient (see Chapter 4 and McAllister-Pavageau, 2013). Knowledge (language and content) will be co-constructed (Hutchins, 1995) from plurilingual sources if necessary.

Learners will face individual difficulties. As a consequence, training tasks will be partly individualised. Our assumption is that training corresponds to intrapsychological work (see Part 1). The need for it should preferably emerge from tasks that are socially relevant in order for learners to understand why they need to go through it. Learning will need to be organised in a flexible way along the lines of what Spear and Mocker (1984) call *organising circumstances*. The environment is preorganised, ready to adapt but no linear organisation of tasks and content is pre-established.

The theme and content of the sequences are determined by the curriculum and explained to the students, but preferably negotiated with them. In some university courses, the students actually determine the contents of the course and discuss it with the lecturer and a compromise is reached (e.g. Narcy-Combes & Narcy-Combes, 2014). All TBLT features and phases mentioned in Ellis (2003) or in Park (2012), for instance, are observable in such learning environments but not in a regular order. Research results (Andronova, 2016; Bozhinova *et al.*, 2017; Brudermann, 2010; McAllister *et al.*, 2012) show that this type of work leads to developments that (1) satisfactorily meet institutional demands, (2) compensate for the unspecific objectives of some courses and (3) can be adapted to the different learning cultures.

Belonging to a 'real' community of discourse seems to have a positive influence on the motivation to participate in the task and negotiate the norms expected. Such tasks have positive effects on how individuals face what is new or different and reduce teacher interference. The learning environments and tasks we advocate give more responsibility to the learners in their construction of knowledge and may help maintain the complexity and relational effects of such episodes at a dynamic and manageable level.

A Flexible Approach to CLIL-Oriented TBLT

Socioeconomic and identity issues have to be taken on board (see Chapter 5). The learner should be taken into consideration from the beginning. Instead of focusing exclusively on linguistic, social and institutional behaviours, tasks should be embedded into an ecology of learning. We should start with the expectations of learners based on their past experiences of interaction with various fields (Kramsch & Narcy-Combes, 2017). They have 'memorised' these experiences in their habitus, they (re)construct them at each interaction and give meaning to their lives by a constant search for relationality between people and events. The cases in Nepal and Cambodia described by Sandberg (2017) are very convincing examples.

Both learners and teachers need to engage with different kinds of expectations:

- The teacher's and learners' expectations of their roles and power.
- The learners' expectations of what the world is like, which may lead to misunderstandings of how they are expected to behave, which may not correspond to what others expect.
- The teacher's expectations of learner's language production.
- The learner's expectations of the addressees (peers and teacher) both as individual interlocutors/readers and as members of a historical collectivity.

Peer mediation can help, but discussion groups online or in the classroom may shy away from confronting or even challenging each other's views in some cultural environments. Adequate mediation will necessitate a tutor aware of how to deal with such discussions.

Teacher Education and Language Awareness

Where bilingual or multilingual schools have been organised, teachers often teach only in one language (Hélot & Erfurt, 2016). It may sometimes be the case in two-way immersion programmes (see Buser, 2015). Recognising the beneficial influence of bilingual or plurilingual teachers would help them play their mediating role. Relying on peer scaffolding (Gibbons, 2002) and collaborating with content colleagues (or being able to teach content and language) will also help. Teacher education and training will have to adapt with an adequate balance between theoretical and practical content. Teachers in particular need to be aware of what plurilingual education entails (Ziegler, 2013). When local institutions are not in a position to deliver adequate teacher training and education, teachers could organise and set up networks to share their experience (see OEP, Chapter 6, and refer to TESS-India as an example or to *le français de l'histoire*, Case 10).

García *et al*. (2017) with Freire (1970), Cummins (2007) and other transformative educators, believe in a critical pedagogy that is situated in practice. They base transformative pedagogy on the four elements developed by the New London Group (1996) for their multiliteracies pedagogy:

- **Authentic situated practice** and immersion of *students* in such practice.
- **Overt instruction** to develop awareness and understanding of practice.
- **Critique of practices** as socially particular through critical framing.
- **Transformed practice** through experimentation with innovative practices that are a result of reflection, overt instruction and critical framing.

We have seen (Chapter 3) that theoretical courses on plurilingual learning need to be combined with authentic situated practice, and self-critique of that practice, for effective change to take place (e.g. Narcy-Combes & Xue, forthcoming 2018).

Practical Framework

Table 17.1 takes into account and summarises the main points of our approach and relies on all the crystals described in Table 15.1. Specifically oriented to the design and running of LLEs, it shows how the crystals can be applied concretely. The purely cognitive and affective crystals should not be overlooked even if it is more difficult to deal with them explicitly in such practical suggestions.

Table 17.1 Implications for setting up LLEs

Key parameters	Suggested approach
Knowledge co-construction	Flipped schooling may not always be an adequate solution, but collaborative or individual construction of knowledge is to be encouraged. Informal learning should be exploited. The work should be both process and product oriented.
Definition of tasks	A task involves real-world meaningful processes of language use in any or all of the four language skills. It has a clearly defined socially realistic outcome. It triggers cognitive processes and involves the learner personally (individual outcome) in an interaction (cf. project-based or problem-based learning).
Why tasks?	Linguistic syllabi are not effective in promoting acquisition because they do not conform to developmental processes, whereas task-based language learning corresponds to our understanding of what language is. The learners' real-life experiences recreate a natural context which is personalised and relevant for them.
Evolution of tasks	The task-based learning tradition has moved from an emphasis on negotiation of meaning to an investigation of a number of issues related to form-focused instruction (FFI). The action-based approach has remained purely interactive so far. Multilingual tasks can help learners reach their objectives more rapidly and develop a sense of the social validity of a task (translanguaging and ICT tools can prove very helpful when writing tasks are concerned). Multiliteracies research provides interesting insights.
Action-based approach	The aim is to engage in collective/collaborative actions both in the classroom and in the 'real' world.
Social/macro and training/micro tasks	Social tasks are 'real'-world tasks with a truly social outcome, macro tasks are realistic simulations. Micro tasks result from cognitive or constructive hypotheses that assume that the results of practice can transfer to real-life activities; doing them should respond to actual difficulties arising in the social/macro tasks rather than result from the tutor's assumptions.
Taxonomy of tasks	Types of tasks will be selected in relation to the objectives assigned to each task (implicit or explicit processing, approach, timing, specific focus, type of material, similarity with real-life tasks, etc.). In order for the learners to reach the objectives, a combination of features will be selected. Bilingual or multilingual/intercomprehension tasks, tasks with no production in the target language (AL) and tasks with production in the AL will not rely on the same features. Micro tasks may require specific development expertise as will Computer-Mediated Communication (CMC)-based social/macro tasks. Tasks will be designed to encourage pair or small (multilingual) group work. Facilities for such work must then be implemented in the course structure. Micro tasks will either be predetermined and preselected or devised as needs arise.
Task sequencing	It can be done based on the criteria of complexity, 'chronological' ordering or conceptual difficulty in the content matter.
Level of task difficulty	An appropriate level of task difficulty will be ensured especially when the learners collect the materials (webquest, informal search, etc.) or design the tasks. A multilingual approach may reduce the difficulty especially in developing receptive skills.
Task-based sequence/course sequence	Clear goals will be established for each task-based sequence if the course is sequenced or for the course if the work results from constant negotiation. The link with the curriculum must be discussed and maintained.

(*Continued*)

Table 17.1 (*Continued*)

Key parameters	Suggested approach
Thematic content/ CLIL	The materials are determined and collected according to situations and themes set in the curriculum. The tasks will be designed or suggested as a compromise between the learning opportunities provided by the material, the curriculum and the present level of proficiency of the learners. Content and language integrated or content-based courses (possibly bi- or multilingual) will be advocated, even if this may prove easier in the macro tasks than in the micro tasks, and content expertise of some the tutors will have to be adequate.
Content, culture and language-related instructions	Specific instructions in more than one language if necessary will be given to learners in relation to content, language and culture according to the requirements of the curriculum and to what is known of their learning needs and of their context of work. These instructions will focus learners on meaning, while ensuring that this focus on meaning will provide opportunities for focusing on form. Receptive tasks in a given language may lead to productive tasks in another language or in the schooling language. Preparing clear, coherent instructions that are related to the curriculum and that do not hinder the learners' creativity remains a challenge and may be facilitated by a bi or multilingual approach.
Learner as course designer	The advantages of empowering learners with aspects of the design of the course and of the tasks may be facilitated by support tools and unobtrusive instructions.
CMCL settings	They provide useful and motivating social/macro tasks. Instructions need to be carefully devised (not necessarily in the AL). Feedback will have to be carefully implemented in order to suggest micro tasks if and when necessary. Multilingual tasks will be suggested.
Equipment	This is determined by the institutional context. When computers and/ or CMC are not possible, photocopying and using paper support will be feasible, but will be more time-consuming for the teacher and more complex for the learners. Personal mobile telephones may prove successful.
Assessment	Key element in learning, especially if the environment is seen as an organising circumstances. Collaborative work can supplement tutor assessment and self-evaluation has a role to play. Regular assessment of the course can help adjust to the needs the course has created.
Learner involvement	Learners will be encouraged to maintain an active role and to take risks. Guidance will lead learners to evaluate their performance and progress.
Role of tutors	Multi/bilingual tutors will ensure that investment in the tasks is rewarding so that learners feel motivated. This will include appropriateness of organisation, recourse to macro tasks and to micro tasks as needed and easy access to the (virtual) resource centre and adequate support and supplements. Blended learning environments and classroom-based work will require team work.
Translanguaging	This enables learners to express themselves and to understand content information and avoids oversimplifications and slow progression in receptive work.
Conditions for translanguaging	The objective is providing opportunities for students to develop linguistic practices for academic contexts and becoming aware of the role of academic language as a specific part of their repertoire. Teachers do not have to be plurilingual and need not speak all the languages the learners speak as exemplified in the case studies. Learners can collaborate on the basis of their languages. If input is in different languages, this collaboration will prove valid. Resorting to ICT tools (dictionaries, spellcheckers, translators, etc.) will help learners to determine how to use them.
Assessment and translanguaging	Translanguaging helps teachers separate language-specific performances in the named language from general linguistic performances (the ability to argue a point, communicate complex ideas, etc.) which do not really vary from one language from the other.

Source: Adapted and synthesised from Bertin *et al.* (2010).

18 Modelling the Work

In this chapter, building on the cases we saw in Chapters 9–13, we are now going to see how all the crystals can be taken into account in setting up multilingual and multicultural learning environments and tasks.

Tasks

In this book, we favour a flexible, task-based approach (Bertin *et al.*, 2010) in blended environments whenever possible (see Figure 18.1). Interactions leading to the final tasks and the work documents will be in as many languages as useful. The final task will be in the language and register that corresponds to the social (institutional) expectations.

Central to the work will be tutor–learner relations (see Figure 18.1: intersection of the two orbits *Teacher/Learner*). A social or realistic macro task (Ma) is proposed:

- If (1) it is validated, then another such task is started.
- If (2) difficulties emerge (as is likely), a number of training/micro tasks (Mi) will be either improvised or turned to if preorganised on the required problems until the social/macro task can be validated (Mi orbits around the Ma task).

Training phases may then take place during the social/macro task, or after, or before the next social/macro task as necessary, in agreement with the learners. Some of these training/micro tasks may be predictable in some situations, they may be preorganised in physical or virtual resource centres (see Brudermann [2010] and http://www.taskbasedenglish.eu/useful-links/ for the actual online resource centre). Tutor and learners validate the different tasks (follow-up and evaluation, which can also lead to micro tasks) in collaboration with other teachers and people from outside such as parents and specialists, in order to ensure the social validity and to legitimise the work (e.g. Narcy-Combes [2005] and Cases 1–5, 16 and 18). This follow-up can lead to specific training work, in the form of micro tasks, detached from the macro/social task if the learner feels the need for it (orbits around the follow-up planet at the top). More than one macro task can take place at the same time in the group since there are individual and/or group activities. Follow-up can also take place simultaneously (only two macro tasks have been represented). The dotted line shows the connection between one of the macro tasks and the follow-up.

Tables 18.1 and 18.2 summarise the way tasks can be designed and implemented. Referring back to the case studies in Chapters 9–13 will help see how they can be implemented in actual learning situations.

Type A macro or social tasks and micro or training tasks can be performed without any production in the target language (TL), whereas Type B tasks will eventually lead to TL production.

Evaluation in such environments is essentially formative and shared, and if possible social. Summative evaluation is linked to certification, which may be organised by each institution but outside the actual learning group.

The theories developed in Part 1 explain why the social/macro task is used to trigger the language processes by creating the need for the necessary interactions and, hopefully, the necessary intention to take part. Micro/training tasks should be turned to in a bottom-up way in order to respond to students' individual needs. Khalil (2011) had to deconstruct specific problems in an unknown context (adult education in Egypt) and her research has shown how helpful it was to have a complex, but flexible, approach to learning environments and tasks.

More generally, reconstructing the learning environment necessitates

- Determining the cause of the problems and what can help to overcome them (social/affective, cognitive, technical, institutional).
- Knowing who the learners are (histories, language biographies, individual/cultural differences, etc.).

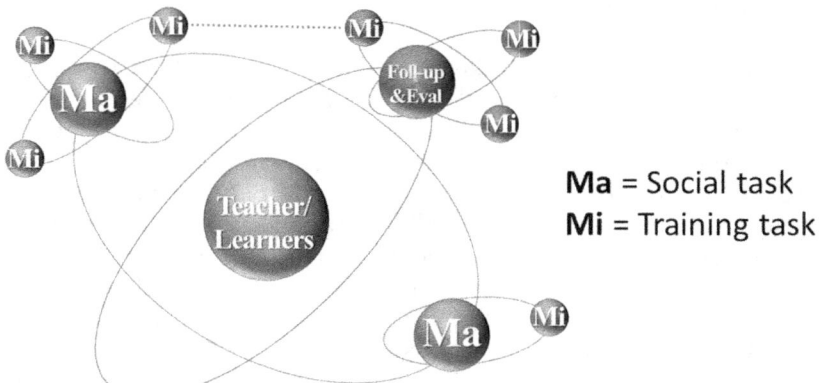

Ma = Social task
Mi = Training task

Figure 18.1 A model of a flexible task-based approach at time *t*

Table 18.1 Key characteristics of social/macro tasks

Social/macro tasks	Nature of the tasks	Objectives	Task features	Work organisation	Media
Type A Tasks with target language (TL) or plurilingual input and no production in TL	• Possible plurilingual collaborative work to share understanding of information • No TL output, output in known languages or other non-linguistic forms • (Co) construction of knowledge (disciplinary or linguistic)	• Access to new knowledge • Sensitisation to obstacles • Awareness of inter and intralingual gaps • Will reveal learning needs • Assessment of outcome (content)	• Realistic/ social/ academic tasks • Material outcome • Individually measurable outcome • Closed tasks • Heuristic tasks • Projects • Problem-solving tasks	• Individual, pair or group work • Telecollaborative from time to time if class is monolingual • Collaborative/cooperative work	• Multimedia support (wiki/blog but not in TL) • Internet • Mobile phones + Instructions and monitoring
Type B Tasks with TL and/or plurilingual input and TL production	• Possible plurilingual collaborative work to share understanding of information • TL social interaction • Production of social documents	• Meaningful activities • Socially realistic outcome • Implicit AL production • Assessment of noticing • Assessment of process • Assessment of product • Assessment of needs • Complexity and its influence on accuracy and fluency	• Social/ realistic/academic tasks • Material outcome individually measurable outcome • Open tasks • Projects • Problem-solving tasks • Unpredictable content (information, opinion or knowledge) • Pair or tutor feedback included in the task (realistic interaction)	• Best in pairs or groups • Telecollaborative from time to time if class is monolingual • Collaborative/cooperative work	• Multimedia support in TL (wiki/blog, mobile phones) • Microworld task • MOOC • Problem-solving tasks • Webquest • Lecture/lesson (slide or paper presentations) • Tandem work with precise social task, project or problem-solving activity+ Instructions and monitoring

Source: Adapted from Bertin et al. (2010).

Table 18.2 Key characteristics of micro/training tasks

Micro/training tasks	Nature of the tasks	Objectives	Task features	Work organisation	Media
Type A Tasks with target language (TL) or plurilingual input and no production in TL	• (Pre, during or post macro task)Plurilingual or monolingual, but not TL output • Awareness raising or recall • Collective work can be in language of schooling or common language(s)	• (Re)creation of 'adequate' explicit knowledge:Phonology • Morphosyntax • Lexis/instances • Concepts • Cultures, etc. • Accuracy	• Closed tasks leading to implicit knowledge:Low cognitive load • No output in TL • Predictable content in order to notice the gaps	• Individual/group work possibly in physical or virtual resource centre • Possibly collective for metareflection	• Incorporated monitoring and feedback
Type B Tasks with TL and/or plurilingual input and TL production	• Output in TL (pre, during or post macro task) • Controlled practice	• Practice of controlled automatic production:Accuracy • Fluency	• Imposed meaning with an element of creativity:Closed tasks (practice) • Predictable content (reduced cognitive load) • Pertinent and automatic choice of problematic features	• Individual or pair • Individual/group work possibly • In physical or virtual resource centre	• Listening and speaking • Reading and writing • ICT tools (audio, video, pictures, voice recording, etc.) • Mobile phones • Incorporated monitoring and feedback (pedagogic agent), etc.

Source: Adapted from Bertin et al. (2010).

- Knowing the language and educational specificities of the context that will influence the expected language development (phonology, grammar, educational culture, etc.).
- Adapting the environment by taking contextual influences into account without adopting practices that would run counter to the objectives.

Learning Environments and the Teacher's Role

Learning environments result from *a priori* educational engineering work in order to reach specific objectives with specific groups in a given context. This makes it possible for course tutors to run a course and adapt to the learners' evolving learning needs. Learning environments are complex systems in which different complex systems are interrelated and respond to each other. We have tried to represent this complex interrelation in Figure 18.2, adapted from Bertin *et al.* (2010), which helps us to visualise this interplay of systems which all have different characteristics.

If we simplify things, we will say that our systemic model is organised around six poles:

- The four traditional poles: language, cultures/content, learner(s) and tutor/teacher.
- The technology pole which includes not only information and communications technology (ICT) tools but also all technological devices in the classroom, including the blackboard.
- The context, at the micro, meso and macro levels.

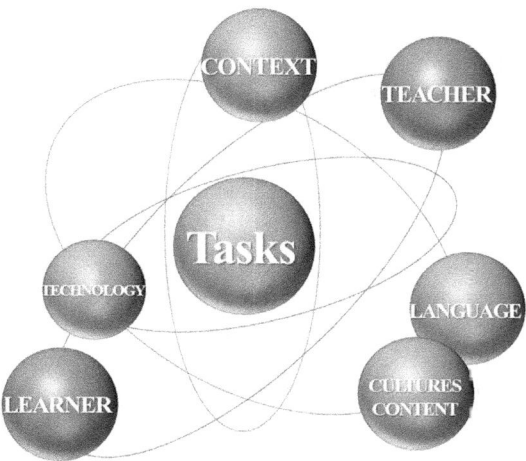

Figure 18.2 The model: Poles in interaction

A network of interactions (mediated or not) develops between the poles. Their interfaces may be identified, but the nature of these interactions often escapes our capacity for observation.

In spite of being simplified, this model helps to visualise:

- how it may vary in an emergentist perspective;
- how it can be deconstructed to better trace specific actions (teaching, learning, follow-up, monitoring, etc.) and see specific roles (teacher, tutor, learner) and people from outside the institution (parents, etc.).

The adequate variables of the environment will be identified and defined before the course. However, educational engineering is not sufficient to totally encompass the learning situation which eventually depends on how the participants will actually experience it. Furthermore, the tutor and the teaching team will never be able to control all the elements of the situation. The evolution of the environment will depend not only on human constraints linked to individual living and learning differences but also on social, material and institutional constraints that may or may not facilitate the process. For instance, Sandberg (2017) mentions agricultural demands in Cambodian projects.

Our choice of the collocation *language learning environment* (LLE) is not fortuitous. 'Classroom' or even 'course' seems to refer to a closed space, cut off from the world outside. Environment implies that the connection with the whole world is possible (physically or digitally). The materials and supports of the social/macro tasks may/will be collected by the learners (formally or informally) and they will preferably co-construct their language and content knowledge as seen in *flipped schooling* (see e.g. Knewton, 2017). Flipped schooling sometimes relies on transmissive practices (videos, etc.) and we would prefer the term 'inverted pedagogy' (see Chapter 6).

The learning environment is no longer teacher centred, but relies on the learners–tutor relation. They all co-construct the course as they co-construct the tasks in a network and reveal individual learning needs that will necessitate specific training/micro tasks (see Case 24).

Teacher/Tutor's Role and Community of Learners

At the teacher level, all over the world, the greatest barriers appear to be time, institutional constraints, assessment requirements, as well as a need for training and support. Having a well-established syllabus and project is one way of relieving educators of some of the time burden that the organisation of blended projects imposes and would also facilitate integration into curricula and recognition with credits. Research needs to be carried out on the development, piloting and evaluation of such projects.

The tutor (the teacher may be the tutor, but they have dissociated roles in some instances) is in charge of following the different stages in the course and sees with the teacher how to adapt when problems occur

(Bygate *et al.*, 2001). The teacher (supported by an engineer sometimes in complex VLEs) organises the learning environment and sees to the necessary adaptations. Adaptations will result from events having different origins (inside or outside the environment). These events may disrupt the apparent linearity of the work.

Individualisation/Socialisation of Learning

The emergentist and sociocultural theories we refer to make us revisit the notion of the individualisation of learning. Language development is discontinuous in an unpredictable and individual way. Individual activities will enable learners to go through their periods of discontinuity at their own pace while still contributing to the collaborative work.

This implies that:

- Content is organised with reference to the curriculum and the objectives (determined in levels, e.g. Common European Framework of Reference for Languages [CEFRL], and negotiated with learners whenever possible). It will be neither necessary nor possible to ensure total correspondence.
- Correspondence with the curriculum will be ensured initially if the teachers are in charge. Adjustments will be made when learners are in charge.
- Course documents/materials/sites will be collected by the teachers and/or by the learners (with clear instructions in this case).
- Criteria for the selection of the documents/materials/sites will be defined according to the specificity of the course (Content and Language Integrated Learning [CLIL] or not, etc.).
- Specific tasks/actions with precise outcomes will be suggested in order for learners to face obstacles and not rely on avoidance strategies.
- Micro/training tasks will be identified before the course if they can be predicted, created or imported as needed. The resource centre can be physical (a simple filing cabinet or shelves may do) or virtual.

Learning languages cannot be effective if learners do not feel and understand their social, cultural and affective meaning. A course that only offers collective activities and training exercises will only satisfy learners who see beyond the tasks. Learning environments will take all the phenomena involved on board in ways that will differ with the contexts as evidenced in the case studies in Part 2. Taking into account the complementarity and responsibility of all participants to a system makes its management easier (Lewin, 1947).

Discontinuity and Changes in LLEs

As illustrated in Figure 18.3, the changes between states N and $N + 1$ symbolise how the environment was reorganised between the two states

174 Part 3: Designing Contextualised Language Learning Environments

and then on (N + 2). As we have seen, the poles and how they relate should not change drastically, but they will not remain identical. How they change and what the consequences are should be assessed regularly.

Accepting the dynamic nature of the environment and the resulting discontinuity results from our emergentist position (see Chapter 4). The initial stage is only a starting point. It will constantly evolve as seen in Figure 18.3 sometimes in very simple ways: changing the layout of the tables or having an internet connection may have more important repercussions on the environment than a governmental decision. Such changes mean that the respective weight of each pole has to be reconsidered as have the relations between the poles (a new layout in a classroom changes tutor/learner relations, as some learners may no longer face the teacher). Research results (e.g. Khalil, 2011) show these changes. In her case, what had been planned to be done in class was eventually done at home, as the learners thought they preferred to do the training tasks when she was present and the macro tasks at home. This clearly shows how the actors take over the environment (or some of its aspects) leading to significant discrepancies between what was initially intended and what is actually done (Fischer, 2007). The model can help us, if we keep in mind its constituents and ensure that they keep interacting in ways that are congruent with the objectives and our theoretical positions while meeting the learners' needs and accepting unavoidable changes.

This model reflects:

- The construct of *organising circumstances* as defined by Spear and Mocker (1984).
- The underlying organisation of the inter/retroactions at play in the environment without unduly reducing its essential complexity and without making it too complex with which to work.

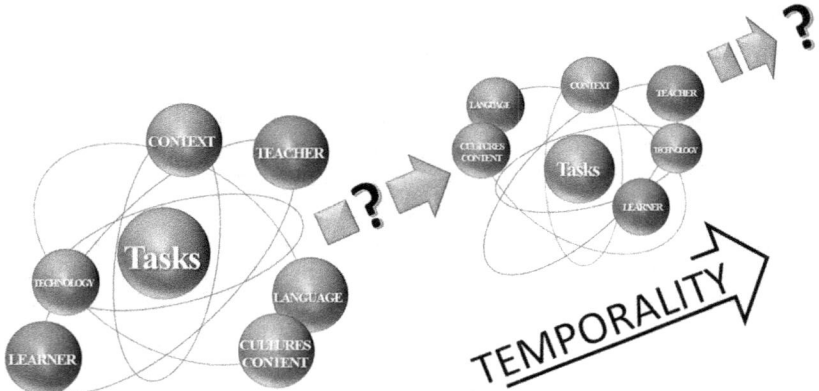

Figure 18.3 Discontinuities in the LLE

Synthesis

The model enables the teacher/tutor to ensure that the whole system of inter/retroactions is taken into account. We assume that it can be applied everywhere but, of course, implementing the learning environment will be context dependent and will vary with how the respective roles and responsibility of learners and teacher/tutor have been decided in relation to the pedagogical traditions. The pertinence of such traditions may need to be questioned. This reflection will imply reflecting on how the various systems evolve and on their emergentist properties. In order to respond quickly and effectively, the team will need to be able to grasp the essential of what is happening without having too simplistic a view.

Andronova (2016), Brudermann (2010) and Khalil (2011), among others have applied this model. Their research confirms its validity and underscores the pertinence of turning to so many theories in order to monitor, understand and respond to the problems. As we have already stressed, associative networks of researchers and teachers are helpful in sharing the experience.

Blended learning environments make it easy to dissociate the teachers' roles (designer, organiser, mediator/tutor). They no longer have to transmit knowledge, nor will they feel the same weight of pedagogic immediacy (Perrenoud, 1998). If learning is not linear, content presentation may be. Training tasks can often be predicted (pro-active mediation) with experience if their assignment cannot come before the need arises (Arthaud, 2009). Even with a pre-established curriculum, the learning environment will constantly have to be adapted. It will have to make it possible for teachers to anticipate and respond to permanent variability. Flexibility is the keyword, but with constant monitoring, which is not always easy to maintain in some contexts. Khalil (2011) experienced it in Egypt when power cuts made recourse to ICT more complex than she had expected. If her course had taken place in the winter, she would not have experienced the same problems, but would not have realised that learners preferred to do the macro tasks at home (collaborating on the internet) and the training tasks at school when she could help them individually on the spot.

Organising circumstances and tutor and peer mediation make it possible to run non-coercive learning environments where learners feel empowered. These environments will each be very different depending on the contexts as seen in the case studies or as shown by Andronova (2016), Brudermann (2010), Khalil (2011), Narcy-Combes and Narcy-Combes (2014), among others.

Concluding Remarks

This book has approached language learning in multilingual contexts initially from a theoretical perspective, highlighting not only the language-related theories, but also what other human sciences tell us. Case studies then showed multilingualism enacted in specific settings and contexts and a general worldwide outlook was then proposed. Building on this, an approach to setting up appropriate learning environments was described. However, many issues are still unresolved, in particular (Narcy-Combes *et al.*, 2015):

- A better understanding of the link between language/discourse/norms in multilingual academic settings is necessary, as well as a clearer view of the social and individual consequences of undermining the influence of the code and of undermining the dominance of centrality.
- The issue of learning vs. teaching should be tackled in order to understand the link between individual development and teacher mediation in specific cultural situations (which means giving greater importance to process than product initially, contrary to traditional school evaluation).
- The question of how structures, ideology and beliefs interact with face and self-esteem should be examined, which would help to better understand individual or collective so-called 'resistance' to schooling or to top-down projects.
- The role of 'variation' should be investigated in order to understand how it could be coped with without ignoring more 'universal' parameters.

Epistemologically speaking, finding solutions to the problems listed above implies that complementarity and not superiority of research findings is valued. Very local research can be just as enlightening as research carried out in well-known research centres, especially when dealing with variation. The dissemination of results and planned partial duplication when applicable are still badly needed to avoid unnecessary and costly repetition of research. However, there are many domains that we cannot access because they are too far from language education and we need to work with them in collaborative projects. Political decision-making will remain problematic, if we do not take part in it and allow it to escape our influence; this situation forces us to admit that the object of research cannot be problematised 'objectively'. It depends on the rapport between the researcher and what Corijn (2006) calls the 'City', in terms of ethics, individual posture and deontology. Commitment is obviously linked to how individual researchers see their position in that 'City'. A balance has obviously to be found between commitment and scientific distantiation, but it would be difficult to say that there is no hidden political agenda in research on education. Researchers become more and more aware of their eventual political involvement (see i.e. Beacco, 2013; Corijn, 2006; Douglas Fir Group, 2016; Medioni & Narcy-Combes, 2016), which may be a good sign. As a consequence, we will conclude by suggesting more reflection.

Implementing LLEs and designing tasks in multilingual contexts will be facilitated and made more effective by adopting action research, or at least reflective practice (see Dörnyei, 2007; Narcy-Combes, 2005), and by starting with pilot cases rather than decisions at the state level (see Haddad, 2008 and Sandberg, 2017, for instance). We have seen how important it is to distantiate oneself even from theoretical positions as most theories still remain hypothetical. We feel in line with Medin *et al.* (2015) who remind us that epistemologies and cultures have a reciprocal influence that biases our positions.

When teaching/tutoring, an immediate response is often required (Perrenoud, 1996) which necessitates automated know-how that results from education and training. Best practice will never be enough unless we face the very same learners all the time. However, we saw the vast amount of knowledge that was needed (see Ziegler, 2013) and teachers need to check how effective it is. Applied linguistics and research in language education provide incomplete insights for contextualised action (Develay, 2001) and teachers need to distance themselves from social constructs (stereotypes, general opinions) which can cause unavoidable tension.

To be able to work freely and responsibly on a project (Bourdieu, 1987: 127), teachers can:

- assess the problems;
- see how the scientific literature deals with them;
- plan an action project;
- go back to their practice and monitor it with adequate tools to collect data;
- find a balance between their spontaneity and creativity and the scientific validity of the way they act;
- compare the way they feel with the data they have collected;
- interpret the eventual gaps between what they feel and what the data say.

To overcome obstacles to interpretations, the following points must be considered:

- Opinion must be confronted with theoretical knowledge.
- Professional competence results from experience which is sometimes misleading. Self-observation and confrontation may be necessary, a mediator will help (see Chapter 3).

- A tension may be felt between scientific distantiation and engagement (creativity, intuition, initiatic knowledge). Distantiation should not initially hinder engagement, but the people involved should make sure that the effects of engagement correspond to both the values and the objectives of each individual and of the group.

Action research (Ellis, 1997; Narcy-Combes, 2005), or reflective practice (Dörnyei, 2007), will ensure constant validation of the work and will help us understand what happens. This posture implies constant reconsideration of preconceived ideas while taking the beliefs of the various actors into account in order to implement learning environments in accordance with the specific sociocultural parameters of each context. In order to adapt to constantly emerging needs, to steer between scientific, ethical and political positions and to pay attention to individual needs and requirements, a flexible and rigorous methodology will be required to reconsider what is problematic.

Sharing responsibility with everyone involved and negotiating the changes with them has been seen to be of prime importance (see Chapter 5). Such approaches as action research (since Lewin, 1948) and MAG (*Méthode d'analyse en groupe*: group analysis of data; see Chapter 7) (Van Campenhoudt *et al.*, 2009), for instance, will make it possible.

It is best to implement projects where bottom-up decisions have been given a place, thus reducing power effects. Starting from who people actually are and how they feel (teachers and learners) is another key factor as has been repeatedly stressed. It is important to remember that even if beliefs and representations change, this change may not influence behaviours and practices right away (see Chapter 5). Despite the difficulty of influencing such complex situations, this book has tried to describe the interplay between language learning and our multilingual world. The theoretical reflection and the multilingual practices demonstrated in the case studies have led us to propose LLEs that take into account the plurality of cultural and language repertoires, of contexts (at various scales) and, consequently, of individual learning processes. This implied taking into consideration a great number of parameters to define a complex and dynamic approach to designing and managing these LLEs in which different interrelated poles influence and complement each other in a constantly evolving organisation.

Neither the individual teacher nor educational institutions have total control of all the parameters, but distantiation, reflectivity and respect for who the learners are can help to adapt LLEs to renewed demands in order to boost the development of individuals in today's multilingual world.

References

Abdellilah-Bauer, B. (2014) *Le défi des enfants bilingues. Grandir et vivre en parlant plusieurs langues*. Paris: La Découverte.
Abdellilah-Bauer, B. and Bijeljac-Babic, R. (2015) Grandir entre deux langues. Entretien: propos recueillis par Nicolas Journet. *Sciences Humaines* 274, 54–55.
Adam, C. and Calvez, R. (2016) De l'éducation bilingue en Bretagne: breton et gallo à l'école. In C. Hélot and J. Erfurt (eds) *L'éducation bilingue en France: politiques linguistiques, modèles et pratiques* (pp. 183–198). Rennes: Presses Universitaires de Rennes.
Agbefle, K.G. (ed.) (2016) *Plurilinguisme et enseignement du français en Afrique subsaharienne*. Vincennes: Observatoire Européen du Plurilinguisme.
Agence Universitaire de la Francophonie (2017) See http://www.aidenligne-francais-universite.auf.org/spip.php?article1147 (Accessed 10/11/2018).
Aimard, V. (2005) Environnements virtuels et didactique des langues, quelle réalité? PhD thesis, Université Paris III.
Akiyama, Y. (2017) Learner beliefs and corrective feedback in telecollaboration: A longitudinal investigation. *System* 64, 68–73.
Andersen, R. (1983) *Pidginisation and Creolisation as Language Acquisition*. Rowley, MA: Newbury House.
Anderson, J. (1993) *Rules of the Mind*. Hillsdale, NJ: Erlbaum.
Anderson, M.L. (2014) *After Phrenology. Neural Reuse and the Interactive Brain*. Cambridge, MA: MIT Press.
Andrews, L. (2006) *Language Exploration and Awareness. A Resource Book for Teachers*. Mahwah, NJ: Erlbaum.
Andronova, O. (2016) Analyse didactique d'un dispositif d'apprentissage des langues en autonomie dirigée, médiatisé par les technologies en milieu universitaire destiné à des apprenants non spécialistes des langues étrangères en première année de Licence. PhD thesis, Université Paris-Diderot.
Annoot, E. (1996) *Les formateurs face aux nouvelles technologies: le sens du changement*. Paris: Ophrys.
Arnold, J. (2000) *Affect in Language Learning*. Cambridge: Cambridge University Press.
Arthaud, P. (2009) *Anglais: une médiation technologique*. PhD thesis, Université de technologie de Belfort-Montbéliard.
Austin, N., Hampel, R. and Kukulska-Hulme, A. (2017) Video conferencing and multimodal expression of voice: Children's conversations using Skype for second language development in a telecollaborative setting. *System* 64, 87–103.
Auzéau, F. (2017) Pertinences de l'enseignement de la prononciation par le théâtre et par le chant en contexte universitaire. PhD thesis, Université Sorbonne Nouvelle-Paris 3.
Baena, R. (ed.) (2006) *Transculturing Auto/Biography: Forms of Life Writing*. New York: Routledge.

Bailly, S., Boulton, A., Chateau, A., Duda, R. and Tyne, H. (2009) L'anglais langue d'appui pour l'apprentissage du français langue étrangère. In G. Forlot (ed.) *L'Anglais et le plurilinguisme: pour une didactique des contacts et des passerelles linguistiques* (pp. 35–57). Paris: L'Harmattan.
Bakhtin, M.M. (1981) *The Dialogic Imagination: Fours Essays* (M. Holquist ed. and C. Emerson and M. Holquist trans). Austin, TX: University of Texas Press.
Bandura, A. (2001) Social cognition theory: An agentic perspective. *Annual Review of Psychology* 52 (1), 1–26.
Bange, P. (1992) *Analyse conversationnelle et théorie de l'action*. Paris: Didier.
Barreteau, D. (1998) *Politiques linguistiques et éducatives: quelles pistes pour sortir de l'impasse?* Ouagadougou: ORSTOM.
Bascia, N. (2014) *The School Context Model: How School Environments Shape Students' Opportunities to Learn*. Toronto: Measuring What Matters, People for Education.
Beacco, J.-C. (2000) *Les Dimensions Culturelles des Enseignements de Langue*. Paris: Hachette.
Beacco, J.-C. (ed.) (2013) *Ethique et Politique en Didactique des Langues: autour de la Notion de Responsabilité*. Paris: Didier.
Beacco, J.-C., Byram, M., Cavalli, M., Coste, D., Egli Cuenat, M., Goullier, F. and Panthier, J. (Language Policy Division) (2010) *Guide for the Development and Implementation of Curricula for Plurilingual and Intercultural Education*. Strasbourg: Council of Europe.
Bensfia, A., Mabrour, A. and Mgharfaoui, Kh. (2013) L'impact du choix de la langue sur les débouchés et carrières professionnels: points de vue d'étudiants. *Recherches en didactique des langues et des cultures: les cahiers de l'ACEDLE* 10 (3), 55–73.
Berger, P.L. and Luckmann, T. (1966) *The Social Construction of Reality: A Treatise in the Sociology of Knowledge*. New York: Anchor.
Bertin, J.-C., Gravé, P. and Narcy-Combes, J.-P. (2010) *Second Language Distance Learning. Theoretical Perspectives and Didactic Ergonomics*. Hershley, PA: IGI Global.
Bialystok, E. (1993) *Symbolic Representation and Attentional Control in Pragmatic Competence in Interlanguage Pragmatics*. Oxford: Oxford University Press.
Bialystok, E. (2009) Bilingualism. The good, the bad and the indifferent. *Bilingualism, Language and Cognition* 12 (1), 3–11.
Blackledge, A. and Creese, A. (2010) Translanguaging in the bilingual classroom: A pedagogy for learning and teaching? *Modern Language Journal* 94, 103–115.
Blanchet, P., Moore, D. and Asselah Rahal, S. (2008) *Perspectives pour une didactique des Langues contextualisée*. Paris: Editions des Archives Contemporaines.
Blaxton, T. (1989) Investigating dissociations among memory measures: Support for a transfer-appropriate processing framework. *Journal of Experimental Psychology: Learning, Memory, and Cognition* 15, 657–668.
Block, D. (2003) *The Social Turn in Second Language Acquisition*. Washington, DC: Georgetown University Press.
Bolduc, J., Montésinos-Gelet, I. and Boisvert, S. (2014) Perceptions musicales et conscience phonologique: recherche auprès d'enfants francophones d'âge préscolaire. *Psychologie française* 59 (3), 247–255.
Bouchard, R. (2009) Intervention didactique en milieu scolaire et cycle dialogal. In O. Galatanu (ed.) *Intervention didactique en milieu scolaire et cycle dialogal* (pp. 269–288). Bern: Peter Lang.
Boughnim, A. and Narcy-Combes, J.-P. (2011) Télévision et apprentissage de l'italien dans un contexte plurilingue: pistes pour l'enseignement des langues à l'école élémentaire. *Recherches en didactique des langues et des cultures: les cahiers de l'ACEDLE* 8 (1), 147–162. See http://journals.openedition.org/rdlc/2288 (accessed 6 January 2018).
Boukri-Friekh, S. (2011) Le français, langue utilitaire donc concurrencée. Du rapport ambivalent à la langue: concurrence de l'anglais dans l'espace maghrébin. *Les Cahiers de l'Orient* 103 (3), 39–42.

Bourdieu, P. (1966) L'école conservatrice: les inégalités devant l'école et devant la culture. *Revue française de sociologie* 7 (3), 325–347.
Bourdieu, P. (1980) *Le sens pratique*. Paris: Editions de Minuit.
Bourdieu, P. (1987) *Choses dites*. Paris: Editions de Minuit.
Bozhinova, K. (2018) Productions non conformes aux normes et rétroactions correctives dans l'apprentissage de L3. *Revue internationale d'études en langues modernes appliquées* numéro spécial, 55–67.
Bozhinova, K., Narcy-Combes, J.-P. and Zaouali, S. (2017) La production écrite vue comme un processus bilingue: dans quelle mesure les TIC peuvent-elles aider ? *Pratiques* 173–174. See http://journals.openedition.org/pratiques/3426 (accessed 9 May 2017).
Brammerts, H. and Calvert, M. (2002) Apprendre en communiquant. In B. Helmling (ed.) *L'apprentissage autonome des langues en tandem* (pp. 31–41). Paris: Didier.
Bretegnier, A. and Audras, I. (forthcoming 2018) Des langues en relation dans la formation linguistique des adultes en insertion. Quels enjeux? Quels effets? In C. Jeoffrion and M.-F. Narcy-Combes (eds) *Perspectives plurilingues en éducation et formation* (pp. 219–236). Rennes: Presses Universitaire de Rennes.
Brodin, E. (2002) Innovation, instrumentation technologique de l'apprentissage des langues: des schèmes d'action aux modèles de pratiques émergentes. *Alsic* 5 (2). See http://journals.openedition.org/alsic/2070 (accessed 21 December 2017).
Brohy, C., Genoud, P.A. and Gurtner, J.L. (2014) Discourse on multilingualism, language competence, use and attitudes in German-English bilingual vocational schools in Switzerland. In A. Otwinowska and G. De Angelis (eds) *Learning and Teaching in Multilingual Contexts. Conceptual, Sociolinguistic and Educational Perspectives* (pp. 167–198). Bristol: Multilingual Matters.
Bronckart, J.-P. (2004) Pourquoi et comment analyser l'agir verbal et non verbal en situation de travail. In J.-P. Bronckart, E. Bulea and L. Filliettaz (eds) *Agir et discours en situation de travail* (pp. 11–14). Genève: Université de Genève, Cahiers de la section des sciences de l'éducation 103.
Brown, D. (2009) Performance orientation and motivational strategies in high-achievement language learners. *Lidil* 40, 105–121.
Brudermann, C. (2010) From action research to the implementation of ICT pedagogical tools: Taking into account student's needs to propose adjusted online tutorial practice. *ReCall* 22 (2), 172–190.
Bruner, J.S. (1966) *Toward a Theory of Instruction*. Cambridge: Belkapp Press.
Burgen, S. (2015) US Now has More Spanish Speakers than Spain – Only Mexico has More. *The Guardian*. See https://www.theguardian.com/us-news/2015/jun/29/us-second-biggest-spanish-speaking-country (accessed 6 December 2017).
Burston, J. (2015) Twenty years of MALL project implementation: A meta-analysis of learning outcomes. *ReCALL* 27 (1), 4–20.
Buser, M. (2015) Two-way immersion in Biel/Bienne, Switzerland: Multilingual education in the public school Filière Bilingue (FiBi): A longitudinal study of the development of languages of schooling (French & Swiss) German. PhD thesis, Université Sorbonne Nouvelle-Paris 3.
Bygate, M., Skehan, P. and Swain, M. (eds) (2001) *Researching Pedagogic Tasks: Second Language Learning, Teaching and Testing*. Harlow: Longman.
Cahour, B. (2014) Démasquer incompréhensions et désaccords interactionnels avec des entretiens' re-situant'. *Le Français dans le Monde. Recherches et Applications* 56, 151–165.
Cambra Giné, M. (2003) *Une approche ethnographique de la classe de langue*. Paris: Didier.
Canagarajah, A.S. (2007) Lingua franca English, multilingual communities, and language acquisition. *The Modern Language Journal* 91 (1), 923–939.

Canagarajah, A.S. (2008) Language shift and the family: Questions from the Sri Lankan Tamil diaspora. *Journal of Sociolinguistics* 12 (2), 1–34.

Canagarajah, A.S. (2011) Codemeshing in academic writing: Identifying teachable strategies of translanguaging. *The Modern Language Journal* 95 (3), 401–417.

Canagarajah, A.S. (2013) From intercultural rhetoric to cosmopolitan practice: Addressing new challenges in lingua franca English. In D. Belcher and G. Nelson (eds) *Critical and Corpus-Based Approaches to Intercultural Rhetoric* (pp. 381–401). Ann Arbor, MI: University of Michigan Press.

Canagarajah, S. and Ashraf, H. (2013) Multilingualism and education in South Asia: Resolving policy/practice dilemmas. *Annual Review of Applied Linguistics* 33, 258–285.

Candalot, A. (2005) Rôle et enjeux du système éducatif en Mauritanie dans l'évolution politique. *Le Portique, Archives des cahiers de la recherche, Cahier* 3. See http://journals.openedition.org/leportique/760 (accessed 23 December 2017).

Candelier, M. (ed.) (2003) *L'éveil aux langues à l'école primaire*. Bruxelles: De Boeck.

Candelier, M. (2008) Approches plurielles, didactiques du plurilinguisme: le même et l'autre. *Recherches en didactique des langues et des cultures: les cahiers de l'ACEDLE* 5 (1), 65–90.

Cappellini, M. and Rivens Mompean, A. (2013) Positionnements culturels dans un tandem sino-français par visioconférence. *Synergies Chine* 8, 137–149.

Cappellini, M. and Zhang, M. (2013) Étude des négociations du sens dans un tandem par visioconférence. *Recherches en didactique des langues et des cultures: les cahiers de l'ACEDLE* 10 (2), 27–59.

Carrasco Perea, E. and Pishva, Y. (2007) Comment préparer et accompagner l'émergence d'interactions en ligne dans une approche plurilingue axée sur l'intercompréhension romane? *Lidil* 36, 141–162. See http://lidil.revues.org/2523 (accessed 30 September 2016).

Carson, L. (2012) The role of drama in task-based learning: Agency, identity and autonomy. *Scenario* 6 (2), 47–60.

Carstensen, L.L. (1995) Evidence for a life-span theory of socioemotional selectivity. *Psychological Science* 4, 151–156.

Castellotti, V. and Moore, D. (2008) Contextualisation et universalisme. Quelle didactique des langues pour le 21ème siècle? In P. Blanchet, D. Moore and S. Asselah-Rahal (eds) *Perspectives pour une didactique des langues contextualisée* (pp. 183–203). Paris: Editions des Archives Contemporaines.

Castellotti, V. and Moore, D. (2010) *Représentations sociales des langues et enseignements*. Strasbourg: Conseil de l'Europe.

Catroux, M. (2006) L'apprentissage collaboratif médiatisé par Internet: conditions de mise en œuvre chez de jeunes apprenants d'anglais. *Recherches en didactique des langues et des cultures: les cahiers de l'ACEDLE* 2, 52–73.

Causa, M. (2002) *L'alternance codique dans l'enseignement d'une langue étrangère*. Bern: Peter Lang.

Cavalli, M. (2005) *Education bilingue et plurilinguisme: le cas du Val d'Aoste*. Paris: Didier.

Cenoz, J. (2009) *Towards Multilingual Education: Basque Educational Research in International Perspective*. Bristol: Multilingual Matters.

Cenoz, J. (2015) Content-based instruction and content and language integrated learning: The same or different? *Language, Culture and Curriculum* 28 (1), 8–24.

Cenoz, J. and Gorter, D. (2011) A holistic approach in multilingual education: Introduction. *The Modern Language Journal* 95 (3), 339–343.

Channouf, A. (2004) *Les influences inconscientes*. Paris: Armand Colin.

Chapelle, C.A. (2003) *English Language Learning and Technology*. Philadelphia, PA: John Benjamins.

Chazot, D. (2017) La télécollaboration à travers un scénario pédagogique ludique. *Les Langues Modernes* 1-2017, 42–49.

Chen, Y.H. and Baker, P. (2010) Lexical bundles in L1 and L2 academic writing. *Language Learning and Technology* 14 (2), 30–49. See http://llt.msu.edu/vol14num2/chenbaker.pdf (accessed 6 January 2018).

Chen, J.F., Warden, C.A. and Chang, H. (2005) Motivators that do not motivate: The case of Chinese and EFL learners and the influence of culture on motivation. *TESOL Quarterly* 39 (4), 609–633.

Chini, D. (2002) La situation d'apprentissage: d'un lieu externe à un espace interne. *ASp* 37/38, 95–108. See http://asp.revues.org/1507 (accessed 17 September 2017).

Christenson, S.L., Reschly, A.L. and Wylie, C. (eds) (2012) *Handbook of Research on Student Engagement*. New York: Springer Science.

Churchland, B. (2002) *Brain-Wise: Studies in Neurophilosophy*. Cambridge: The MIT Press.

Cicurel, F. and Narcy-Combes, J.-P. (2014) Quelle complémentarité entre les savoirs d'action et les savoirs théoriques ? Quelques significations à attribuer à l'action enseignante. In J. Aguilar, C. Brudermann and M. Leclère (eds) *Langues, cultures et pratiques en contexte: interrogations didactiques* (pp. 347–367). Paris: Riveneuve éditions.

Clougherty, R. and Wells, M. (2008) Use of Wikis in chemistry instruction for problem-based learning assignments: An example in instrumental analysis. *Journal of Chemical Education* 86 (10), 1446–1448.

Collentine, J. and Freed, B. (2004) *Learning Context and Its Effects on Second Language Acquisition*. Cambridge: Cambridge University Press.

Collins, B.A. and Cioè-Pena, M. (2016) Declaring freedom: Translanguaging in the social studies classroom to understand complex texts. In O. García and T. Kleyn (eds) *Translanguaging with Multilingual Students: Learning from Classroom Moments* (pp. 118–139). New York: Routledge.

Cook, V.J. (ed.) (2003) *Effects of the Second Language on the First*. Clevedon: Multilingual Matters.

Cook, V.J. (2007) The goals of ELT: Reproducing native-speakers or promoting multi-competence among second language users? In J. Cummins and C. Davison (eds) *Handbook on English Language Teaching* (pp. 237–248). Amsterdam: Kluwer.

Cook, V.J. (2008) *Second Language Learning and Language Teaching*. Abingdon: Routledge.

Cope, B. and Kalantzis, M. (2007) Language education and multiliteracies. In S. May and N.H. Hornberger (eds) *Encyclopedia of Language and Education* (2nd edn; pp. 195–211). Boston, MA: Springer Science and Business Media LLC.

Cope, B. and Kalantzis, M. (2009) A grammar of multimodality. *International Journal of Learning* 16 (2), 361–425.

Corijn, E. (2006) *Eléments d'un projet pour Ixelles. Une contribution citoyenne*. Bruxelles: Parcours Citoyen.

Coroama, L. (2013) Contribution à la réflexion sur les apprentissages formels et informels dans un environnement plurilingue et pluriculturel: le cas de l'anglais dans la région du Banat en Roumanie. PhD thesis, Université du Maine.

Cortier, C., Kaaboub, A., Kherra, N. and Benaoum, M. (2013) Français langue d'enseignement et prise en compte du bi-plurilinguisme dans les études universitaires en Algérie: quelles compatibilités avec la didactique du FOS? *Recherches en didactique des langues et des cultures: les cahiers de l'ACEDLE* 10 (3), 75–98.

Coste, D. (2001) *D'une langue à d'autres: pratiques et représentations*. Rouen: Publications de l'Université de Rouen.

Council of Europe (1992) *European Charter for Regional or Minority Languages*. See https://www.coe.int/en/web/conventions/full-list/-/conventions/treaty/148. (Accessed 10/12/2018).

Council of Europe (1995) Council resolution of 31 March 1995 on improving and diversifying language learning and teaching within the education systems of the European Union. *Official Journal of the European Union*, C 207, 1–5.

Council of Europe (2001) *Common European Framework of Reference for Languages*. Cambridge: Cambridge University Press.

Coyle, D., Hood, P. and Marsh, D. (2010) *CLIL: Content and Language Integrated Learning*. Cambridge: Cambridge University Press.

Coyos, J-B. (2016) L'enseignement scolaire bilingue basque-français: avancées et limites. In C. Hélot and J. Erfurt (eds) *L'éducation bilingue en France* (pp. 168–182). Limoges: Lambert Lucas.

Cross, J. (2006) *Informal Learning*. San Francisco, CA: Pfeiffer.

Cuet, C. (2011) Enseigner le français en Chine, méthodologies nouvelles, perspectives. *Synergies Chine* 6, 95–103.

Cummins, J. (1979) Cognitive/academic language proficiency, linguistic interdependence, the optimum age question and some other matters. *Working Papers on Bilingualism* 19, 121–129.

Cummins, J. (1984) *Bilingualism and Special Education: Issues in Assessment and Pedagogy*. Clevedon: Multilingual Matters.

Cummins, J. (1994) Knowledge, power, and identity in teaching English as a second language. In F. Genesee (ed.) *Educating Second Language Children: The Whole Child, the Whole Curriculum, the Whole Community* (pp. 33–58). Cambridge: Cambridge University Press.

Cummins, J. (2000) *Language, Power and Pedagogy: Bilingual Children in the Crossfire*. Clevedon: Multilingual Matters.

Cummins, J. (2005) A proposal for action: Strategies for recognizing heritage language competence as a learning resource within the mainstream classroom. *The Modern Language Journal* 89 (4), 585–592.

Cummins, J. (2007) Rethinking monolingual instructional strategies in multilingual classrooms. *Canadian Journal of Applied Linguistics* 10, 221–240.

Cunningham, D.J. (2017) Methodological innovation for the study of request production in telecollaboration. *Language Learning & Technology* 21 (1), 75–98. See http://llt.msu.edu/issues/february2017/cunningham.pdf (accessed 6 January 2018).

Cuq, J.-P. (2004) *Dictionnaire de Didactique du Français Langue Etrangère et Seconde*. Paris: CLE International/Asdifle.

Cutler, A. (2000) Listening to a second language through the ears of a first. *Interpreting*, 5, 1, Amsterdam: John Benjamins Publishing Company. 1–23.

Dagenais, D. (2012) Littératies multimodales et perspectives critiques. *Les Cahiers de l'Acedle* 9 (2) 16–46.

Dalton-Puffer, C. (2007) *Discourse in Content and Language Integrated Learning (CLIL) Classrooms*. Philadelphia, PA: John Benjamins.

Damasio, A.R. (1994) *Descartes' Error: Emotion, Reason, and the Human Brain*. New York: Putnam Books.

Damasio, A.R. (2003) *Spinoza avait raison. Joie et tristesse, le cerveau des émotions*. Paris: Odile Jacob.

Daryai-Hansen, P., Barford, S. and Schwarz, L. (2017) A call for (trans)languaging: The language profiles at Roskilde University. In C.M. Mazak and K.S. Carroll (eds) *Translanguaging in Higher Education: Beyond Monolingual Ideologies* (pp. 29–49). Bristol: Multilingual Matters.

De Angelis, G. (2005) Multilingualism and non-native lexical transfer. An identification problem. *International Journal of Multilingualism* 2, 1–25.

De Bot, K. and Jaensch, C. (2015) What is special about L3 processing? Bilingualism: Language and Cognition 18 (2), 130–144.

De Bot, K., Lowie, W. and Verspoor, M. (2007) A dynamic systems theory to second language acquisition. *Bilingualism: Language and Cognition* 10, 7–21.

De Boysson-Bardies, B. (2005) *Comment la parole vient aux enfants*. Paris: Odile Jacob.
de Leersnyder, J., Kim, H. and Mesquita, B. (2015) Feeling right is feeling good: Psychological well-being and emotional fit with culture in autonomy- versus relatedness-promoting situations. *Frontiers in Psychology* 6, 630. See https://doi.org/10.3389/fpsyg.2015.00630 (accessed 6 January 2018).
de Pietro, J.-F., Matthey, M. and Py, B. (1989) Acquisition et contrat didactique: les séquences potentiellement acquisitionnelles dans la conversation exolingue. *Actes du troisième Colloque Régional de Linguistique Strasbourg des 28–29 avril 1988* (pp. 99–119). Strasbourg: Université des Sciences Humaines et Université Louis Pasteur.
de Putter-Smits, L.G.A., Taconis, R. and Jochems, W.M.G. (2013) Mapping context-based learning environments: The construction of an instrument. *Learning Environments Research* 16 (3), 437–462.
Deakin Crick, R., Green, H., Barr, S., Shafi, A. and Peng, W.J. (2013) *Evaluating the Wider Outcomes of Schooling: The Oasis ECHO Project. Technical Report*. Bristol: University of Bristol.
Deci, E. and Ryan, R. (2008) Self-determination theory: A macrotheory of human motivation, development and health. *Canadian Psychology* 49 (3), 182–185.
Degache, C. and Garbarino, S. (dir.) (2017) *Itinéraires pédagogiques de l'alternance des langues. L'intercompréhension*, Grenoble, UGA Editions, Didaskein.
Degache, C. (2018) Enjeux des modalités télécollaboratives dans un scénario pour l'intercompréhension: chronique d'un changement annoncé. In C. Jeoffrion and M.-F. Narcy-Combes (eds) *Perspectives plurilingues en éducation et formation* (pp. 179–199). Rennes: Presses Universiraires de Rennes.
Dehaene, S. (2007) *Les neurones de la lecture*. Paris: Odile Jacob.
Demaizière, F. and Narcy-Combes, J.-P. (2007) Du positionnement épistémologique aux données de terrain. *Recherches en didactique des langues et des cultures: les cahiers de l'ACEDLE* 4, 1–20.
Démonet, J.-F., Thierry, G. and Cardebat, D. (2005) Renewal of the neurophysiology of language: Functional neuroimaging. *Physiological Reviews* 85 (1), 49–95.
Derix, J., Iljina, O., Weiske, J., Schulze-Bonhage, A., Aertsen, A. and Ball, T. (2014) From speech to thought: The neuronal basis of cognitive units in non-experimental, real-life communication investigated using ECoG. *Frontiers in Human Neuroscience* 8, 383. See https://doi.org/10.3389/fnhum.2014.00383 (accessed 9 January 2018).
Dervin, F. (2011) *Les identités des couples interculturels. En finir vraiment avec la culture?* Paris: L'Harmattan.
Develay, M. (2001) *Propos sur les Sciences de l'Éducation: Réflexions épistémologiques*. Paris: ESF éditeur.
Dewaele, J.-M., Petrides, K.V. and Furnham, A. (2008) Effects of trait emotional intelligence and sociobiographical variables on communicative anxiety and foreign language anxiety among adult multilinguals: A review and empirical investigation. *Language Learning* 58 (4), 911–960.
Di Meglio, A. and Cortier, C. (2016) La langue corse comme socle d'une éducation bi-plurilingue. In C. Hélot and J. Erfurt (eds) *L'éducation bilingue en France* (pp. 215–230). Limoges: Lambert Lucas.
Dompmartin, C. (forthcoming 2018) Un atelier d'écriture expérientielle en FLE comme parcours de sécurisation entre l'ici et l'ailleurs linguistique et culturel. In C. Jeoffrion and M.-F. Narcy-Combes (eds) *Perspectives plurilingues en éducation et formation*. Rennes: Presses Universitaires de Rennes.
Dornisch, M. (2013) The digital divide in classrooms: Teacher technology comfort and evaluations. *Computers in the Schools Interdisciplinary Journal of Practice, Theory, and Applied Research* 30 (3), 210–228.
Dörnyei, Z. (2001) New themes and approaches in L2 motivation research. *Annual Review of Applied Linguistics* 21, 43–59.

Dörnyei, Z. (2007) *Research Methods in Applied Linguistics: Quantitative, Qualitative and Mixed Methodologies*. Oxford: Oxford University Press.

Dörnyei, Z. (2009) *The Psychology of Second Language Acquisition*. Oxford: Oxford University Press.

Dörnyei, Z. and Ushioda, E. (2009) Motivation, language identities and the L2 self: A theoretical overview. In Z. Dörnyei and E. Ushioda (eds) *Motivation, Language Identity and the L2 Self* (pp. 1–42). Bristol: Multilingual Matters.

Dörnyei, Z., Henry, A. and Muir, C. (2016) *Motivational Currents in Language Learning: Frameworks for Focused Interventions*. New York Routledge.

Doughty, C.J. and Long, M.H. (eds) (2005) *The Handbook of Second Language Acquisition*. Oxford: Blackwell.

Douglas Fir Group (2016) A transdisciplinary framework for SLA in a multilingual world. *The Modern Language Journal* 100 (S1), 19–47.

Doyde, P. (2005) 'L'intercompréhension', Guide pour l'élaboration des politiques linguistiques éducatives en Europe. De la diversité linguistique à l'éducation plurilingue. Étude de référence. Division des politiques linguistiques. Conseil de l'Europe Strasbourg. See http://www.coe.int/t/dg4/linguistic/Source/DoyeFR.pdf (accessed 6 January 2018).

Duclos, A.M. (2015) Resistance to change: An outdated and invalid concept in education. *Psychologie & Éducation* 2015 (1), 33–45.

Duffau, H. (2016) *L'erreur de Broca*. Paris: Lafon.

DuFon, M.A. (2010) The acquisition of terms of address in a second language. In A. Trosborg (ed.) *Pragmatics across Languages and Cultures: Handbooks of Pragmatics* (pp. 309–332). Berlin: Walter de Gruyter.

Dulay, H., Burt, M. and Krashen, S. (1982) *Language Two*. New York: Oxford University Press.

Durus, N. (2009) Discourse strategies in learner inhabited talk. Unpublished scientific master's thesis, University of Luxembourg.

Egeth, H.E. and Yantis, S. (1997) Visual attention: Control, representation, and time course. *Annual Review of Psychology* 48 (1), 269–297.

Eisele-Henderson, A. (2000) La lecture de textes en anglais langue étrangère chez des étudiants en sociologie: Implications didactiques d'une perspective socio-cognitive. PhD thesis, Université de Savoie.

Ellis, N.C. (1993) Rules and instances in foreign language learning: Interactions of explicit and implicit knowledge. *European Journal of Cognitive Psychology* 5 (3), 289–318.

Ellis, N.C. (1998) Emergentism, connectionism and language learning. *Language Learning*, 48 (4), 631–664.

Ellis, N.C. (2008) Usage-based and form-focused language acquisition: The associative learning of constructions, learned-attention, and the limited L2 end state. In P. Robinson and N.C. Ellis (eds) *Handbook of Cognitive Linguistics and Second Language Acquisition* (pp. 372–405). London: Routledge.

Ellis, R.S. (1994) *The Study of Second Language Acquisition*. Oxford: Oxford University Press.

Ellis, R.S. (1997) *SLA Research and Language Teaching*. Oxford: Oxford University Press.

Ellis, R.S. (2001) Investigating form-focused instruction. *Language Learning* 51, 1–46.

Ellis, R.S. (2003) *Task-Based Language Learning and Teaching*. Oxford: Oxford University Press.

Ellison, N.B. (2013) What is, and will be, the impact of social media on identity? Report commissioned by the UK Government Office for Science for a Foresight project on The Future of Identity. See https://www.gov.uk/government/collections/future-of-identity (accessed 30 December 2017).

Elorza, I. and Muñoa, I. (2008) Promoting the minority language through integrated plurilingual language planning: The case of the Ikastolas. In J. Cenoz (ed.) *Teaching*

Through Basque: Achievements and Challenges (pp. 85–101). Clevedon: Multilingual Matters.

Escudé, P. (2016) Le bilinguisme scolaire français-occitan: histoire et avenir. In C. Hélot and J. Erfurt (eds) L'éducation bilingue en France (pp. 87–99). Limoges: Lambert Lucas.

European Commission (2012) First European Survey on Language Competences: Final Report. See http://ec.europa.eu/dgs/education_culture/repository/languages/policy/strategic-framework/documents/language-survey-final-report_en.pdf (accessed 4 January 2018).

European Council (1995) Council Resolution of 31 March 1995 on improving and diversifying language learning and teaching within the education systems of the European Union, Official Journal C 207 of 12.08.1995.

Eurydice (2005) Chiffres clés de l'éducation en Europe 2005. See http://www.indire.it/lucabas/lkmw_file/eurydice///Key_Data_2005_FR.pdf (accessed 4 January 2018).

Fantognon, C. (2014) De la conceptualisation à la contextualisation du projet IFADEM au Bénin. In S. Babault, M. Bento, L. Le Ferrec and V. Spaëth (eds) Actes du Colloque international contexte global, contextes locaux – Tensions, convergences et enjeux en didactique des langues (pp. 203–221). See https://www.ifadem.org/sites/default/files/divers/actes_colloque_0.pdf (accessed 5 November 2017).

Ferguson, G. (2009) What next? Towards an agenda for classroom codeswitching research. International Journal of Bilingual Education and Bilingualism 12 (2), 231–241.

Filliettaz, L. (2005) Discours, travail et polyfocalisation de l'action. In L. Filliettaz and J.-P. Bronckart (eds) L'analyse des actions et des discours en situation de travail. Concepts, méthodes et applications (pp. 155–175). Louvain-La-Neuve: Peeters.

Fillol, V. and Colombel, C. (2016) Langue française et cultures océaniennes: quelle éducation plurilingue pour la Nouvelle-Calédonie? In C. Hélot and J. Erfurt (eds) L'éducation bilingue en France (pp. 118–129). Limoges: Lambert Lucas.

Finn, E.S., Shen, X., Scheinost, D., Rosenberg, M.D., Huang, J., Chun, M.M., Papademetris, X. and Constable R.T. (2015) Functional connectome fingerprinting: Identifying individuals using patterns of brain connectivity. Nature Neurosciences 18 (11), 1664–1671.

Fischer, T.B. (2007) The Theory & Practice of Strategic Environmental Assessment: Towards a More Systematic Approach. London: Earthscan Publications.

Fisher, G. (2012) Effectuation, causation, and bricolage: A behavioral comparison of emerging theories in entrepreneurship research. Entrepreneurship Theory and Practice 36 (5), 1019–1051.

Fishman, Joshua (1971) La Sociolinguistique. Paris: Nathan.

Flores, N. and García, O. (2013) Multilingualism and common core state standards in the United States. In S. May (ed.) The Multilingual Turn: Implications for SLA, TESOL, and Bilingual Education (pp. 147–166). New York: Routledge.

Fodor, J. (1986) La modularité de l'esprit. Essai sur la psychologie des facultés. Paris: Editions de Minuit.

Freire, P. (1970) Pedagogy of the Oppressed. New York: Continuum.

Gajo, L. (2001) Immersion, bilinguisme et interaction en classe. Paris: Didier.

Gajo, L. (2003) Approche comparative des données suisses et valdôtaines. In M. Cavalli, D. Coletta, L. Gajo, M. Matthey and C. Serra (eds) Langues, bilinguisme et représentations sociales au Val d'Aoste (pp. 518–558). Aoste: IRRE-VDA.

Galisson, R. (1991) De la langue à la culture par les mots. Paris: CLE International.

Gaonac'h, D. (2006) Apprentissage précoce des langues étrangères. Paris: Hachette.

García, O. (2009) TESOL Quarterly: A Journal for Teachers of English to Speakers of Other Languages and of Standard English as a Second Dialect, v.43 n.2 p322–326 June 2009.

García, O. (2014) Countering the dual: Transglossia, dynamic bilingualism and translanguaging in education. In R. Rubdy and L. Alsagoff (eds) *The Global–Local Interface and Hybridity: Exploring Language and Identity* (pp. 100–118). Bristol: Multilingual Matters.

García, O and Sylvan, C. (2011) Pedagogies and practices in multilingual classrooms: Singularities in pluralities. *The Modern Language Journal* 95 (3), 385–400.

García, O. and Wei, L. (2014) *Translanguaging: Language, Bilingualism and Education*. New York: Palgrave Macmillan.

García, O. and Kleyn, T. (eds) (2016) *Translanguaging with Multilingual Students: Learning from Classroom Moments*. New York: Routledge.

García, O., Kleifgen, J.A. and Falchi, L. (2008) *From English Language Learners to Emergent Bilinguals. A Research Initiative of the Campaign for Educational Equity*. New York: Teachers College, Columbia University.

García, O., Johnson, J. and Seltzer, K. (2017) *The Translanguaging Classroom: Leveraging Student Bilingualism for Learning*. Philadelphia, PA: Caslon.

Gardner, H. (1985) *The Mind's New Science*. New York: Basic Books.

Gardner, R. (2010) *Motivation and Second Language Acquisition: The Socio-Educational Model*. New York: Peter Lang.

Gass, S.M. (1997) *Input, Interaction, and the Second Language Learner*. Hillsdale, NJ: Erlbaum.

Gauthier, P.-L. (1998) Diversité culturelle et plurilinguisme en Asie du Sud-Est. *Revue internationale d'éducation de Sèvres* 17, 61–68. See http://ries.revues.org/2949; doi: 10.4000/ries.2949 (accessed 1 October 2016).

Gavins, J. (2007) *Text World Theory: An Introduction*. Edinburgh: Edinburgh University Press.

Genesee, F. (1987) *Learning through Two Languages: Studies of Immersion and Bilingual Education*. Cambridge: Newbury House.

Gentner, D., Özyürek, A., Gürcanli, Ö. and Goldin-Meadow, S. (2013) Spatial language facilitates spatial cognition: Evidence from children who lack language input. *Cognition* 127, 318–330.

Gibbons, P. (2002) *Scaffolding Language, Scaffolding Learning: Teaching ESL Children in the Mainstream Classroom*. Portsmouth: Heinemann.

Gibbs, G. (1999–2000) Changing student learning behavior outside of class. *Essays on Teaching Excellence* 11 (1). See https://podnetwork.org/content/uploads/99-00_v11.pdf (accessed 6 January 2018).

Giles, H. and Johnson, P. (1987) Ethnolinguistic identity theory: A social psychological approach to language maintenance. *International Journal of the Sociology of Language* 68, 69–99.

Gleason, J. and Suvorov, R. (2011) Learner perceptions of asynchronous oral computer-mediated communication tasks using Wimba Voice for developing their L2 oral proficiency. In S. Huffman and V. Hegelheimer (eds) *The Role of CALL in Hybrid and Online Language Courses*. Ames, IA: Iowa State University. See https://apling.engl.iastate.edu/alt-content/uploads/2015/05/tsll_gleason_and_suvorov_2011.pdf (accessed 6 January 2018).

Goodman, B.A. (2017) The ecology of language and translanguaging in a Ukrainian university. In C.M. Mazak and K.S. Carroll (eds) *Translanguaging in Higher Education: Beyond Monolingual Ideologies* (pp. 50–69). Bristol: Multilingual Matters.

Gorter, D. (ed.) (2006) *Linguistic Landscape: A New Approach to Multilingualism*. Clevedon: Multilingual Matters.

Gorter, D. (2013) Linguistic landscapes in a multilingual world. *Annual Review of Applied Linguistics* 33, 190–212.

Gorter, D. (2015) Multilingual interaction and minority languages: Proficiency and language practices in education and society. *Language Teaching* 48, 82–98.

Grenfell, M. (ed.) (2000) *Modern Languages across the Curriculum*. Abingdon: Routledge/Falmer.

Grosbois, M. (2006) Projet collectif de création d'une ressource numérique comme levier d'apprentissage de l'anglais. PhD thesis, Université Sorbonne Nouvelle-Paris 3.

Grosbois, M. (2011) CMC-based projects and L2 learning: Confirming the importance of nativisation. *ReCALL* 23 (3), 294–310.

Grosjean, F. (1989) Neurolinguists, beware! The bilingual is not two monolinguals in one person. *Brain and Language* 36, 3–15.

Grosjean, F. (2008) *Studying Bilinguals*. Oxford: Oxford University Press.

Grosjean, F. (2010) *Bilingual: Life and Reality*. Harvard, MA: Harvard University Press.

Grosjean, F. and Li, P. (2013) *The Psycholinguistics of Bilingualism*. Malden, MA: Wiley-Blackwell.

Guiora, A.Z. (1983) The dialectic of language acquisition *Language Learning* 33 (5), 3–12.

Guyomard Guihard, C. (2017) Dispositif multimodal interculturel: quelle plus-value pour la communication orale en anglais dans le secondaire ? *Les Langues Modernes* 1/2017, 73–82.

Haddad, C. (ed.) (2008) *Improving the Quality of Mother Tongue-Based Literacy and Learning: Case Studies from Asia, Africa and South America*. Bangkok: UNESCO.

Hall, G.E. and Hord, S.M. (2014) *Implementing Change: Patterns, Principles, and Potholes*. Boston, MA: Pearson/Allyn & Bacon.

Halliday, M.A.K. (1975) *Learning How to Mean: Explorations in the Development of Language*. London: Edward Arnold.

Hammarberg, B. (2014) Problems of defining the concepts of L1, L2, L3. In A. Otwinowska and G. De Angelis (eds) *Teaching and Learning in Multilingual Contexts: Sociolinguistic and Educational Perspectives* (pp. 27–43). Bristol: Multilingual Matters.

Hamon, Y. and Cervini, C. (2015) La formation des enseignants de langue en Italie: espaces pour l'innovation didactique? *Synergies Italie* 11, 107–122.

Hampel, R. (2006) Rethinking task design for the digital age: A framework for language teaching and learning in a synchronous online environment. *ReCALL* 18 (1), 105–121.

Helm, F. (2015) The practices and challenges of telecollaboration in higher education in Europe. *Language Learning & Technology* 19 (2), 197–217. See http://llt.msu.edu/issues/june2015/helm.pdf (accessed 29 July 2017).

Helmling, B. (ed.) (2007) *L'apprentissage autonome des langues en tandem*. Paris: Didier.

Hélot, C. and Erfurt, J. (eds) (2016) *L'éducation bilingue en France: politiques linguistiques, modèles et pratiques*. Rennes: Presses Universitaires de Rennes.

Herdina, P. and Jessner, U. (2006) *A Dynamic Model of Multilingualism, Perspectives of Change in Psycholinguistics*. Clevedon: Multilingual Matters.

Hernandez, P.J., Andrzejewski, M.E., Sadeghian, K., Panksepp, J.B. and Kelley, A.E. (2005) AMPA/kainate, NMDA, and dopamine D1 receptor function in the nucleus accumbens core: A context-limited role in the encoding and consolidation of instrumental memory. *Learning Memory* 12, 285–295.

Hopkins, M. (2014) Through a glass, darkly: Processes and effects of teaching L3 through L2. Centre for Languages, Linguistics and Area Studies (LLAS) Conference, Southampton. See http://cle.ust.hk/staff/lcmark/presentations/ (accessed 9 July 2018).

Hoppe, C. (2017) MOOC et didactique des langues. *Synergies France* 11, 77–89.

Horgues, C. and Tardieu, C. (forthcoming 2018) Positionnement correctif dans les interactions orales en tandem anglais-français *Recherches en didactique des langues et cultures: les cahiers de l'ACEDLE*.

Horgues, C., Debras, C. and Scheuer, S. (2015) The multimodality of corrective feedback in tandem interactions. *Procedia: Social and Behavioral Sciences* 212, 16–22.

Horwitz, E.K. (1999) Cultural and situational influences on foreign language learners' beliefs about language learning: A review of BALLI studies. *System* 27 (4), 557–576.

Hulstijn, J. (2002) Towards a unified account of the representation, processing and acquisition of second language knowledge. *Second Language Research* 18, 193–223.

Hutchins, E. (1995) *Cognition in the Wild*. Cambridge: MIT Press.

Huver, E. (2015) Prendre la diversité au sérieux en didactique/didactologie des langues. Contextualisation – universalisme: Des notions en face à face ? *Recherches en didactique des langues et des cultures: les cahiers de l'ACEDLE* 12 (1), 3–21. See https://acedle.org/old/IMG/pdf/2__Editorial_E-_Huver.pdf (accessed 28 September 2017).

Hymes, D.H. (1972) On communicative competence. In J.B. Pride and J. Holmes (eds) *Sociolinguistics. Selected Readings* (pp. 269–293). Harmondsworth: Penguin.

Jack, A.I., Boyatzis, R.E., Khawaja, M.S., Passarelli, A.M. and Leckie, R.L. (2013) Visioning in the brain: An fMRI study of inspirational coaching and mentoring. *Social Neurosciences* 8, 369–384.

Jacquier, V. (2017) Approche télécollaborative de la mise en place d'un dispositif d'apprentissage des langues MoDiMEs à l'Université de Nantes. Comment enclencher le processus de distanciation culturelle dans le cadre d'une préparation à la mobilité internationale ? PhD thesis, Université de Nantes.

Jarvis, S. and Pavlenko, A. (2008) *Crosslinguistic Influence in Language and Cognition*. New York/London: Routledge.

Jeannot-Fourcaud, B., Delcroix, A. and Poggi M.-P. (2014) Introduction. In B. Jeannot-Fourcaud, A. Delcroix and M.-P. Poggi (eds) *Contextes, effets de contexte et didactique des langues* (pp. 9–37). Paris: L'Harmattan.

Jenkins, J. (2007) *English as a Lingua Franca: Attitude and Identity*. Oxford: Oxford University Press.

Jessner, U. (2006) *Linguistic Awareness in Multilinguals*. Edinburgh: Edinburgh University Press.

Jonsson, C. (2017) Translanguaging and ideology: Moving away from a monolingual norm. In B.A. Paulsrud, J. Rosen, B. Straszer and A. Wedin (eds) *New Perspectives on Translanguaging and Education* (pp. 20–37). Bristol: Multilingual Matters.

Jørgensen, J.N. (2008) Polylingual languaging around and among children and adolescents. *International Journal of Multilingualism* 5 (3), 161–173.

Kail, M. (2012) *L'acquisition du langage*. Paris: PUF.

Kail, M. (2015) *L'acquisition de plusieurs langues*. Paris: PUF.

Kail, M. (2016) La plasticité: une clé pour les apprentissages langagiers tout au long de la vie. *Administration & Éducation* 2016/4 (152), 41–48.

Karimvand, P.N. (2011) Psycholinguistic perspectives on comprehension in SLA. *Journal of Language Teaching and Research* 2 (6), 1268–1273.

Kay, R. (2011) Exploring the influence of context on attitudes toward web-based learning tools (WBLTs) and learning performance. *Interdisciplinary Journal of E-Learning and Learning Objects* 7, 125–142.

Kem, R.G. (1994) The role of mental translation in second language reading. *Studies in Second Language Acquisition* 16, 441–461.

Kervran, M. (2006) *Les langues du monde au quotidien*, Vol. 1: Cycle 2, Vol. 2: Cycle 3. Rennes: SCEREN/CRDP.

Khalil, A. (2015) L'efficacité de l'informel dans le développement langagier: Le passage de l'input à la construction de l'output. *Langues, Cultures et Sociétés* 1 (2), 29–51.

Khalil, H. (2011) Exploitation du potentiel d'Internet pour consolider l'intake dans l'apprentissage du FLE (Français Langue Étrangère): Quelles tâches proposer sur Internet pour améliorer l'acquisition chez des apprenants arabophones de FLE en Égypte. PhD thesis, Université Sorbonne Nouvelle-Paris 3.

Khreim, J.-M. (2008) Apport des technologies de l'information et de la communication (TIC) sur la dénativisation d'apprenants arabophones de l'anglais langue étrangère dans un contexte syrien. PhD thesis, Université Sorbonne Nouvelle-Paris 3.

Kim, K.H.S., Relkin, N.R., Lee, K.M. and Hirsch, J. (1997) Distinct cortical areas associated with native and second languages. *Nature* 388, 171–174.

Kitayama, S., Markus, H.R., Matsumoto, H. and Norasakkunkit, V. (1997) Individual and collective processes in the construction of the self: Self-enhancement in the United

States and self-criticism in Japan. *Journal of Personality and Social Psychology* 72, 1245–1267.
Knewton (2018) Flipped, tipped or traditional: Adaptive technology can support any blended learning model. https://www.knewton.com/tag/flipped-classroom/ (accessed 10/11/2018).
Knight, C. and Power, C. (2011) Social conditions for the evolutionary emergence of language. In M. Tallerman and K. Gibson (eds) *Handbook of Language Evolution* (pp. 346–349). Oxford: Oxford University Press.
Komorowska, H. (2014) Analyzing linguistic landscapes. A diachronic study of multilingualism in Poland. In A. Otwinowska and G. De Angelis (eds) *Teaching and Learning in Multilingual Contexts: Sociolinguistic and Educational Perspectives* (pp. 19–31). Bristol: Multilingual Matters.
Kramsch, C. (1993) *Context and Culture in Language Teaching*. Oxford: Oxford University Press.
Kramsch, C. (2000) *Language and Culture*. Oxford: Oxford University Press.
Kramsch, C. (2006) From communicative competence to symbolic competence. *Modern Language Journal* 90 (2), 249–252.
Kramsch, C. (2009) *The Multilingual Subject: What Foreign Language Learners Say about Their Experience and Why it Matters*. Oxford: Oxford University Press.
Kramsch, C. and Whiteside, A. (2008) Language ecology in multilingual settings. Towards a theory of symbolic competence. *Applied Linguistics* 29 (4), 645–671.
Kramsch, C. and Narcy-Combes, J.-P. (2017) From social tasks to language development: coping with historicity and subjectivity. In M.J. Ahmadian and M. García Mayo (eds) *Recent Perspectives on Task-Based Language Learning and Teaching: Trends in Applied Linguistics* (pp. 195–215). Berlin: De Gruyter Mouton.
Krashen, S. (1982) *Principles and Practice in Second Language Acquisition*. Oxford: Oxford University Press.
Kukulska-Hulme, A. and Bull, B. (2009) Theory-based support for mobile language learning: Noticing and recording. *International Journal of Interactive Mobile Technologies* 3 (2), 12–18.
Kumashiro, K.K. (2012) *Bad Teacher!: How Blaming Teachers Distorts the Bigger Picture*. New York: Teachers College Press.
Kurek, M. and Müller-Hartmann, A. (2017) Task design for telecollaborative exchanges: In search of new criteria. *System* 64, 1–104.
Kusyk, M. and Sockett, G. (2013) L'apprentissage informel en ligne: nouvelle donne pour l'enseignement-apprentissage de l'anglais. *Recherche et pratiques pédagogiques en langues de spécialité* 32 (1), 75–91.
Kuteeva, M. (ed.) (2011) Academic English in parallel-language and ELF settings. *Ibérica: Journal of the European Association of Languages for Specific Purposes* 22, 5–12.
Labov, W. (2006) *The Social Stratification of English in New York City* (2nd edn). Cambridge/New York: Cambridge University Press (original work published 1966).
Lachaux, J.-P. (2011) *Le cerveau attentif. Contrôle, maîtrise et lâcher-prise*. Paris: Odile Jacob.
Lachaux, J.-P. (2015) *Le cerveau funambule. Comprendre et apprivoiser son attention grâce aux neurosciences*. Paris: Odile Jacob.
Lamy, M.-N. and Hampel, R. (2007) *Online Communication in Language Learning and Teaching*. New York: Palgrave.
Lancien, T. (1998) *Le multimédia*. Paris: Clé international.
La Politique des langues officielles du gouvernement fédéral (2017) See http://www.axl.cefan.ulaval.ca/amnord/cndpollng.htm (Accessed 10/11/2018).
Larsen-Freeman, D. and Cameron, L. (2008) *Complex Systems and Applied Linguistics*. Oxford: Oxford University Press.

Lave, J. and Wenger, E. (1991) *Situated Learning: Legitimate Peripheral Participation.* Cambridge: Cambridge University Press.

Le Besnerais, M. and Cortier, C. (2012) Langues régionales et minoritaires, pratiques intercompréhensives dans l'éducation bi-/plurilingue (EBP-ICI): un terrain privilégié? In C. Degache and S. Garbarino (eds) *Actes du colloque IC2012. Intercompréhension: compétences plurielles, corpus, intégration.* See http://ic2012.u-grenoble3.fr/OpenConf/papers/43.pdf (accessed 15 February 2017).

Leconte, F., Badrinathan, V. and Forlot, G. (eds) (2018) *Le plurilinguisme en contextes asiatiques: dynamiques et articulations.* GLOTTOPOL 30.

LeDoux, J. (2003) *Neurobiologie de la personnalité.* Paris: Odile Jacob.

Leichsering, T. (2014) Rethinking urban schools: A sociolinguistic analysis of multilingualism in Frankfurt/M, Germany. In A. Otwinowska and G. De Angelis (eds) *Teaching and Learning in Multilingual Contexts. Sociolinguistic and Educational Perspectives* (pp. 98–123). Bristol: Multilingual Matters.

Lenoir, Y. (2007) L'habitus dans l'œuvre de Pierre Bourdieu: un concept central dans sa théorie de la pratique à prendre en compte pour analyser les pratiques d'enseignement. Document du CRI et de la CRCIE n°1. Université de Sherbrooke.

Leplat, J. (2001) La gestion des communications par le contexte. *Perspectives interdisciplinaires sur le travail et la santé* 3 (1). See http://journals.openedition.org/pistes/3755 (accessed 22 June 2017).

Lerner, J.S., Li, Y., Valdesolo, P. and Kassam, K.S. (2015) Emotion and decision making. *Annual Review of Psychology* 66, 799–823.

Levelt, W. (1989) *Speaking: From Intention to Articulation.* Cambridge: Cambridge University Press.

Levy, J. (1969) Possible basis for the evolution of lateral specialization of the human brain. *Nature* 224, 614–615.

Lewin, K. (1947) Group decision and social change. In T. Newcomb and E. Hartley (eds) *Readings in Social Psychology* (pp. 197–211). New York: Holt, Rinehart and Winston.

Lewin, K. (1948) *Resolving Social Conflicts.* New York: Harper.

Liaw, M.L. and English, K. (2017) Identity and addressivity in the 'Beyond These Walls' program. *System* 64, 74–86.

Lightbown, P.M. and Spada, N. (2006) *How Languages are Learned.* Oxford: Oxford University Press.

Lin, H. (2014) Establishing an empirical link between computer-mediated communication (CMC) and SLA. *Language Learning and Technology* 18 (3), 120–147.

Lin, H. (2015) Computer-mediated communication (CMC) in L2 oral proficiency development: A meta-analysis. *ReCALL* 27 (3), 261–287.

Lindholm-Leary, K. (2001) *Dual Language Education.* Clevedon: Multilingual Matters.

Little, D. (1991) *Learner Autonomy 1: Definitions, Issues and Problems.* Dublin: Authentik.

Little, D., Dam, L. and Legenhausen, L. (2017) *Language Learner Autonomy: Theory, Practice and Research.* Bristol: Multilingual Matters.

Logan, G.D. (1990) Repetition priming and automaticity: Common underlying mechanisms? *Cognitive Psychology* 22, 1–35.

Long, M. (1991) Focus on form: A design feature in language teaching. In K. de Bot, R. Ginsberg and C. Kramsch (eds) *Foreign Language Research in Cross-Cultural Perspective* (pp. 39–52). Amsterdam: John Benjamins.

Long, M.H. (1996) The role of the linguistic environment in second language acquisition. In W. Ritchie and T. Bhatia (eds) *Handbook of Second Language Acquisition* (pp. 413–468). New York: Academic Press.

Lowie, W. (2017) Emergentism: Wide ranging theoretical framework or just one more meta-theory? *Recherches en didactique des langues et des cultures: les cahiers de l'ACEDLE* 14 (1). See http://rdlc.revues.org/1140 (accessed 31 January 2017).

Lowie, W., Plat, R. and de Bot, K. (2014) Pink noise in language production: A nonlinear approach to the multilingual lexicon. *Ecological Psychology* 26 (3), 216–228.

Lupyan, G. (2012) Linguistically modulated perception and cognition: The label-feedback hypothesis. *Frontiers in Psychology* 3, 1–13.

Mabrour, A. and Narcy-Combes, M.-F. (forthcoming 2018) Observer pour former les enseignants de français en contexte marocain. *Relais 5*, publication du LERIC-Urac 57, Université Chouaïb Doukkali, El Jadida, Maroc.

Maingueneau, D. (2009) *Les termes clés de l'analyse du discours*. Paris: Editions du Seuil.

Maizonniaux, C., Deraîche, M. and Saffari, H. (2017) Télécollaboration et autobiographie: un projet croisé FLS/FLE. *Les Langues Modernes: La télécollaboration interculturelle* 1/2017, 59–64.

Mangenot, F. (ed.) (2001) Interactivité, interactions et multimédia. *Notions en Questions, No. 5*. Lyon: ENS Editions.

Mangenot, F. (2002) Produits multimédias: médiation ou médiatisation ? *Le Français dans le Monde* 322, 34–35.

Mangenot, F. (2014) Heurs et malheurs de l'intégration des TIC dans l'apprentissage des langues. *Les Cahiers de l'ASDIFLE* 25, 17–25.

Mangenot, F. (2017) *Formation en ligne et MOOC: apprendre et se former en ligne avec le numérique*. Paris: Hachette.

Mangiante, J-M. and Parpette, C. (2011) *Le français sur objectifs universitaires*. Grenoble: Presses Universitaires de Grenoble.

Manoïlov, P. and Tardieu C. (2015) Feedback correctif et uptake dans le contexte de l'apprentissage en tandems Français-Anglais à l'université. *Recherches en didactique des langues et des cultures: les cahiers de l'ACEDLE* 12 (3), 91–116. See http://journals.openedition.org/rdlc/986 (accessed 16 November 2017).

Marchive, A. (1997) L'interaction de tutelle entre pairs: approche psychologique et usage didactique. *Psychologie et éducation* 30, 29–43.

Marendaz, C. (2015) *Peut-on manipuler notre cerveau?* Paris: le Pommier.

Marneffe, M. (2017) E-tandem et «interculturation»: un archipel en chantier. *Les Langues Modernes: La télécollaboration interculturelle* 1/2017, 50–58.

Marquilló Larruy, M. (2012) Littératie et multimodalité ici & là-bas... En réponse à Diane Dagenais. *Recherches en didactique des langues et des cultures: les cahiers de l'ACEDLE* 9 (2), 15–46.

Martin-Beltrán, M. (2010) Positioning proficiency: How students and teachers (de)construct language proficiency at school. *Linguistics and Education* 21 (4), 257–281.

Marx, N. (2012) Reading across the Germanic languages. Is equal access just wishful thinking? *International Journal of Bilingualism: Interdisciplinary Studies of Multilingual Behaviour* 16 (4), 467–483.

Maslow, A. (1954) *Motivation and Personality*. New York: Harper.

Masperi, M. and Quintin, J.-J. (2007) Modèle de scénario pédagogique pour la pratique de la compréhension croisée plurilingue à distance: élaboration, usage et effets. In *Actes du colloque Scénario 2007 – Scénariser les activités de l'apprenant: une activité de modélisation* (pp. 113–120). Montreal: Centre de Recherche LICEF.

Matthey, M. (ed.) (1997) *Les langues et leurs images*. Neuchâtel: IRDP/Le Mont-sur-Lausanne: LEP/Perros-Guirrec: AELPL.

Maurer, B. (2010) Éléments de réflexion pour une didactique du plurilinguisme en Afrique francophone. *Recherches en didactique des langues et des cultures: les cahiers de l'ACEDLE* 7 (1). See http://journals.openedition.org/rdlc/2036 (accessed 26 December 2017).

Maurer, B. (ed.) (2011) LASCOLAF et ELAN-Afrique: d'une enquête sur les langues de scolarisation en Afrique francophone à des plans d'action nationaux. *Le Français à l'Université*, 16 (1). See http://www.bulletin.auf.org/index.php?id=276 (accessed 4 January 2018).

Maurer, B. (ed.) (2016) *Les approches bi-plurilingues d'enseignement-apprentissage: Autour du programme ELAN en Afrique*. Paris: Editions des Archives Contemporaines.

Mazak, C.M. and Carroll, K.S. (eds) (2017) *Translanguaging in Higher Education: Beyond Monolingual Ideologies*. Bristol: Multilingual Matters.

Mazak, C.M., Fiorelys, M. and Pérez Mangonéz, L. (2017) Professors translanguaging in practice: Three cases from a bilingual university. In C.M. Mazak and K.S. Carroll (eds) *Translanguaging in Higher Education: Beyond Monolingual Ideologies* (pp. 70–90). Bristol: Multilingual Matters.

McAllister, J., Narcy-Combes, M.-F. and Starkey-Perret, R. (2012) Language teachers' perceptions of their roles, self-identity and teaching practices in a large-scale task-based blended learning programme in a French university. In A. Shehadeh and C.A. Coombe (eds) *Task-Based Language Teaching in Foreign Language Contexts: Research and Implementation* (pp. 313–342). Amsterdam: John Benjamins.

McAllister-Pavageau, J. (2013) Évaluation d'un dispositif hybride d'apprentissage de l'anglais en milieu universitaire: potentialités et enjeux pour l'acquisition d'une L2. PhD thesis, Université de Nantes.

McAndrew, M. and Ciceri, C. (2003) L'enseignement des langues d'origine au Canada: réalités et débats. *Revue Européenne des Migrations Internationales* 19 (1), 173–194.

McIlwraith, H. (ed.) (2013) *Multilingual Education in Africa: Lessons from the Juba Language-in-Education Conference*. London: British Council.

McNamara, T. (2012) Language assessments as Shibboleths: A poststructuralist perspective. *Applied Linguistics* 33, 564–581.

McWhinney, B. (2006) Emergentism: Use often and with care. *Applied Linguistics* 27 (4), 729–740.

McWhinney, B. and O'Grady, W. (eds) (2015) *The Handbook of Language Emergence*. Malden, MA: Wiley-Blackwell.

Medin, D.L., Ojalehto, B., Waxman, S.R. and Bang M. (2015) Relations: Language, epistemologies, categories, and concepts. In E. Margolis and S. Laurence (eds) *The Conceptual Mind: New Directions in the Study of Concepts* (pp. 349–378). Cambridge: MIT Press.

Médioni, M.-A. and Narcy-Combes, J.-P. (eds) (2016) Ethique et enseignement des langues. *Les Langues Modernes*. 4/2016. Paris: APLV.

Meirieu, P. (2015) *Comment aider nos enfants à réussir à l'école, dans leur vie, pour le monde*. Paris: Bayard.

Mercer, S. and Dörnyei, Z. (forthcoming) *Engaging Students in Contemporary Classrooms*. Cambridge: Cambridge University Press.

Midgley, C., Kaplan, A. and Middleton, M. (2001) Performance approach goals: Good for what, for whom, under what circumstances and at what cost? *Journal of Educational Psychology* 93, 77–86.

Miller, E.K. and Cohen, J.D. (2001) An integrative theory of prefrontal cortex function. *Annual Review of Neurosciences* 24, 167–202.

Miras, G. (2014) Approche plurielle des liens musique parole pour la didactique de la prononciation du français en contexte de langue étrangère/seconde. PhD thesis, Université Sorbonne Nouvelle-Paris 3.

Mitchell, R. and Martin, C. (1997) Rote learning, creativity and 'understanding' in classroom foreign language teaching. *Language Teaching Research* 1, 1–27.

Moore, D. (2010) Multilingual literacies and third script acquisition: Young Chinese in French immersion in Vancouver, Canada. *International Journal of Multilingualism* 7, 322–342.

Morley, D.A. (2012) Enhancing networking and proactive learning skills in the first year university experience through the use of wikis. *Nurse Education Today* 32 (3), 261–266. See http://dx.doi.org/10.1016/j.nedt.2011.03.007 (accessed 12 December 2017).

Morsly, D. (2016) Revisiter le(s) plurilinguisme(s) algérien(s). In M. Auzanneau, M. Bento and M. Leclère (eds) *Espaces, mobilités et éducation plurilingues: Éclairages d'Afrique et d'ailleurs* (pp. 173–182). Paris. Éditions des Archives Contemporaines.
Muni Toke, V. (2016) Les politiques éducatives bilingues dans les outremers situation postcoloniale et rhétorique de l'expérimentation. In C. Hélot and J. Erfurt (eds) *L'éducation bilingue en France: politiques linguistiques, modèles et pratiques* (pp. 45–51). Limoges: Lambert-Lucas.
Musser, J., O'Reilly, T. and the O'Reilly Radar Team (2007) *Web 2.0 Principles and Best Practices*. Sebastopol: O'Reilly.
Narcy, J.-P. (1990) *Apprendre une langue étrangère*. Paris: Editions d'organisation.
Narcy, J.-P. and Biesse, F. (2003) *Didactique des langues: une recherche-action en Picardie*. Amiens: Conseil Régional/CRDP.
Narcy-Combes, J.-P. (2005) *Didactique des langues et TIC, vers une recherche-action responsable*. Paris: Ophrys.
Narcy-Combes, J.-P. and Narcy-Combes, M.-F. (2014) Formations hybrides en milieu pluriculturel: comment concilier théories, pratiques et contraintes. In D. Abendroth-Timmer, and E-M. Hennig (eds) *Plurilingualism and Multiliteracies: International Research on Identity Construction in Language Education* (pp. 211–227). Frankfurt: Peter Lang.
Narcy-Combes, J-P. and Xue, L. (forthcoming 2018) L'observation des pratiques enseignantes effectives en relation avec les apprentissages dans des contextes spécifiques et différents pour former les enseignants: approches compréhensives et plurielles. *Relais 5*.
Narcy-Combes, J.-P., Tardieu, C., Le Bihan, J.-C., Aden, J., Delassale, D., Larreya, P. and Raby, F. (2008) L'anglais à l'école élémentaire. *Les Langues Modernes* 4, 72–82.
New London Group (1996) A pedagogy of multiliteracies: Designing social futures. *Harvard Educational Review* 66, 60–92.
Nielsen, J.A., Zielinski, B.A., Ferguson, M.A., Lainhart, J.E. and Anderson, J.S. (2013) An evaluation of the left-brain vs. right-brain hypothesis with resting state functional connectivity magnetic resonance imaging. *Public Library of Science One (PLoS ONE)* 8 (8), e71275. See http://journals.plos.org/plosone/article?id=10.1371/journal.pone.0071275 (accessed 6 January 2018).
Nishihori, Y. (2011) Facilitating collaborative language learning in a multicultural distance class over broadband networks: Learner awareness to cross-cultural understanding. In M. Levy, F. Blin, C.B. Siskin and O. Takeuchi (eds) *WorldCALL: International Perspectives on Computer-Assisted Language Learning* (pp. 70–85). New York: Routledge.
Noels, K.A., Chaffee, K.E., Mantou Lou, N. and Dincer, A. (2016) Self-determination, engagement, and identity in learning German: Some directions in the psychology of language learning motivation. *Fremdsprachen lehren und lernen* 45 (2), 12–29.
Norton, B. (2013) *Identity and Language Learning: Extending the Conversation*. Bristol: Multilingual Matters.
Norton Peirce, B. (1995) Social identity, investment, and language learning. *TESOL Quarterly* 29 (1), 9–31.
Noyau, C. (2016) Transferts linguistiques et transferts de connaissances à l'école bilingue, recherches de terrain dans quelques pays subsahariens. In B. Maurer (ed.) *Les approches bi-plurilingues d'enseignement-apprentissage: autour du programme Ecole et langues nationales en Afrique (ELAN-Afrique)* (pp. 55–82). Paris: Editions des Archives Contemporaines.
O'Dowd, R. (2016) Emerging trends and new directions in telecollaborative learning. *Calico Journal* 33 (3), 291–310.
O'Dowd, R. and Ritter, M. (2006) Understanding and working with 'failed communication' in telecollaborative exchanges. *Calico Journal* 23 (3), 623–642.

Okon-Singer, H., Hendler, T., Pessoa, L. and Shackman, A.J. (2015) The neurobiology of emotion–cognition interactions: Fundamental questions and strategies for future research. *Frontiers in Human Neuroscience* 9, article 58. See https://doi.org/10.3389/fnhum.2015.00058 (accessed 10 December 2017).

Ollivier, C. (2013) Tensions épistémologiques en intercompréhension. *Recherches en didactique des langues et cultures: les cahiers de l'ACEDLE* 10 (1), 5–27.

O'Rourke, B. (2007) Models of telecollaboration (1): eTandem. In R. O'Dowd (ed.) *Online Intercultural Exchange. An Introduction for Foreign Language Teachers* (pp. 41–61). Clevedon: Multilingual Matters.

Ortega, L. (2010) Research synthesis. In B. Paltridge and A. Phakiti (eds) *Companion to Research Methods in Applied Linguistics* (pp. 111–126). London: Continuum.

Otheguy, R., Garcia, O. and Reid, W. (2015) Clarifying translanguaging and deconstructing named languages: A perspective from linguistics. *Applied Linguistics Review* 6 (3), 281–307.

Otsuji, E. and Pennycook, A. (2010) Metrolingualism: Fixity, fluidity and language in flux. *International Journal of Multilingualism* 7 (3), 240–254.

Otwinowska, A. and De Angelis, G. (eds) (2014) *Teaching and Learning in Multilingual Contexts: Sociolinguistic and Educational Perspectives*. Bristol: Multilingual Matters.

Ouoba, B.B. (2016) Construction des premières compétences linguistiques en langues négro-africaines de la famille Oti-Volta comme langues premières dans une perspective de transfert et la langue française comme langue seconde d'enseignement. In B. Maurer (ed.) *Les approches bi-plurilingues d'enseignement-apprentissage: autour du programme ELAN en Afrique* (pp. 3–11). Paris: Editions des Archives Contemporaines.

Pacteau, B. (1999) Penser: de la logique à l'expérience. In J-F. Dortier (ed.) *Le Cerveau et la Pensée* (pp. 335–343). Auxerre: Sciences Humaines.

Paia, M. and Vernaudon, J. (2016) Le défi de l'éducation bilingue en Polynésie française. In C. Hélot and J. Erfurt (eds) *L'éducation bilingue en France: politiques linguistiques, modèles et pratiques* (pp. 215–230). Limoges: Lambert Lucas.

Pallier, C., Dehaene, S., Poline, J.-B., LeBihan, D., Argenti, A.-M., Dupoux, E. and Mehler, J. (2003) Brain imaging of language plasticity in adopted adults: Can a second language replace the first? *Cerebral Cortex* 13, 155–161.

Paradis, J. (2004) On the relevance of specific language impairment to understanding the role of transfer in second language acquisition. *Applied Psycholinguistics* 25, 67–82.

Park, M. (2012) Implementing computer-assisted task-based language teaching in the Korean context. In A. Shehadeh and C.A. Coombe (eds) *Task-Based Language Teaching in Foreign Language Contexts. Research and Implementation* (pp. 215–241). Amsterdam: John Benjamins.

Paulsrud, B.A., Rosen, J., Straszer, B. and A. Wedin (2017) *New Perspectives on Translanguaging and Education*. Bristol: Multilingual Matters.

Pecher, D. and Zwaan, R. (eds) (2005) *Grounding Cognition: The Role of Perception and Action in Memory, Language, and Thinking*. Cambridge: Cambridge University Press.

Penloup, M.-C. (2012) Littératies numériques: quels enjeux pour la didactique de l'écriture-lecture? Réponse à Jeannine Gerbault. *Recherches en didactique des langues et des cultures: les cahiers de l'ACEDLE* 9 (2), 129–140.

Perani, D., Abutalebi, J., Paulesu, E., Brambati, S., Scifo, P. and Cappa, S.F. (2003) The role of age of acquisition and language usage in early, high-proficient bilinguals: An fMRI study during verbal fluency. *Human Brain Mapping* 19 (3), 170–182.

Pereltsvaig, A. (2011) 'On official languages of sub-Saharan Africa'. Languages of the World: Exploring the Rich Diversity of Human Languages (blog post, 9 December 2011). See http://www.languagesoftheworld.info/student-papers/on-official-languages-of-sub-saharan-africa.html#ixzz4rb7KcIkT (accessed 6 January 2018).

Perregaux, C., De Goumoëns, C., Jeannot, D. and De Pietro, J-F. (eds) (2003) Éducation et ouverture aux Langues, EOLE 1 & 2. Neuchâtel: SG/CIIP. See http://eole.irdp.ch/eole/presentation.html (accessed 29 July 2017).
Perrenoud, Ph. (1996) *Enseigner. Agir dans l'urgence, décider dans l'incertitude.* Paris: ESF.
Perrenoud, Ph. (1998) *L'évaluation des élèves. De la fabrication de l'excellence à la régulation des apprentissages.* Bruxelles: De Boeck.
Pessoa, L. (2015) Précis on the cognitive-emotional brain. *Behavioral and Brain Sciences* 38, e71. See https://doi.org/10.1017/S0140525X14000120 (accessed 6 January 2018).
Piaget, J. (1970) *Psychologie et épistémologie. Pour une théorie de la connaissance.* Paris: Gonthier Denoël.
Pica, T., Kang, H.-S. and Sauro, S. (2006) Information gap tasks: Their multiple roles and contributions to interaction research methodology. *Studies in Second Language Acquisition* 28 (2), 301–338.
Piccardo, E. (2006) Les TIC et les langues à l'école primaire: pour une démarche créative. *Spirale-Revue de Recherche en Education* 38, 111–121.
Piccardo, E. (2016) Créativité et complexité: quels modèles, quelles conditions, quels enjeux? In I. Capron Puozzo (ed.) *La Créativité en éducation et en formation. Perspectives théoriques et pratiques* (pp. 47–64). Bruxelles: de Boeck.
Porquier, R. and Py, B. (2004) *Apprentissage d'une langue étrangère: contextes et discours.* Paris: Didier.
Price, C.J., Seghier, M.L. and Leff, A.P. (2010) Predicting language outcome and recovery after stroke: The PLORAS system. *Nature Reviews Neurology* 6 (4), 202–210.
Puozzo Capron, I. and Piccardo, E. (2013) Au commencement était l'émotion: Introduction. *Lidil* 48, 5–16.
Puren, C. (2002) Perspectives actionnelles et perspectives culturelles en didactique des langues-cultures: vers une perspective co-actionnelle co-culturelle. *Les Langues Modernes* 3, 55–71.
Py, B. (1989) L'acquisition vue dans la perspective de l'interaction. *DRLAV Revue de Linguistique* 41, 83–100.
Quéré, L. (1999) Action située et perception du sens. In M. Fornel and L. Quéré (eds) *La logique des situations* (pp. 301–338). Paris: Editions de l'EHESS.
Rancillac, A. (2014) *AlicE 2630: Expérience humaine.* Palo Alto, CA: Clonitech.
Randall, M. (2007) *Memory, Psychology and Second Language Learning.* Amsterdam/Philadelphia, PA: John Benjamins.
Rees, D. (2003) Analyse socioculturelle du discours de négociation au sein de dyades LNN-LNN. PhD thesis, Université de Montpellier 3.
Reeve, J. (2014) *Psychologie de la motivation et des émotions.* Louvain la Neuve: De Boeck.
Robert, J.M. (2016) L'anglais, langue de transfert pour la compréhension écrite du français écrit par des étudiants allemands. *Synergies Pays Germanophones* 9, 107–116. See https://gerflint.fr/Base/Paysgermanophones9/robert.pdf (accessed 9 July 2018).
Rodrigues, C. (2012) Intercompréhension: quelles stratégies pour l'apprentissage du vocabulaire en anglais à l'IUT? In C. Degache and S. Garbarino (eds) *Actes du colloque IC2012. Intercompréhension: compétences plurielles, corpus, intégration.* Université Stendhal Grenoble 3 (France), 21–23 June 2012. See http://ic2012.u-grenoble3.fr/OpenConf/papers/13.pdf (accessed 2 June 2018).
Rodríguez-Fornells, A., Cunillera, T., Mestres-Missé, A. and de Diego-Balaguer, R. (2009) Neurophysiological mechanisms involved in language learning in adults. *Philosophical Transactions of the Royal Society B: Biological Sciences* 364, 3711–3735.
Roehr, K. (2006) Metalinguistic knowledge in L2 performance: A verbal protocol analysis, *Language Awareness* 15 (3), 180–198.
Rogers, C. (1969) *Freedom to Learn.* Columbus, OH: Charles Merill.
Romero, L.P. (2001) Why English-only notice to Spanish-only speakers is not enough: The argument for enhancing procedural due process in New Mexico. *New Mexico Law*

Review 41 (603). See http://digitalrepository.unm.edu/nmlr/vol41/iss2/11 (accessed 6 January 2018).

Rosen, J. (2017) Spaces for translanguaging in Swedish education policy. In B.A. Paulsrud, J. Rosen, B. Straszer and A. Wedin (eds) *New Perspectives on Translanguaging and Education* (pp. 38–55). Bristol: Multilingual Matters.

Salomon, G. (1997) *Novel Constructivist Learning Environments and Novel Technologies: Some Issues to be Concerned.* Invited keynote address presented at the EARLI conference, Athens, 26–30 August.

Sandberg, A. (2017) *Mother Tongue-Based Multilingual Education among Linguistic Minorities: Review of Finland's Development Cooperation and UPR Recommendations 2006–2016.* Helsinki: Felm. See https://felm.suomenlahetysseura.fi/wp-content/uploads/2017/12/Kielioikeusselvitys-englanniksi.pdf (accessed 17 July 2018).

Santos, A., Cenoz, J. and Gorter, D. (2017) Communicative anxiety in English as a third language. *International Journal of Bilingualism and Bilingual Education* 20 (7), 823–336. See https://doi.org/10.1080/13670050.2015.1105780 (accessed 6 January 2018).

Schachter, J. (1990) On the issue of completeness in second language acquisition. *Second Language Research* 6 (1), 205–214.

Schenker, T. (2017) Synchronous telecollaboration for novice language learners: Effects on speaking skills and language learning interests. *Alsic* 20. See http://alsic.revues.org/3068 (accessed 28 July 2017).

Schmidt, R. (2001) Attention. In P. Robinson (ed.) *Cognition and Second Language Instruction* (pp. 3–32). Cambridge: Cambridge University Press.

Schultz, W., Tremblay, L. and Hollerman, J.R. (2000) Reward processing in primate orbitofrontal cortex and basal ganglia. *Cerebral Cortex* 10 (3), 272–283.

Schurmans, M.-N. (2001) *La construction sociale de la connaissance comme action.* Brussels: De Boeck Supérieur.

Schwarzer, R. and Knoll, N. (2007) Functional roles of social support within the stress and coping process: A theoretical and empirical overview. *International Journal of Psychology* 42 (4), 243–252.

Seidlhofer, B. (2003) *Controversies in Applied Linguistics.* Oxford: Oxford University Press.

Seidlhofer, B. (2007) Common property: English as a lingua franca in Europe. In J. Cummins and C. Davison (eds) *International Handbook of English Language Teaching* (pp. 137–153). New York: Springer.

Selinker, L. (1972) Interlanguage. *International Review of Applied Linguistics in Language Teaching* 10, 219–231.

Seltzer, K., Collins, B.A. and Angeles, K.M. (2016) Navigating turbulent waters: Translanguaging to support academic and socioemotional well-being. In O. García and T. Kleyn (eds) *Translanguaging with Multilingual Students: Learning from Classroom Moments* (pp. 140–159). New York: Routledge.

Sevinç, Y. and Dewaele, J.-M. (2016) Heritage language anxiety and majority language anxiety among Turkish immigrants in the Netherlands. *International Journal of Bilingualism.* See http://journals.sagepub.com/doi/pdf/10.1177/1367006916661635 (accessed 6 January 2018).

Sheeren, H. (2016) L'intercompréhension: un nouveau souffle pour les langues romanes minoritaires et pour les dialectes? *Lengas* 79. See http://lengas.revues.org/1060 (accessed 1 January 2018).

Shohamy, E. (2001) *The Power of Tests: A Critical Perspective on the Uses of Language Tests.* New York: Longman.

Shohamy, E. and Gorter, D. (eds) (2009) *Linguistic Landscape: Expanding the Scenery.* New York: Routledge.

Siemens, G. (2005) Connectivism: A learning theory for the digital age. *International Journal of Instructional Technology and Distance Learning* 2 (1), 3–10. See http://www.itdl.org/journal/jan_05 (accessed 6 January 2018).

Siguan, M. and Mackey, W. (1986) *Educación y bilingüismo*. Madrid: Santillana UNESCO.

Singleton, D. (2005) The critical period hypothesis: A coat of many colours. *International Review of Applied Linguistics in Language Teaching* 43 (4), 269–285.

Slamecka, N.J. and Graf, P. (1978) The generation effect: Delineation of a phenomenon. *Journal of Experimental Psychology: Human Learning and Memory* 4 (6), 592–604.

Sockett, G. (2012) Le web social – La complexité au service de l'apprentissage informel de l'anglais. *Alsic* 15 (2). See http://alsic.revues.org/2505 (accessed 26 July 2017).

Sockett, G. (2014) *The Online Informal Learning of English*. Basingstoke: Palgrave Macmillan.

Souliou, L. (2014) L'activation d'une autre langue que celle attendue: pratiques et représentations des apprenants d'une troisième langue. PhD thesis, Université Sorbonne Nouvelle-Paris 3.

Spear, G.E. and Mocker, D.W. (1984) The organizing circumstance: Environmental determinants in self-directed learning. *Adult Education Quarterly* 35 (1), 1–10.

Spoelman, M. and Verspoor, M. (2010) Dynamic patterns in development of accuracy and complexity: A longitudinal case study in the acquisition of Finnish. *Applied Linguistics* 31 (4), 532–553. See https://doi.org/10.1093/applin/amq001 (accessed 16 November 2017).

Springer, C. (2009) La dimension sociale dans le CECR: pistes pour scénariser, évaluer et valoriser l'apprentissage collaboratif. *Le français dans le monde Recherches et Applications* 45, 25–34.

Starkey-Perret, R. and Narcy-Combes, M.-F. (2016) Implementing a plurilingual program in a university in a monolingual region of France: Strengths, weaknesses, opportunities and threats. *Language, Culture and Curriculum* 30 (2), 174–197. See http://www.tandfonline.com/action/doSearch?AllField=Starkey&SeriesKey=rlcc20 (accessed 20 October 2017).

Statistical Atlas (2015) Languages in New York State. See https://statisticalatlas.com/state/New-York/Languages. (Accessed 10/11/2018).

Sweller, J. (1988) Cognitive load during problem solving: Effects on learning. *Cognitive Science* 12, 257–285.

Tan, L.H., Chan, A.H.D., Kay, P., Khong, P.L., Yip, L.K.C. and Luke, K.K. (2008) *Language affects patterns of brain activation associated with perceptual decision*. Proceedings of the National Academy of Sciences of the United States of America 105, 4004–4009.

Tissot, P. (2004) *Terminology of Vocational Training Policy. A Multilingual Glossary for an Enlarged Europe*. Luxembourg: CEDEFOP.

Toffoli, D. and Sockett, G. (2015) L'apprentissage informel de l'anglais en ligne (AIAL): quelles conséquences pour les centres de ressources en langues? *Recherche et pratiques pédagogiques en langues de spécialité* 34 (1), 147–165.

Tomasello, M. (2003) *Constructing a Language*. Cambridge: Harvard University Press.

Tricot, A. and Amadieu, F. (2014) *Apprendre avec le numérique. Mythes et réalités*. Paris: Retz.

Troadec, B. (2007) *Psychologie culturelle. Le développement cognitif est-il culturel?* Paris: Belin Sup.

Troubetzkoy, N.S. (1939) *Principes de phonologie*. Paris: Klincksieck.

Turnbull, B. (2016) Reframing foreign language learning as bilingual education: Epistemological changes towards the emergent bilingual. *International Journal of Bilingual Education and Bilingualism*. See https://www.tandfonline.com/doi/full/10.1080/13670050.2016.1238866 (accessed 9 July 2018).

Turula, A. (2017) Teaching presence in telecollaboration. Keeping an open mind. *System* 64, 21–33.
US Department of Education (2015) *Dual Language Education Programs: Current State Policies and Practices*. Washington, DC: US Department of Education.
Ushioda, E. (2008) Motivation and good language learners. In C. Griffiths (ed.) *Lessons from Good Language Learners* (pp. 19–34). Cambridge: Cambridge University Press.
Valdés, G. (2005) Bilingualism, heritage learners, and SLA research: Opportunities lost or seized? *Modern Language Journal*, 89(3), 410–26.
Valdès, J.M. (1986) *Culture Bound*. Cambridge: Cambridge University Press.
Valk, J.H., Ahmed, T.R. and Elder, L. (2010) Using mobile phones to improve educational outcomes: An analysis of evidence from Asia. *International Review of Research in Open and Distance Learning* 11 (1), 117–140.
Van Campenhoudt, L., Franssen, A. and Cantelli, F. (2009) La méthode d'analyse en groupe. *SociologieS, théories et recherches*. See http://sociologies.revues.org/2968 (accessed 4 May 2014).
Van Lier, L. (1996) *Interaction in the Language Curriculum: Awareness, Autonomy and Authenticity*. London/New York: Longman.
Van Lier, L. (2004) *The Ecology and Semiotics of Language Learning: A Sociocultural Perspective*. Boston, MA/Dordrecht/London: Kluwer Academic.
Van Lier, L. (2008) Agency in the classroom. In J. Lantolf and M. Poehner (eds) *Sociocultural Theory and the Teaching of Second Languages* (pp. 207–226). London: Equinox.
Varela, F. (1993) *L'Inscription corporelle de l'esprit*. Paris: Seuil.
Villemonteix, F. (2016) Technologies numériques et pratiques enseignantes: permanences ou évolutions de la forme scolaire? *Revue suisse de sciences de l'éducation* 38 (2), 221–240.
Vlad, M. (2017) Télécollaboration et apprentissage de la réflexivité enseignante. *Les Langues Modernes* 1, 14–21.
Vosloo, S. and West, M. (2012) *Mobile Learning for Teachers in Asia. Exploring the Potential of Mobile Technologies to Support Teachers and Improve Practice*. Paris: UNESCO.
Vygotsky, L.S. (1962) *Thought and Language* (E. Hanfmann and G. Vakar eds and trans). Cambridge: MIT Press.
Vygotsky, L.S. (1978) *Mind in Society: The Development of Higher Psychological Processes*. Cambridge: Harvard University Press.
Wang, J., Zou, B., Wang, D. and Xing, M. (2013) Students' perception of a wiki platform and the impact of wiki engagement on intercultural communication. *System* 41 (2), 245–256.
Warschauer, M. (1999) *Electronic Literacies: Language, Culture and Power in Online Education*. Mahwah, NJ: Erlbaum.
Wehbe, O. (2017) Questions que pose une didactique plurilingue au Liban, pratiques et représentations. PhD thesis, Université Sorbonne Nouvelle-Paris 3.
Wei, L. (2011) Moment analysis and translanguaging space: Discursive construction of identities by multilingual Chinese youth in Britain. *Journal of Pragmatics* 43, 1222–1235.
Wei, L. (2017) Translanguaging as a practical theory of language. *Applied Linguistics* 39 (1), February 2018, 9–30.
Wei, L. and Martin, P.W. (eds) (2009) Conflicts and tensions in classroom code-switching. *International Journal of Bilingual Education and Bilingualism* 13 (2), 117–122.
Wheeler, S., Yeomans, P. and Wheeler, D. (2007) The good, the bad and the wiki: Evaluating student-generated content for collaborative learning. *British Journal of Educational Technology* 39 (6), 987–995.
White, C. (2003) *Language Learning in Distance Education*. Cambridge: Cambridge University Press.

Whyte, S. (2015) *Implementing and Researching Technological Innovation in Language Teaching. The Case of Interactive Whiteboards for EFL in French Schools*. Basingstoke: Palgrave Macmillan.
Williams, C. (1996) Secondary education: Teaching in the bilingual situation. In C. Williams, G. Lewis and C. Baker (Dir.) *The Language Policy: Taking Stock* (pp. 193–211). Llangefni: CAI Language Studies Center.
Williams, S. and Hammarberg, B. (1998) Language switches in L3 production: Implications for a polyglot speaking model. *Applied Linguistics* 19 (3), 295–333.
Willis, D. and Willis, J. (2007) *Doing Task-Based Teaching*. Oxford: Oxford University Press.
Woodrow, L. (2006) Anxiety and speaking English as a second language. *RELC Journal* 37 (3), 308–328. See http://dx.doi.org/10.1177%2F0033688206071315 (accessed 6 January 2018).
Wray, A. (2002) *Formulaic Language and the Lexicon*. Cambridge: Cambridge University Press.
Wright, W.E. (2015) *Foundations for Teaching English Language Learners: Research, Theory, Policy and Practice* (2nd edn). Philadelphia, PA: Caslon.
Xu, H. (2010) From EFL to ESL: The influence of context on learners' motivational profiles. *123 Arizona Working Papers in SLA & Teaching* 17, 123–142.
Xue, L. (2016) Aspects évolutifs de l'agir professoral dans le domaine de l'enseignement des langues. Une étude à travers les discours de verbalisation de six enseignants de français langue étrangère et de chinois langue étrangère. PhD thesis, Université Sorbonne Nouvelle-Paris 3.
Yetkin, O., Zerrin Yetkin, F., Haughton, V.M. and Cox, R.W. (1996) Use of functional MR to map language in multilingual volunteers. *American Journal of Neuroradiology* 17, 473–477.
Zhou, W., Simpson, E. and Pinette Domizi, D. (2012) Google Docs in an out-of-class collaborative writing activity. *International Journal of Teaching and Learning in Higher Education* 24 (3), 359–375.
Ziegler, G. (2013) Multilingualism and the language education landscape: Challenges for teacher training in Europe. *Multilingual Education* 3 (1), 1–23.
Zourou, K. (2016) Social networking affordances for open educational language practice. *Alsic* 19 (1). See http://journals.openedition.org/alsic/2903 (accessed 6 January 2018).

Index

action, 8, 23–24, 26, 30, 35–36, 38, 41, 44–45, 61, 63, 65, 67, 69–70, 72, 74, 76–78, 80, 82, 84–88, 90–92, 94, 96, 98, 100, 102, 104, 106, 108, 110, 112–114, 116–118, 120, 122–124, 126, 128–130, 132, 134, 136, 138–140, 142, 144–148, 150, 165, 177–178, 180–181, 183–184, 187, 193, 195–198
additive bilingualism, 14–15, 87
affects, 16, 31, 35–39, 41, 43, 45, 60
agency, 40–41, 43–45
agent, 43, 170
anxiety, 34, 37–39, 118–119, 141, 158
assessment, 13, 24, 44, 53, 61, 73, 78, 81, 88, 93, 95, 99, 111–112, 115–116, 123, 142, 154–155, 157–158, 166, 169, 172
attention, 6, 8, 16, 23, 26, 29, 31–32, 37, 41, 56, 62, 74, 76, 80, 123, 125, 128, 132, 135, 140, 144–145, 154–155, 178
autonomy, 42, 44–45, 53, 108, 137, 149

bilingual education, 19–20, 70, 79, 85, 160
bilingualism, 10, 14–16, 19, 39, 72, 74–75, 87, 103, 130, 134–135, 137, 160
brain plasticity, 5, 9

CLIL, 20–22, 57, 69, 72, 82, 91, 95, 104, 108, 110, 139–140, 142, 149, 160–161, 163, 166, 173
codemeshing, 10–12, 161
codeswitching, 10–12, 14, 19, 122
cognition, 3–5, 7–8, 30, 35–37, 41, 59

collaboration, 7, 23, 48, 51–52, 61, 86, 115, 121–123, 148–149, 153, 166–167
collaborative writing, 51–52, 71, 96, 100
common underlying proficiency, 19
community, 17, 24, 39–40, 45, 50, 58–59, 61–62, 64, 77, 79, 81, 119, 129, 139, 153, 160, 163, 172
competence, 10–13, 15, 20, 24–25, 33, 39, 41–42, 46, 53, 61, 71, 90, 115, 120, 124, 128, 150, 154, 158, 177
competition, 8, 28–29, 98
computer-mediated communication, 36, 48, 50, 117, 149, 153, 160, 165
connection, 4, 28, 62, 141, 147, 149, 168, 172, 174
connectionist, 3, 28–29
context, 6–7, 11, 14–16, 24, 30, 32, 34, 37–39, 42–43, 45, 48–51, 54–65, 72–75, 78–79, 82, 87–88, 90–91, 96, 101, 106, 108, 111, 114, 119–120, 123, 126, 130–131, 135–138, 145, 148–149, 157–160, 165–166, 168, 171, 175, 178

diglossia, 90
dynamic bilingualism, 14–16, 75

emergentism, 29–30
emotions, 8, 30, 35–42, 82, 148, 158
engagement, 40, 42, 45, 54, 61, 80, 95, 100, 107, 112, 114, 121, 142–143, 157, 162, 178
evaluation, 19, 73, 82, 108–109, 142–143, 149, 161, 166–168, 172, 176
exemplar-based production, 28

homoglot, 62

ICT 21, 23, 47–50, 53–54, 70, 96, 100–101, 106–107, 122–123, 153–155, 157, 165–166, 170–171, 175
identity, 11, 16–17, 24–25, 35, 38–39, 44–45, 50, 72, 112, 124, 129–130, 138, 143, 163
individualisation, 173
informal learning, 49–50, 58, 60, 62, 64, 70, 89, 141, 162, 165
interaction, 7–8, 11, 15, 24, 26–27, 29–30, 32–33, 44, 48, 50–51, 53, 56, 59, 81, 92, 96, 101, 109, 124, 148–150, 154–155, 159, 161–163, 165, 169, 171, 187–188, 193, 197, 200
interactionist, 26–27, 91
intercomprehension, 10, 12–13, 27, 70–72, 90–93, 95–97, 99, 115, 119, 121–122, 128, 132, 136, 138–139, 141–142, 154–155, 165
interlanguage, 25, 33
intervention, 96, 132

language acquisition, 4, 6, 15, 29–30, 33, 55, 91, 106, 120, 127
language development, 6–7, 26, 30, 33, 35, 46, 53, 65, 73, 89, 93, 95, 100–102, 106, 114–115, 117, 120, 142–143, 145, 148–149, 155, 158, 160, 162, 171, 173
language learning, 6, 11–12, 26, 31, 45, 47–49, 51, 53–55, 57, 59, 69, 106, 108, 110, 114, 121, 127–128, 134–135, 139–141, 147–149, 151, 153–158, 160–162, 164–168, 170, 172, 174, 176, 178
language learning environment, 172
language production, 5, 11, 28, 163
language proficiency, 21, 39, 91, 93
learning system, 138

macro level, 64, 73, 145
macro task, 167–168, 170
mediation, 11, 31–33, 41–42, 48–49, 52, 71, 118, 122, 125, 146, 148–149, 153, 160, 163, 175–176
memory, 4, 6–7, 16, 18, 27, 29, 34, 37, 52, 128
meso level, 58, 64, 73

metareflection, 31, 33, 36, 48, 70–71, 105–106, 108, 141, 170
micro level, 58, 64–65, 73, 114, 138–140, 145
modularity, 5
monolingual ideologies, 82, 108
monolingual mode, 10
monolingual stance, 125
motivation, 13, 33, 40–45, 53, 57, 59, 109, 118, 123, 148, 163
motive, 41, 121
multiculturalism, 12
multilingual education, 19, 136
multilingual practices, 14–15, 18–21, 23, 25, 67, 69–70, 72, 74, 76, 78, 80, 82, 84–86, 88, 90–92, 94, 96, 98, 100, 102, 104, 106, 108, 110, 112, 114, 116–118, 120, 122, 124, 126, 128–130, 132, 134, 136, 138, 140, 142, 144, 146–148, 150, 154, 156, 178
multilingualism, 12, 15, 18–20, 22–23, 25, 36, 72, 97, 110, 130, 136, 176
multiliteracy, 15, 19, 22–23
multimodality, 15, 20, 22, 126–127

native speaker, 15, 25, 96, 133
nativisation, 5, 29, 31, 118, 149, 154, 156
network, 3, 5, 8–9, 28, 50, 54, 62, 97, 128, 172

perception, 4, 8, 11, 30–31, 35, 38, 45, 61, 110, 123, 126, 144
performance, 7, 21, 25, 34, 40–42, 45, 50, 53, 59, 74, 135, 166
plasticity, 4–5, 9
plurilingual approach, 26, 88, 115, 117
plurilingual competence, 13, 15, 20, 25, 90, 115
plurilingual mode, 10
plurilingual repertoire, 18
plurilingualism, 9, 15–16, 18–19, 23, 29, 72, 87, 90, 104, 107, 112–113, 115, 130–131, 137–138, 141, 143–144, 148
procedural memory, 27
proficiency, 7, 9, 19, 21–22, 25, 33, 39, 53–54, 75, 89, 91, 93, 125–127, 130, 135, 144, 166

representations, 11, 16, 22, 29, 37, 56, 63–64, 88, 97, 108, 110, 123, 144, 178
rule-based production, 28

scaffold, 74
scaffolding, 13, 52, 59, 77, 81, 162, 164
situated cognition, 7
situation, 6, 10, 13–14, 27–28, 31–32, 35, 38–39, 41, 45, 54–58, 62, 73, 86, 89–90, 97, 101, 104, 111, 118, 122–123, 128–132, 134, 136–137, 140, 145, 149, 172, 176
social contexts, 41
social situation, 39
social task(s), 23, 27, 48, 100, 114, 118, 158, 162, 165, 167, 168, 169
socialisation, 45, 173
subtractive bilingualism, 14, 16, 87, 134

tandem learning, 53, 71, 128, 155
tasks, 16, 18, 21, 23, 26–27, 31, 33–34, 36–38, 45, 48, 53–54, 69, 77, 80, 89, 91, 93–95, 97–102, 104, 106–107, 110, 115, 117–118, 120–124, 126, 128, 141–142, 147–151, 153–163, 165–170, 172–175, 177
teacher, 13, 20, 22, 24–25, 27, 33, 42–43, 48, 57–61, 65, 69–71, 77–81, 85, 88, 91–92, 96, 101–102, 104, 109, 118, 122–124, 132, 136–137, 139–140, 142, 144–145, 147, 149–150, 154, 156–158, 162–164, 166–167, 171–176, 178
telecollaboration, 53–54, 71–72, 97, 117–125, 127–128, 155
training tasks, 21, 34, 100, 115, 149, 162, 168, 170, 173–175
transculturing, 36
translanguaging, 7, 9–16, 19–20, 30, 70–72, 74–76, 78–84, 88–89, 100, 104, 108–111, 117–119, 127, 140, 148–149, 154–155, 165–166
translation, 18–19, 38, 115, 149

For Product Safety Concerns and Information please contact our EU Authorised Representative:

Easy Access System Europe

Mustamäe tee 50

10621 Tallinn

Estonia

gpsr.requests@easproject.com